D0098588

UN-TRUMPING AMERICA

ALSO BY DAN PFEIFFER

Yes We (Still) Can: Politics in the Age of Obama, Twitter, and Trump

UN-TRUMPING AMERICA

A Plan to Make America a Democracy Again

DAN PFEIFFER

TWELVE

New York Boston

Cover design by Jarrod Taylor
Cover photographs: Supreme Court © Bob Huberman, all others © Getty images
Author photograph © Sarah Deragon
Cover copyright © 2020 by Hachette Book Group, Inc.

Twelve
Hachette Book Group
1290 Avenue of the Americas, New York, NY 10104
twelvebooks.com
twitter.com/twelvebooks

First edition: February 2020

Twelve is an imprint of Grand Central Publishing. The Twelve name and logo are trademarks of Hachette Book Group, Inc.

The publisher is not responsible for websites (or their content) that are not owned by the publisher.

The Hachette Speakers Bureau provides a wide range of authors for speaking events. To find out more, go to www.hachettespeakersbureau.com or call (866) 376-6591.

Library of Congress Control Number: 2019952660

ISBNs: 978-1-5387-3355-4 (hardcover), 978-1-5387-3356-1 (ebook)

Printed in the United States of America

LSC-C

10 9 8 7 6 5 4 3 2 1

For Kyla, who makes every day brighter

"This is one of those pivotal moments when every one of us, as citizens of the United States, needs to determine just who it is that we are, just what it is that we stand for."

—Barack Obama

CONTENTS

INTRODUCTION

"Could this be it?" I thought to myself at the beginning of the scandal that sparked the fourth impeachment proceedings in American history.[1] "Would this be the thing that finally caused some in the Republican Party to break with Trump?"[2]

If it was true—as the *Washington Post* and others were reporting—that during a call with the newly elected Ukrainian president, Trump used the specter of military aid to extort the Ukrainian government to investigate Joe Biden, then Trump would be guilty of a crime more serious than anything Nixon was accused of during Watergate.

To date, Trump's presidency had been far from successful. His poll numbers had vacillated between mediocre and historically terrible. He had few legislative accomplishments, and most of his executive orders were caught up in the courts because they were poorly thought out and even more poorly executed. But Trump had escaped true political accountability despite saying and doing things on a near-daily basis that would have ended most presidencies.

---

1 Three impeachment trials and counting Nixon, who resigned.
2 Also, I'm doing the footnote thing again.

As I have done every day since the 2016 election, I tempered my optimism. There was no upside to getting my hopes up. After the much-anticipated Mueller report landed with a thud, I—like most Democrats—had conditioned myself to expect disappointment in the scandal department. The problem with the Mueller report wasn't that it didn't include ample evidence of wrongdoing by the president; the report was a none-too-subtle road map for impeachment. But it went nowhere. The press treated it as old news, the Democrats seemed ready to move on before the ink was dry, and Republicans just lied about it. I feared the same thing would happen again. Don't get me wrong, I had little doubt Trump was guilty of wrongdoing—it was just a question how explicit his crime was and how definitive the evidence. Trump's efforts to collude with Russia and obstruct the Mueller probe had been so ham-handed that the lines between his criminality and his incompetence were blurred.

My preemptive sense of disappointment deepened the next morning when Trump announced that he would be releasing the transcript of the call. To say Trump is not the sharpest knife in the drawer is an insult to butter knives, but even he is not dumb enough to release a transcript of a call that would implicate him in global criminal conspiracy to interfere in an American election.

Right?

Wrong.

In the transcript, Trump sounded like a crooked capo trying to pressure a local businessman. Trump called his conversation with the Ukraine President—the "perfect call," but it was an imperfect crime.[3]

In the following days, we would learn that the efforts to cover up this obviously impeachable offense involved the White House,

---

3 Trump is like Nixon, but instead of erasing the eighteen minutes, he tweeted them out.

the National Security Council, the intelligence community, and the Department of Justice. As an example, Attorney General Bill Barr who helped cover up the Mueller report played a similar role in this affair. Barr didn't recuse himself from the investigation even though Trump names him in the call with Ukraine as a participant in the criminal conspiracy.

Additionally, the witnesses to the crimes were not partisan actors but decorated veterans, career diplomats and national security professionals, as well as Trump's own staff. It's easy to miss the historical significance of what Trump did. Our national attention span is so short and the pace of events so frenetic that it's nearly impossible to step back and take stock of the moment.

Trump handled the beginning of an impeachment inquiry with his usual aplomb. In a period of about 96 hours, Trump

- called for the execution of the whistleblower and the administration officials that corroborated their account;
- referred to six members of Congress as "savages"—the six members Trump chose were two Jews and four women of color which wasn't a coincidence.
- suggested a second civil war would be an appropriate response to impeachment;[4]
- posted eighteen tweets[5] in five minutes attacking the weekend anchor of *Fox & Friends* for having the audacity to ask a barely tough question of one of Trump's defenders[6]
- said that the Democratic chair of the Intelligence Committee should be arrested for treason, which happens to be a crime punishable by death; and

---

4 I'm 90 percent sure Trump thinks civil war is an *Avengers* plotline and not the bloodiest war in US history.

5 One of the accounts Trump retweeted was a bot account that just added the word "Shark" to Trump's tweets.

6 I support this and wish Trump had sent more tweets about the Fox anchor, who deserves all the shame.

- reportedly committed another crime by agreeing to back off legislation to mandate background checks for gun sales in exchange for the National Rifle Association contributing to his legal and political defense.[7]

In the early days of the impeachment inquiry, public opinion moved decidedly in the Democrats' direction. Majorities backed the inquiry, and even some Republican voters were troubled by Trump's actions. There was a drumbeat of credible firsthand witnesses. Before long, there could be no doubt about what happened. The call and the extensive effort to cover it up were a crime higher than any of the crimes committed during Watergate.

Yet, Donald Trump is still president.[8] In the end, none of it mattered very much. A few Republicans expressed private concerns. Some even sent a few sad tweets. But no one actually did anything. Large swaths of voters believed he had committed a crime, but few expected him to face any accountability.

As a nation, we were uncomfortably numb to crimes being committed in the Oval Office.

The whole thing was deeply depressing, but it was also final confirmation of something that had been eating at me for years.

The American political system is fundamentally broken—a fact the Republican Party has ruthlessly exploited to rig politics in their favor.

This notion was not a new one to me. The fact that the Republican Party was out of control has been obvious for a long time. They were radical, rabid, and often racist the entire time I worked for Barack Obama. Their approach to government was nihilist on

---

7 These are not the actions of an innocent (or well) individual.

8 If he weren't, I would be rewriting this book. *Un-Penceing America* doesn't really roll off the tongue.

the best day. They were people who just wanted to see the world burn.

At the time, I thought this was a temporary affliction on the body politic. One that would be cured by the passage of time and the 2016 election.

I cockily assumed that Hillary Clinton would defeat Trump in resounding fashion. The Republicans would learn the error of their ways and take a couple of steps back from the brink. My confidence that Clinton would win emanated from an unyielding—and mistaken—belief in the health of our democracy. Instead, Trump rode into office on the back of our broken democracy. He won with fewer votes and benefited from a raft of laws passed by Republicans to make it harder for people to vote.

The future of American democracy now depends on a Democratic Party that is eyes wide open about who the Republican Party is, what they have wrought, and what it takes to undo the damage.

Democrats have spent much of the Trump era engaging in an internal debate about the future of the party. This to be expected and healthy. We have entered the post-Obama era of the party, and we need to figure out what comes next. However, this divide is usually framed on ideological terms: moderates v. progressives. Should the party embrace the bold progressive policies advocated by Bernie Sanders, Elizabeth Warren, and Alexandria Ocasio-Cortez or more centrist solutions? There is often confusion in our political discourse between ideology and policy. In my experience, most voters have policy preferences but rarely view politics through the lens of one specific ideology. A candidate's ability to tell a story about why his or her policies are the right ones is exponentially more consequential than whether those policies are left, right, or center.

The focus on ideology masks the larger issue. The biggest divide in the Democratic Party is not between left and center. It's between those who believe once Trump is gone things will go back to normal, and those who believe that our democracy is under a threat that goes beyond Trump.

Everything flows from this debate. If you believe the former, simply surviving the moment is enough. If you believe the latter—as I do[9]—then you have to be willing to contemplate ideas that were off the table even a few years ago.

I have come to the conclusion that there is nothing more important than beating Trump, but beating Trump is not nearly enough. The Democratic Party needs an aggressive strategy to fundamentally reshape American democracy. We have to come to terms with who the Republican Party is and what they have done. We have to recognize that Donald Trump is not an aberration or an accident. There will be no Republican epiphany during or after Trump. The media won't save us.[10] Bob Mueller didn't save us. And Trump's propensity for committing impeachable offenses won't save us.

It took me a long time to come to this conclusion and to embrace the solutions in this book. I am an institutionalist by nature. I have spent nearly twenty years working in Democratic politics. I have served a president, a vice president, three senators, and the Democratic Party. I spent most of my career working at both ends of Pennsylvania Avenue.

I chose politics for my career because I thought working within the system was the best way to bring change. I believed politics and government got a bad rap. Despite cynical media coverage and reductionist Hollywood portrayals, the politicians I met were not inherently corrupt or incompetent. They were imperfect humans working within an imperfect system to do what they thought was best for the country. I believed this to be true no

---

9 And hopefully you will soon.
10 The media may have done more than not save us, but more on that later.

matter the party.[11] I believed that our democracy was messy but worked. I trusted institutions and believed in norms. I thought the arc of American politics was long but ultimately bent toward democracy.

During the Obama presidency, I viewed it as our responsibility to protect our political institutions because we were the party that believed in the power of government to do good. I believed the filibuster had merit and the Electoral College was a feature, not a bug, of the system. And even if I was deeply skeptical of the motivations of the Republicans in Congress, I remained optimistic that they would one day see the folly of their ways and begin to take governing at least a little more seriously.

But I was wrong. I have been radicalized by Trump's election and everything that has happened since. I believe we need bigger, bolder solutions. The same old politics simply won't do.

Removing Trump is not enough. America is a "democracy" governed by antidemocratic institutions, a country where a growing progressive diverse majority is being governed by a shrinking conservative white minority.

My fear as we sit here on the eve of the 2020 election season is that too many Democrats in Washington remain blind to the stakes of the moment.

If Democrats don't get smarter and tougher about how we conduct politics and embrace the bold activism of the grassroots, we are going to continue to come up short. We might win some battles, but we will lose the war.

I believe that un-Trumping America involves three elements: First, understanding who the Republicans are and what their strategy is. Second, winning in 2020. And finally, using our newfound political power to fix American politics to ensure we never have to deal with someone like Donald Trump ever again.

---

11 The Republicans I met were much more "imperfect."

Tim Geithner, the former Treasury secretary, used to have a saying that became a mantra in the Obama White House—"Plan beats no plan." My version of Geithner's saying was "Memo beats no memo." In the first few days in the White House, there was a staff meeting to discuss whether Obama should do a press conference. In the room were all of the new president's top advisors and me. As the then deputy communications director, I was the lowest ranking person in the room. By title alone, I shouldn't have made the cut. I think I was invited out of habit. On the campaign, which was much less hierarchical than the White House, I was always around for a meeting like this. I didn't really agree with the idea of the press conference, but no one asked my opinion and I wasn't sure I should offer it. The group quickly decided the press conference was a good idea. As everyone was gathering their things, Rahm Emanuel, the new White House chief of staff and one of the few people around the table who had worked in the White House before, said, "If we are going to do this, the president needs to be prepared. Who's writing the briefing memo with possible questions and answers?"

Everyone looked at each other in silence for a moment. No one was volunteering for this seemingly mundane and time-consuming task.

All of a sudden, I felt the collective gaze turning to me. I tried not to make eye contact, but it was too late.

"Pfeiffer?" someone said.

"Great idea," someone else said.

The rest of the room concurred, with a palpable sense of relief that they had avoided a homework assignment.[12]

---

12 During the campaign, Obama was answering press questions so often that he felt little need for briefing memos to be prepared for him. Donald Trump is more likely to read *Infinite Jest* than Obama was to peruse a memo for a series of local TV interviews. (I would bet Trump thinks David Foster Wallace is a member of the *Morning Joe* roundtable.)

Before I knew it, everyone was gone and I was stuck writing a memo. I was pissed. No one had acknowledged my presence in the meeting until it came time to assign some work.

As I trudged back to my new office, I ran into Stephanie Cutter, who had been Michelle Obama's chief of staff on the campaign and was now working as a top advisor at the Treasury Department. I told her how annoyed I was that I was going to be at the office all night working on the memo. Stephanie told me I was looking at it the wrong way: "In the White House, you always want to be the person who writes the memo. Being the one who holds the pen gives you the most influence on what the president says and does. Plus, they have to invite the author of the memo to the meeting."

That encounter opened my eyes. Being the person who wrote the memo, whether it was prep for a press conference or the strategic plan for the next quarter, became my golden ticket. It gave me a voice larger than my station. It gave me the opportunity to drive the strategy in the direction that I thought best. Over the next six years, I always volunteered to write the strategy memos and learned the tremendous value of being the one with the pen.

Un-Trumping America is my much longer, post–White House memo to the Democratic Party and the millions of activists that have joined the fight since Trump won. It lays out my ideas on how to defeat Trump and restore American democracy while staying true to who we are as Democrats.

This book is informed by the lessons learned in the Obama White House as we watched the rise of Trumpism and the humility of not fully understanding the danger we were facing. It's also inspired by the next generation of activists who were born out of Trump's victory—people who channeled their anger into activism and helped lead the Democrats to victories in 2018 and have pushed bolder and more progressive policies. They are the present and future of the party—if it embraces them.

And while the White House taught me the importance of being

the one with the pen, *Pod Save America* has taught me the importance of talking (and writing) about politics in an accessible and (hopefully) entertaining way. Too often political discussions are filled with jargon and indecipherable acronyms. This isn't an accident. It's designed to separate those in the "know" from the masses. Too much political messaging is about serving spinach and then wondering why people aren't coming back for seconds and thirds. There is a reason Jon Stewart is a more influential figure than the folks who host the nightly news. There's no law[13] that says politics can't be fun. So my hope is that this book is more fun than spinach.[14]

While the premise that Trumpism will outlast Trump can seem dark, I remain hopeful.[15] Despite everything that has happened since Election Day 2016, I know we can relegate Donald Trump and this version of the Republican Party to the dustbin of history. But it's going to take a lot of work, and that work starts with understanding how we got into this mess and who we are up against.

---

13 Yet.
14 Really setting the bar high with this one.
15 And you should, too!

UN-TRUMPING AMERICA

PART ONE

HOW REPUBLICANS TRUMPED AMERICA

CHAPTER 1

TRUMP: AN ABOMINATION, NOT AN ABERRATION

Let's do a little visualization exercise:[1]

It's January 20, 2021. It's a freezing but sunny day in Washington, DC. The National Mall is packed with over a million Americans of all ages, races, and backgrounds. It is the largest audience to witness an inauguration, period. A palpable sense of joy and relief pulsates throughout the crowd.

After a beautiful rendition of the national anthem[2] and an opening prayer that spoke to diversity and inclusion, the official proceedings begin.

Seated on the platform are all of America's living former presidents and their wives—the Obamas, the Bushes, Clintons, and the Carters. All of them are smiling and appear pleased to be in attendance despite the cold.

The crowd erupts as the newly elected president makes his or her way to the podium to take the oath of office on a Bible held by Chief Justice John Roberts, who seems less excited than everyone else in attendance.

---

1 It's possible this is a piece of evidence I have lived in California a little too long.

2 Probably Lizzo.

Watching the speech from the front row to the left of the new president is Donald Trump. He has a scowl affixed to his face, he can't stop fidgeting, and the wind has done no favors to his bird's nest of a hairdo. He is seated next to Ivanka because Melania decided not to come for reasons the Trump White House declined to disclose (but we could all guess).

At the conclusion of the inaugural address, which included no references to "American Carnage," Trump—now a *former* president—makes a beeline for the exits. He skips the congressional luncheon and heads directly to Mar-a-Lago, where he will spend the rest of his days tweeting about "voter fraud" and doing infomercials for a sketchy line of masculine virility supplements.[3]

Seems appealing, huh? As you can probably tell, I spend way too much time imagining Trump's political demise and national humiliation. Almost nothing would give me more joy and be better for the country than Trump's defeat in 2020. But that beautiful, hypothetical day in 2021 is the beginning, not the end, of the fight against Trumpism. Defeating Trump is not enough; defeating Trumpism must be the goal.

WTF IS TRUMPISM?

Trumpism is a somewhat ambiguous concept. Trump is not a philosopher. He doesn't have a political theory or any underlying beliefs. The only *-isms* that he has ever been associated with are racism and narcissism. The best summary of Trumpism is "billionaire-funded racial grievance politics." It's plutocracy in populist clothing.

---

3 There is an alternative scenario in which Trump disembarks Air Force One in Florida and is greeted by New York state troopers to be escorted back to New York to face justice for the many, many crimes he committed before and during his presidency.

Ultimately, Trumpism is more a political playbook than anything else:

- Sowing racial division to turn out the base is acceptable.
- Lying is not only okay, it's encouraged.
- The press is the enemy of the people.
- The will of the people is at best an annoying speed bump on the path to maintaining power.
- Propaganda is the preferred method of communication.
- Winning at all costs is okay no matter the morals, laws, or consequences to the country.

Many of these tactics were used before Trump, but never so explicitly or successfully. His win supercharged the worst instincts of the Republican Party and wrote a playbook for the party that will be around for years after Trump has been defeated, retired, or imprisoned.

WHY TRUMPISM IS HERE TO STAY

Back when we all slept soundly with false confidence about Trump's political demise,[4] I got a preview of the near future of American politics. I was hanging out at the Republican National Convention in Cleveland. This was not a choice.[5] CNN had sent me to do political analysis from the Democratic perspective—and who turns down a free trip to Cleveland?[6] All in all, it was a very odd experience. I had been to a lot of national conventions

---

4 Historians will refer to this period as "the era before bed-wetting."

5 No shit. It was like being stuck in a very large elevator with three thousand of the worst people in America.

6 I'm kidding...I like Cleveland. It's way better than a handful of cities in the former Russian republics. I really am kidding. I do like Cleveland. I swear.

over the years—this wasn't even the first Republican convention I had been to. But at this Republican convention, you could cut the awkward tension with a knife. The whole gathering felt like a wedding where everyone in attendance knew the union was a bad idea but no one had the guts to tell the bride and groom. In another sense, it felt like a celebration of the worst people in American politics[7]—a reunion of rejected guests from the C block on a Fox News daytime show. There was a class of pundits and Republican political strategists whose only path to relevance was to be one of the few Republicans willing to publicly defend Trump's indefensible conduct.[8] People like Jeffrey Lord, a midlevel aide in the Reagan administration who had been in the political wilderness since the 1980s;[9] David Clarke, a sheriff from Wisconsin with a troubling record; and Paul Manafort, a former aide to Bob Dole who would go on to prison. Their bet had paid off. Trump was now the nominee and they were—at least for a moment—celebrities.[10]

Needless to say, I didn't fit in and for that I was grateful. The whole experience was leavened by my rock-solid belief that Trump was going to lose the election and then all of these folks would return to life under whatever rock they crawled out from.

On the last day of the convention, I was waiting for a CNN appearance while some dim-witted Trump surrogate was vomiting dishonest talking points on set. I was sitting next to a former aide to George W. Bush and Mitt Romney who was firmly in the Never Trump camp.

"I bet you can't wait to be done with all of these Trump people," I asked, presupposing a Trump defeat in November.

---

7 This is only a minor difference from most Republican gatherings.
8 We now call these people Republicans.
9 Jeffrey Lord would return to the political wilderness after being fired from CNN for tweeting "Sieg Heil," which in the end was probably inevitable.
10 Celebrities in the *Jersey Shore* sense of the word.

I was just making conversation and passing the time. The question was almost rhetorical in nature.

"Are you fucking kidding me? These people aren't going anywhere. Win or lose, they are here to stay. We [Republicans][11] are stuck with them. This is the Republican Party now. Hell, Don Jr. will be running for governor of New York before too long,"[12] the Republican aide responded with equal parts anger and sadness.

I was shocked by his answer. It hadn't even occurred to me that Trump and his brand of politics were here to stay. I believed that he was an accidental nominee—the product of an insane set of strategic decisions by an abnormally large field of bad candidates with worse campaigns. I viewed Trump as the natural end to the Obama-era downward spiral of Republicanism. The unfunny punch line to an even unfunnier joke.

I was wrong, and this Republican was right.[13] Trump is the beginning of the next era of the Republican Party, not the end of the last era.

Win or lose in 2020, Trumpism and what it has wrought will be here for a very long time.[14]

There are two primary reasons why Trumpism will last longer than Trump.

First, the absolutely shocking nature of Trump's win imbued him with a sort of political magic in the eyes of a lot of observers who proudly predicted that he was doomed. Believing Trump is a political genius because he won the 2016 election is almost certainly confusing correlation and causation. But perception is often more important than reality in politics, and Trump not only beat Clinton, but he was also seen as besting the Obama political

11 But also everyone else.
12 More likely, Don Jr. will be in prison or a nonextradition country by 2024.
13 If there is a theme to my 2016 political predictions, it's a stunning consistency of incorrectness.
14 If you just threw your book, e-reader, or tablet out the window, I hope you retrieved it and finish the rest of the book.

machine. Trump taught Republicans that the best way to win was to be like Trump. His victory didn't just produce supplicants. It produced replicants.

Many of Trump's biggest critics transformed into his biggest supporters. He demanded blind allegiance, and 99 percent of Republican politicians agreed.[15]

There is now a generation of mini-Trumps working their way up the ranks of the Republican Party. Some of them are Trump-lite figures that Trump backed in contentious primaries in 2018. People like Florida governor Ron DeSantis, a frequent Fox News guest who literally ran an ad about teaching his young daughter to say, "Make America great again." Others like Lindsey Graham changed their personality to act more like Trump because they believed it was necessary to succeed in Republican politics in the Trump era.

It taught the politicians that shame was weakness, truth was unnecessary, and democracy was the enemy. Trump also got the Republican base hooked on a particularly high dosage of racial resentment.

The larger political forces of demographic and technological change may have pushed the Republicans to this place eventually, but the shocking nature of Trump's win catalyzed the process. The political lessons continued once he was in office. Mark Sanford, a Republican congressman from South Carolina, fashioned himself a mild Trump critic. Trump endorsed his primary opponent, and Sanford lost.[16] Senators Jeff Flake and Bob Corker spoke out repeatedly against Trump. They were forced to retire rather than lose a primary. Standing with Trump amid his racism, incompetence, and corruption became a requirement for membership in the Republican Party.

---

15 The other 1 percent left the party and took jobs at MSNBC.
16 Notably, the Trump endorsee lost that very Republican seat to a Democrat.

Second, Trump's win resolved a long-running tension within the Republican Party. The last decade of Republicanism has been defined by a battle between the establishment and an upstart group of members who rose up in opposition to Obama. The former were raised on Reagan and Bushes, read *National Review*, and were annoyed America elected a liberal president. The latter were raised on Rush, read Breitbart, and were apoplectic America elected a black president. This new group—often called Tea Partyers—represented the energy in the Republican base. They were part of the conservative zeitgeist and spoke the language of Fox News, which had become the Republican native tongue. They were also pretty bad at politics and knew nothing about government. These Tea Partyers—who rebranded as the Freedom Caucus[17]—repeatedly pushed the party into a bunch of losing confrontations over budget issues and Obamacare. They were a problem to be managed by the "adults" in the party. I witnessed this battle time and again in the Obama administration. John Boehner would agree to a budget or tax deal with Obama only to have the Freedom Caucus kill it by threatening to oust Boehner as Speaker.[18] The Freedom Caucus would then force Boehner to adopt a position that was politically damaging with zero chance of passing the Senate. The most notable example is when the newly elected Republicans forced a confrontation over a budgetary maneuver known as the debt ceiling. The debt ceiling sounds benign. In a rational political world, it would be. It's a simple vote to grant the federal government the authority to pay the bills it has incurred. It's a vote no one likes taking, and the minority party usually makes the majority pass it on their own so they can make political hay and posture about who is more fiscally

---

17 Freedom from common sense.

18 Boehner cared about his own job security a lot more than anyone else's, including the American people.

responsible. But it passes without drama.[19] For something so simple, the consequences of not passing it are devastating. Essentially, the US would no longer be able to spend money on anything, including paying out Social Security. If the US stopped paying its bills, it could lead to a global financial crisis. In 2010, the Republicans under pressure from their radical, newly elected members decided to use the debt-ceiling vote as leverage. The Republicans declared that they would only lift the debt ceiling with corresponding cuts in spending. So, if you wanted to raise the debt ceiling and spend $500 billion, you would need to cut $500 billion from the budget—reducing the federal investment in education, health care, or the military. This proposal was insane—it made zero economic sense, betrayed a radical ignorance about how the federal budget worked, and put America on a dangerous path. Because the Republicans controlled the House of Representatives, they had all the power. If they didn't put a debt-ceiling vote on the floor and pass it, the economy was going to go off a cliff.

I have sat in the Situation Room[20] during meetings about credible terrorist threats on the homeland, the Boston Marathon bombing, and a potential swine flu pandemic. But I was never more afraid than during the debt-ceiling showdown. This was legislative terrorism.

Crisis was eventually averted but not before the stock market plunged, the economy took a hit, and the United States had its credit rating downgraded.

As damaging and terrifying as this incident was, it revealed the fundamental tension at the heart of the Republican Party. On one side, you have a Republican establishment that exists to serve the corporate titans and Wall Street barons that fund the

---

19 When Obama was in the Senate minority, he voted against a debt ceiling increase that was certain to pass and didn't need his vote. He later said he regretted the vote (so don't @ me).

20 White House, not CNN.

party that opposed the debt ceiling confrontation. On the other side, you have a rabid base raised on right-wing red meat and fueled by racial paranoia. One source of real tension was antitrade, anticorporate populism that emerged from the financial crisis. Obama's election changed the Republican base. It became whiter and more rural. This shift led to a growing antitrade, anti-immigrant, and anti–Wall Street sentiment. This populism stood in stark contrast to the corporatism that had defined Republican economic policy since Reagan.

During my time working in the White House, I believed that this tension was irreconcilable and that the GOP was due for a fundamental reckoning. One side had to win. My money was on the radical Right defeating the establishment—always bet on the side with the energy. Either way, the party was headed toward disaster—a civil war where the only winner would be the Democrats.

But that didn't happen.

The reckoning between the billionaire-loving elites and the racist base never happened, because America elected a racist billionaire.[21] When he came to office, Trump decided to keep the racist rhetoric and inflammatory tweets that endeared him to the base, but he also decided to adopt the policy agenda of the donor class. Trump showed the party that they could have their racism and their tax cuts, too.

In this union lies the core of Trumpism—billionaire-funded racial grievance politics.

Trump united the billionaires and the bigots. That union will continue after he is gone because they need each other to maintain their political power.

Understanding how to remove Trumpism root and branch begins with understanding where it came from and how it took hold in the Republican Party.

---

21 "Alleged" billionaire.

CHAPTER 2

YES WE CAN V. BECAUSE WE CAN: WHY DEMOCRATS ARE BETTER BUT WIN LESS

Democrats and Republicans in Washington are playing two different games with different sets of rules. A tweet by Ben Rosen, a writer for the comedy website Funny or Die, perfectly summarizes this dynamic:

> **CHUCK SCHUMER (carefully reading rule book):** ok let's see how this monopoly game works . . .
>
> **MITCH MCCONNELL:** *steals all the monopoly money and also some real money and also throws schumer's dog out the window*
>
> **CHUCK SCHUMER:** so apparently one [of] us gets to be a thimble.

This tweet, while very funny, is unfair to Schumer, who has done an admirable job herding the cats of a fractious caucus that spans the ideological spectrum from Democratic Socialist[1] to

1 Bernie Sanders.

Republican lite.[2] But it does reflect a larger truth that congressional Democrats are unwilling or unable to see this ment for what it is and the Republicans for who they are.

Democrats and Republicans are not opposite sides of the same coin. The great asymmetry in American politics is that Democrats view political power as a means to an end, and Republicans view political power as an end in and of itself. In other words, Democrats want to do the right thing and Republicans want to win. Modern politics is a contest between two different philosophies. It's "Yes We Can" versus "Because We Can."

MCCONNELLISM: BECAUSE WE CAN

There is an amoral (and often immoral) nihilism to an approach that strives for political power for political power's sake. All of a sudden everything is on the table to maintain and expand that power.

That is the approach of the modern Republican Party, and no one embodies that approach more than Mitch McConnell.

For these last many years, we have bemoaned Trump as an existential threat to American life and as an aspiring authoritarian. We have blamed everyone from the Russians to James Comey for Trump becoming president.

But the true threat, the real person undermining democracy, and the real reason Trump is president is Mitch McConnell. He fostered the political environment where someone like Trump could thrive and helped deliver the election for Trump.

Let's take a tour of McConnell's terribleness to learn who he is and why he is the worst person in American politics.[3]

---

2 Joe Manchin.
3 Yes, even worse than Paul Ryan.

First, when the Obama administration uncovered that the Russians were interfering in the 2016 election to help Donald Trump, McConnell was the one who protected Trump. The Obama administration had a dilemma: The public had a right to know about Russia's efforts before they voted, but how would it be possible for a Democratic administration to share that information without appearing to put their thumb on the scale? They hatched a plan to release a letter signed by all of the bipartisan congressional leadership and the administration detailing what they knew. The process was off to a good start. Paul Ryan's staff was reportedly supportive of an initial draft.

McConnell refused to sign the letter.

There was not a question about the validity of the information. There was a strong consensus in the US Intelligence Community that Russia had initiated the hack and that they were doing it with the express purpose of helping Donald Trump. The latter was obvious since it was only the Democrats whose emails were being strategically released for maximum political impact.[4] McConnell refused to sign the letter because he thought it would hurt Trump and the Republicans at the ballot box. This is not to say that McConnell was some sort of Trump superfan. He wasn't, but there were several key Senate races in battleground states like Pennsylvania, Wisconsin, and New Hampshire. If Trump did poorly, there was a good chance the Republicans would lose control of the Senate. McConnell would rather remove his appendix with a dull spoon than give up an ounce of his political power.

On one level, McConnell's actions might seem rational. He is a Republican and he wants Republicans to win elections, so why would he do something that would make it less likely for Republicans to win elections? But on the other hand,

---

4 The Russians released John Podesta's emails within hours of the *Access Hollywood* tape surfacing.

AMERICA HAD JUST BEEN ATTACKED BY A FOREIGN POWER TRYING TO SUBVERT OUR DEMOCRACY IN ORDER TO INSTALL THE PRESIDENT OF THEIR CHOICE.[5]

McConnell put his party and his political power ahead of what was best for America. Party above country. McConnell's decision to help cover up the Russia scandal is even more notable because by all reports McConnell found Trump to be a numbskull of epic proportions.[6]

Second, when Barack Obama came into office during the worst financial crisis since the Great Depression, McConnell had a choice: work with the new president to try to save the American economy or exploit the crisis for partisan gain. He chose the latter. As Alec MacGillis reported in *The Cynic*,[7] his biography of McConnell, the then Senate minority leader told his fellow Republicans, "We begin to take him down, one issue at a time. We create an inventory of losses, so it's Obama lost on this, Obama lost on that." That's exactly what McConnell did. He refused to work with Obama on the economic recovery package that was designed to pull America out of the financial crisis. McConnell made a decision to make the economy worse to improve his political prospects. People lost their jobs, their homes, and their retirement savings because McConnell opposed any action that would help the economy if he thought it would also help Obama. It is one of the most brazen examples of political cynicism in American history. Imagine if after 9/11, Democrats had refused to pass measures to provide aid to the victims and help New York City and the airlines recover to score political points against George W. Bush.

Later on, McConnell was asked about his top priority. Think

---

5 Seriously, WTF?????
6 McConnell being terrible but far from stupid is a theme of this chapter.
7 Great title.

about the possible answers to this question—creating jobs, cutting taxes, fixing health care, helping the troops, or improving education.

Nope.

McConnell responded by saying, "The single most important thing we want to achieve is for President Obama to be a one-term president." When McConnell said this, unemployment was in the double digits, American troops were fighting in two wars, and Osama bin Laden was still walking the earth. It's not just the cynicism of the statement; it's the chutzpah to say it out loud.

McConnell is not dumb. This was not a slip of the tongue. It was whatever the opposite of virtue signaling is. He was sending a message to everyone in the Republican Party that winning elections was more important than helping America.

Finally, the best example of McConnell's "win at all costs" philosophy is his decision to swing the Supreme Court by holding Antonin Scalia's seat open until after the 2016 election. The fact that this isn't one of the greatest scandals in American history is a sign that McConnell and the Republicans have succeeded in convincing the media that cynicism is a virtue. Think about it this way—with support from nearly every Republican senator, McConnell rendered the Supreme Court potentially unable to rule for an entire year.

McConnell wrapped his decision to steal a Supreme Court seat in the faux principle that Supreme Court vacancies should not be filled in election years. He argued that the voters should get to weigh in before a justice is given a lifetime appointment. He showed tremendous umbrage when anyone dared to question this incredibly important, completely made-up principle. In 2019, McConnell was asked by right-wing talk show host Hugh Hewitt[8] whether he would support filling a vacancy in 2020 if one arose.

---

8 Hewitt is a microcosm of the Republican Party. He was a one-time Trump opponent who became a Trump supporter to save his failing radio show. He defended a corrupt Trump cabinet member with whom he had a secret financial relationship and now broadcasts from inside Trump's posterior.

McConnell didn't miss a beat.

"Absolutely."

Most people would be embarrassed by such naked cynicism. McConnell believes it was his greatest accomplishment. In an interview with *Kentucky Today*, McConnell said, "The decision I made not to fill the Supreme Court vacancy when Justice Scalia died was the most consequential decision I've made in my entire public career."

McConnell is right. It may even be one of the most consequential decisions of the decade, but not for the reason he thinks. McConnell potentially rigged the court for generations. But McConnell stealing a Supreme Court seat also changed politics—it laid bare the Republican strategy and gave Democrats an opportunity to respond.

YES WE CAN

An optimism about America summarized by the slogan "Yes, We Can" powered Barack Obama's rise to the White House. Obama had tremendous faith in the American people and a sincere belief in the possibility of better politics. The politics of "Yes, We Can" is a bet on an inherent idealism in the American people that emanated from his own life. The son of a single mother from Kansas with an absent father from Kenya rising to the White House is a story Obama believed could only come true in America.

The optimism of Obama's campaign can feel quaint and perhaps naive with the knowledge of what would happen to American politics in the years to come.

However, it's important to remember the political and historical context for Obama's White House run. By 2007, Democrats were coming off two losing presidential elections and a growing amount of grassroots frustration at poll-tested cautious centrism. This frustration came from several things.

- The Clintonian[9] strategy of triangulation where politicians adopt the position equidistant between liberal Democrats and conservative Republicans. This strategy helped Clinton win some elections but led to policy atrocities like welfare reform and the Defense of Marriage Act, both of which were needlessly cruel in order to appeal to "swing voters."
- An obsession with poll testing everything from the policy agenda to where the Clintons should go on vacation.[10]
- A Democratic approach to policy making that focused on small-bore, poll-tested issues that appealed to everyone and angered no one—an approach embodied by Bill Clinton relentlessly touting school uniforms and V-chips for televisions.
- Democratic support for the Iraq War. Too many Democrats were willing to put their stamp of approval on George W. Bush's decision to invade the country that did NOT attack us on 9/11 in part because they were afraid of being tarred as "weak on terrorism."

Obama's campaign was in many ways a campaign against this version of "politics as usual." This approach came naturally to him. Obama wasn't a "usual" politician. He was a natural campaigner and the most talented politician of his generation, but he didn't love the transactional nature of politics where everyone wants something in exchange for everything. Obama would often say during that first campaign that while he very much wanted to win,

---

9 Bill, not Hillary.

10 This is a real thing that happened. Clinton went on vacation in the mountains in a red state instead of the beach in a blue state because it polled better.

he was comfortable losing the election.[11] He hadn't planned to run for president. As a relative newcomer on the national political scene, he didn't have the battle scars of endless political wars or the well-worn political caution that comes from too many years in the nation's capital. Therefore, he often embraced politically risky positions like the Affordable Care Act.

This approach makes me proud to be a Democrat and even prouder to have worked for Obama.

Political courage is something to be celebrated in our elected officials, and a return to an era when presidents poll their vacation destinations would be a gigantic mistake. The times we live in call for big, bold action on the economy, health care, immigration, civil rights, voting rights, and so many other issues. Policy incrementalism and mushy-middle centrism as strategies should be permanently retired to the political boneyard.

But politics doesn't have to be a choice between doing the right thing and doing the smart thing.

Democrats like to say that "good policy is good politics." It's a noble idea and one we loved to tell ourselves in the Obama administration. It's also sort of true. At least in the sense that bad policy is bad politics. In 2018, the Republicans suffered mightily at the polls in part because they chose to pass an unpopular and poorly constructed tax cut that primarily benefited the wealthy.[12]

Good policy executed well is better than bad policy executed poorly, but good policy alone isn't a political strategy.

Politics isn't just about policy. It's also about power—who has it, who doesn't, and how it is used.

As Democrats we have traditionally been uncomfortable with actions that are strictly about achieving additional political power.

---

11 Obama is insanely competitive in all things. He talked trash to me about kicking my ass at poker for approximately eight years.

12 Great job, Paul Ryan!

Too often we shy away from ideas that would shift the balance of power in favor of the Democratic Party—even when they are the right thing to do.

The Republican approach to politics is quite different...to say the least.

THE ASSHOLE ADVANTAGE

Democrats must come to terms with the fact that despite some important electoral and political victories, Republicans have been winning the long war for power in American politics.

And this happened despite the fact that:

- Republican policies are less popular than Democratic policies;
- Trump's poll numbers are consistently and historically low;
- McConnell's approval numbers make Trump's look like Oprah's;[13]
- Democrats outnumber Republicans in the country.

There was a time when the Republicans were the party of Reagan.[14] They had "Smaller government, less taxes" tattooed on their political souls. That time is no more. At some point over the last couple of decades, the Republicans officially abandoned conservative policy for consistent power as their reason for being. This shift advantages Republicans because it allows them to pick whatever path is most politically beneficial at the time. They are unburdened by principles, prior positions, morality, and in some cases by a compulsion to follow the law. Republican politicians

---

13 Oprah is popular.

14 To be clear, this is nothing to be proud of. Reagan was objectively terrible on many levels. Unlike Trump, he hid his terribleness with an affable persona and a love for jelly beans.

have trained their voters to root for the jersey no matter what they do on (or off) the field.[15]

Democrats do not have that freedom. We are governed by a set of ideological commitments to which our voters hold us. Obama said he was going to pass a health-care bill, and therefore he felt an obligation—morally and politically—to pass one even though doing so would almost certainly hurt his political prospects in the short term and maybe the long term. Had Obama not taken on the issues he campaigned on, his supporters would have rightly felt betrayed. This is not a burden that Republican politicians feel or one imposed by Republican voters. For Republican voters, winning is often enough.[16] What comes after does not matter so much as long as it's followed by more winning. Policy and ideology are secondary to power.

This ideological flexibility[17] is an advantage and a necessity to keep together a party that is increasingly dependent on the votes of white men who are struggling in this economy and the money of the billionaires who are profiting off that struggle.

The Republican Party transitioned from an organization united by a conservative ideology into an incoherent coalition of conflicting interests bound together by an opposition to a changing America.

George W. Bush ran as a small-government conservative, but when he wanted to secure the votes of senior citizens, he passed a bill to help pay for their prescription drugs. Bush's plan made government much bigger, not smaller, and happened to add hundreds of billions of dollars to the deficit. There was no ideology or policy

---

15 Basically, Republican voters are New England Patriots fans, which makes sense given that the owner, coach, and star quarterback of the Patriots all support Trump (sorry, Tommy and Jon). The fact-checkers tried to stop me from including this footnote, I won't be dissuaded by their nitpicking.

16 The one inviolable Republican principle is giving men more control over women's bodies.

17 Talk about a euphemism.

principle driving this decision. The Bush campaign thought they needed to do better with seniors in Florida, so previous positions be damned.[18]

When Obama proposed the Affordable Care Act, the Republicans were all of a sudden small-government conservatives again. They put on tricornered hats and engaged in Revolutionary War cosplay because Obama was—you guessed it—expanding government. It didn't matter that the ACA, unlike Bush's plan, didn't add a penny to the deficit.

When Bush was president, America had a massive surplus. Vice President Cheney declared that deficits didn't matter and spent the entire surplus on a huge tax cut that primarily benefited the wealthy and did nothing to juice the economy. When Obama was president, the Republicans had a performative panic attack about the deficit. They claimed that the US economy was on the verge of collapse because of a growing mountain of debt (most of which came from unpaid tax cuts and wars enacted by Republicans). When Donald Trump became president, Republicans passed a $1 trillion tax cut. And how much of it did the deficit-conscious, small-government party insist was paid for by cutting spending in other areas?

Zero. And all of the deficit Chicken Littles were nowhere to be found.

There is probably no better example of Republican ideological flexibility than immigration. When George W. Bush was president, Republicans thought it was in their interest to be the party that passed immigration reform. The political logic was simple if cynical—deliver on the top policy priority of the Latino community, which just happens to be the fastest-growing bloc of voters. When Obama was president, they opposed a similar immigration law for the same cynical reason. Obama had promised

18 It worked.

to pass immigration reform early in his term. The Republicans believed that if they could force him to break that promise, it would depress Latino turnout in Obama's reelection campaign. When that strategy failed in 2012, the Republicans decided they needed to be for immigration reform. Everyone from Rupert Murdoch to John Boehner to anti-immigrant crusaders like Sean Hannity[19] endorsed the concept of passing an immigration-reform bill that looked exactly like the one they opposed a few years earlier. But when it became clear that making an appeal to Latino voters would anger their overwhelmingly white base, the Republicans flopped back. When Trump became president, nearly every Republican fell in line with his hard-line policies and inflammatory rhetoric. Not because they believed it, but because they thought it was good for the party politically.

Changing positions is not inherently bad—far from it. Politicians and political parties have "evolved" on issues since the beginning of time. And frankly, we should encourage politicians to revisit their long-held views as new facts emerge and social mores evolve. But that's not what the modern Republican Party has done. It has only one principle and that principle is winning.

Playing the game against people who will do anything to win while you adhere to the rules is a losing proposition. It has put Democrats at a decided disadvantage, especially when too many Democrats remain blind to who the Republicans are and why they do what they do.

Trump's election didn't turn the Republican Party into a nihilistic, win-at-all-costs, political-racketeering scheme. The fact that the Republican Party is a nihilistic, win-at-all-costs, political-racketeering scheme is what led to the election of Trump.

---

19 Hannity and everyone at Fox News have just erased this fact from the national consciousness, *Men in Black* style (the original, not the remake, which also needs to be erased from the national consciousness, *Men in Black* style).

DON'T BE A PALER SHADE OF ORANGE

Time feels like a flat circle in the Trump era. It's almost easy to forget that it wasn't that long ago that Obama was president, Trump was headed to an embarrassing defeat, and millions of Americans had champagne on ice to toast the election of the first woman president of the United States.

It is disorienting to think about where we are, how we got here, and how far we have come from the days of hope and change.[20]

As we are wont to do, Democrats have been in a continuous debate about how to respond to the assholery of Donald Trump and the radicalization of the Republican Party. The debate is never ending and rarely fruitful. It's half wishful thinking and half ax grinding about the 2016 primary.

Should we be Clintonian centrists[21] who can win over "swing voters"? Should we be economically populist and establishment-suspicious Bernie-crats? Obama-like hope meisters? Democratic Socialists? New Democrats? Old Democrats? Fighters? Lovers? Uniters? Dividers?

In the midst of this debate, the most dangerous strain of argument is that we should adopt the strategies of McConnell and Trump. Some argue that the only way to beat Trump is to be Trump. On one hand, you can see the appeal of this argument. Trump and the Republicans smash norms, break laws, and lie through their teeth with seemingly no consequences.

If Democrats keep doing the right thing and losing and Republicans do all the wrong things and win, why not emulate them? Is being able to sleep at night really worth anything if you are sleeping at night in an America ruled by rapacious billionaires on a

---

20 This is going to sound crazy, but units of time changed when Trump became president. Days feel like weeks, weeks feel like months, and so on. His tweets have somehow disrupted the space-time continuum.

21 Bill, not Hillary.

polluted, melting planet with women's health laws that make *The Handmaid's Tale* look like a romantic comedy?

Even if we could put morality and the capacity for shame aside, there is an even more fundamental problem with a paler shade of orange approach to politics: it won't work. The Democratic and Republican bases are very different.[22] They have different desires, different needs, and different fears. An approach that works for Republicans not only won't work for Democrats, but it will likely have the opposite effect. The Republican base responds to fear, and Democrats respond to hope. To win elections, we need to inspire nonvoters to become voters. To win elections, Republicans need to fire up their base while keeping everyone else from voting via cynicism and/or suppression. The most effective Republican strategy is to throw around so much mud that the bright lines of difference between the parties are blurred. Trump and the Republicans pursued this strategy with devastating efficacy in 2016. Somewhere down deep in his dark soul, Trump knows he can't convince people he is good, but he can convince people that his opponent is bad. By hammering Hillary Clinton about her ties to Wall Street, her secrecy, and the donors to the Clinton Foundation, Trump was able to convince enough people that he and Clinton were equally problematic. This led some potential Clinton voters to stay home, some to vote for third-party candidates, and some to take a flyer on Trump.

But we also have to acknowledge that a lot of what we have done hasn't worked. Democrats have won some elections—but not nearly enough. Democrats have accomplished a lot of policy goals—but not close to as many as we should. Republicans have racked up wins with long-term consequences for the Democratic Party and American democracy. To win this battle, we have to stop playing by an old set of rules. We have to adapt to a new

---

22 We are from Mars; they are from Sean Hannity's medulla oblongata.

type of politics that fuses the hopeful idealism of Barack Obama with the realism that comes from the knowledge that someone like Trump can become president of the United States. We have to match the Republicans not in cynicism, but in strategy and toughness. Like John F. Kennedy, Democrats need to become "idealists without illusions."

CHAPTER 3

THE CONFEDERACY OF DUNCES

Here's the story the Washington pundit class and the remnants of the Republican Party establishment would like you to believe:

Up until the day Donald Trump rode down the escalator at Trump Tower brandishing racist bromides and a fiery Twitter account, the Republican Party was a serious, governing institution that believed in lower taxes, less government, a strong national defense, and naming every airport, school, and building after Ronald Reagan. The Republicans were patriots who sincerely wanted what is best for the country. They were the mirror image of Democrats—an imperfect institution operating in good faith.

In this telling, the totally normal Republican Party was upended when Donald Trump executed a hostile but temporary takeover of the party. Once Trump returns to the private sector or becomes an involuntary guest of the federal penal system, the Republican Party we knew and pundits loved would return. The party of Reagan and Bush would again focus on their lifelong passions of making rich people richer and corporations freer to pollute and poison.

There's one problem with this story—it's complete and utter

bullshit. It misunderstands the moment we are in and the role the Republican Party played to pave the way for Trump.

People cling to this story—especially in the Trump era—because it's comforting. The idea that Trump hijacked an otherwise well-functioning and well-meaning political party means that this situation is temporary. People desperately want to believe that Trump is the exception, not the rule, when it comes to twenty-first-century Republicanism.

It's not just the pundits. This debate over who the Republicans are and where Trump came from has divided the Democratic Party. Unlike many of the issues Democrats fight over, this one matters . . . a lot. It's fundamentally a question about the health of our democracy and whether a return to normal is inevitable.

If you believe Trump is an accident of history, you can have an approach that is simply about waiting out the storm. If you believe that Trump is the logical extension of modern Republicanism, then you need a different, more aggressive approach to right the ship. It means that you have to embrace bolder, more radical responses to Trumpism.

Despite the wishful thinking emanating from some in Washington, the evidence is crystal clear. Trump didn't come out of nowhere. The Republican Party has been a force for racial division and anti-Democratic sentiment for decades—long before Trump arrived on the scene.

A BRIEF HISTORY OF REPUBLICAN RACISM

There is this tendency to romanticize the pre-Trump Republican Party on race issues as if Trump's racism falls far outside the tradition of the party of Lincoln. But the fact is that over the last fifty years, it's Lincoln who would be run out of the modern Republican Party. Trump fits right in.

In 1968, Richard Nixon won the White House by appealing to the "silent majority" and executing a Southern strategy that courted white voters angry about desegregation. During his 1980 campaign for president, Ronald Reagan gave a seminal speech on "states' rights" at the Neshoba County Fair, which is a stone's throw from the site of the notorious murder of three civil rights activists. "States' rights" in this location and context was code for "I'm on your side, white people."[1] George H. W. Bush, the prototypical genteel, country club Republican, was responsible for an ad against Michael Dukakis about a furloughed convict named Willie Horton that was so racist that all future racist ads would be described as Willie Horton–style ads.

George W. Bush ran as a kinder, gentler version of previous Republicans. His 2000 campaign platform was the nebulous and overly saccharine "Compassionate Conservatism." Bush went and spoke to the NAACP and talked about reforming schools to help children of color suffering the "soft bigotry of low expectations."[2] It's important to note that Bush wasn't actually trying to appeal to African Americans. Instead, he was trying to signal to white independent voters that he wasn't as racist as other Republicans. Bush won, and despite being the worst president in modern history,[3] he did have moderate views on immigration and pushed back against the strains of post-9/11 anti-Muslim bigotry that are now so dominant in the Republican Party. But before we give Bush the Nobel Prize for being less racist, we must remember that Bush won reelection in 2004 by running one of

---

1 Pig latin is a more complex code than the one Republicans use to appeal to racists.

2 The fact that this strategy worked shows that Republicans benefited from the low expectations for their bigotry.

3 As of the writing of this book, Trump had committed many crimes and embarrassed America on a near daily basis, but he had not (yet?) invaded a country under false pretenses with no plan, nor had he helped precipitate the worst financial crisis since the Great Depression.

the most explicitly bigoted campaigns in decades targeting the LGBTQ community by pushing an intentionally divisive constitutional amendment declaring that marriage must be between a man and a woman.

During the 2008 campaign, Republican vice presidential nominee and eventual national joke Sarah Palin accused Obama of being un-American and "palling around" with terrorists. A comment which of course had nothing to do with his race, his middle name, or the rampant smear campaign falsely alleging that Obama was a radical Muslim in the right wing media.

In fairness to Palin, she didn't invent this strategy. Mark Penn,[4] the chief strategist for Hillary Clinton's 2008 campaign, proposed a strategy of portraying Obama as "foreign" in the primary. In a memo to Clinton, Penn wrote, "I cannot imagine America electing a president during a time of war who is not at his center fundamentally American in his thinking and in his values." Clinton didn't adopt Penn's strategy, but the Republicans did.

As soon as Obama was elected, Republicans and their colleagues at Fox News began pushing racist conspiracy theories that Obama stole the election. One such theory said that Obama won due to voter fraud in the inner cities via a housing advocacy group named ACORN. Another suggested that Obama's campaign was helped by a militant group known as the New Black Panthers dispatched to scare white voters away from the polls, which was covered up by his African American attorney general. Much like the conspiracy theory that Obama was born in Kenya, these ideas were patently absurd but gained currency on the right—sparking calls for investigations from Republican members of Congress. In the racial backlash to the election of Obama, Republicans didn't see a moral crisis; they saw a political opportunity.

---

4 Mark Penn now defends Trump on Fox News, which makes complete sense.

Mitt Romney, Utah senator and the great hope of the #NeverTrump movement, won the 2012 Republican nomination by transforming himself into the sort of anti-immigrant crusader that would make Donald Trump proud. It's amusing in hindsight given how everything turned out, but there was a moment in that campaign when Rick Perry, the then Texas governor,[5] posed the biggest threat to Romney's status as Republican front-runner. Romney quickly dispensed with Perry by viciously attacking him for providing in-state tuition to children of undocumented immigrants. Once in the general election, Romney unsubtly and unsuccessfully tried to paint Obama as the president of the "47 percent of Americans" who don't pay taxes. Newt Gingrich, one of Romney's top surrogates, called Obama the "food-stamp president." You don't need to be a cryptographer to know what he meant.

And then there's Steve King, the Republican congressman from Iowa, who is an explicit white supremacist with a habit of retweeting known Nazis. In any other part of polite society, King would be shunned. If he were your uncle, he wouldn't get an invite to Thanksgiving dinner.[6] In the Republican Party, Steve King was not a pariah; he was the belle of the ball. Every Republican presidential candidate begged for his endorsement, gave to his campaigns, and former Speaker of the House Paul Ryan even made King the chair of the subcommittee on the Constitution.

Yes, the Republican Speaker of the House named a known white supremacist to oversee the Constitution. The Republicans eventually took away his committee seats, but they tossed him overboard not because of what he said. They just thought he

---

5 Perry would go from Texas governor to losing presidential candidate to *Dancing with the Stars* contestant to secretary of energy. This path seems weirdly logical in the Trump era.

6 You would also mute him on Facebook, where he almost certainly spends all his time.

might lose, so they went looking for a more subtle racist to support.

The history is clear. Trump didn't come out of nowhere. He fits right into the trajectory of the Republican Party, especially when you consider the backlash and radicalization along racial lines that resulted from the election of a black man named Barack Hussein Obama. An openly racist Republican president isn't an accident of history; it's a product of that history.

FROM THE DOG WHISTLE TO THE BULLHORN

The pre-Trump Republican Party tried to be subtle with their racism. And to be honest, it wasn't that subtle, but their goal was to send a signal to the racists without letting the nonracists know that they were, in fact, racist. This strategy was known as the "dog whistle"—a racist pitch so high that only racists could hear it. Perhaps the most infamous example occurred in the 1990 re-election campaign of North Carolina's Jesse Helms, a bombastic Republican senator whom legendary *Washington Post* columnist David Broder once called "the last prominent unabashed White racist politician in this country." Helms was in a very tight race against Harvey Gantt, the African American mayor of Charlotte, North Carolina. Late in that campaign, Helms ran a television ad that showed the hands of a white man crumpling a rejection letter that said, "You needed that job, and you were the best qualified. But they had to give it to a minority because of a racial quota. Is that really fair?" The ad then went on to say that Gantt supported racial quotas. There was very little that was subtle about the ad, and no one missed the point, but Helms and the Republicans claimed that it was issue based as opposed to race based—and most people in politics let him get away with it.

The theme that connects Reagan's "states' rights" speech and the demonization of Obama by Palin and Gingrich to Trump is a strategy that has been at the center of the Republican Party since the days of Nixon. Republican political success depends on making white people scared that nonwhite people will take their jobs, waste their taxpayer dollars, and commit crimes and terrorism in their community. They would never say this explicitly, but their goal was for a certain subsection of voters (racists) to infer it while others (nonracists) remained oblivious to it.

Trump changed all of that. From the first moments of his campaign, Trump said the quiet part out loud. He put away the dog whistle and brought out a bullhorn. He called immigrants from Mexico "rapists." He referred to an American judge of Mexican descent as "Mexican" who could not fairly rule in a case against Trump because of his ethnicity. A comment that even noted racism enabler Paul Ryan described as the "textbook definition of a racist comment." Trump proposed banning all Muslims from entering the country because of fears of terrorism. Trump's racist comments made many members of the dog whistle brigade uncomfortable—since they wanted to continue to have their racist cake and eat it, too.

Yet despite dire predictions from pundits and crocodile tears from the Republican establishment, Trump's explicit racism did not hamper his campaign to win the Republican nomination. In fact, it helped. He led the polls from wire to wire and won the nomination with relative ease. Trump's racist rhetoric was cheered by the Far Right of the party and its most prominent talking heads / blowhards—people like Rush Limbaugh, Sean Hannity, and Ann Coulter. Trump was celebrated by a segment of the population for refusing to be "politically correct."[7]

Trump's rhetoric worked because Republican leaders spent

7 Sadly, the segment of the population that cheers racism is a significant portion of the Republican base.

years standing silent as Fox News and right-wing radio fed the base racially divisive propaganda. If you remain silent when Newt Gingrich calls Obama the "food-stamp president" and when Steve King touts white nationalist ideology, then you have no standing to criticize Trump when he calls Mexicans rapists or suggests banning all Muslims from the country.[8]

Trump also knew he could get away with it. The clownish opportunism of Trump's birther crusade against Obama has been discussed to death, but the story is less what Trump said than what Republican leaders didn't say.

Prior to Trump, Democrats were very hesitant to use the r-word even in the face of obvious racism. People even tiptoed around it during the birther crusade. *Racist* was seen as some sort of third rail in politics. The Washington, DC, etiquette referees would throw the flag and say calling someone racist (even if they were obviously racist) was beyond the pale.[9] This notion was based on the dumb idea that racism is a binary choice between woke and white supremacist. If Democrats even walked up to the line of pointing out the racist ideology behind questioning Obama's birthplace or calling him the "food-stamp president," the Republicans would howl like a stuck pig. They would accuse the Democrats of playing the "race card." This brushback pitch almost always worked.

While Trump's obvious racism has given Democrats the permission to do the obvious thing and call it out, the Republicans have developed a different strategy. They just call Democrats racist, too. It's very similar to when Trump responded to Hillary Clinton's accusation in a debate that he was in the thrall of Putin by blurting out, "No, you're the puppet!" Trump loves to accuse Democrats of

---

8 These are things that really happened, and then Trump still got picked to lead the Republican Party.

9 This is still the standard of the *New York Times*.

being racist—taking things they say out of context or bringing up the pre–civil rights era of the Democratic Party. "I'm rubber; you're glue" isn't exactly clever, but neither is Trump.

THE SISTER SOUL-NAH MOMENT

During Bill Clinton's 1992 campaign, there was a moment that eventually became a staple of political commentary. Sister Souljah was a rapper who performed with the rap group Public Enemy. After the Los Angeles riots in 1992, she was quoted as saying, "If black people kill black people every day, why not have a week and kill white people?" She also once rapped that "if there are any good white people, I haven't met them." These remarks sparked a media firestorm despite the fact that Souljah was a fairly unknown figure.

Souljah and Clinton were scheduled to appear at a conference hosted by the Reverend Jesse Jackson's Rainbow Coalition. During his speech, Clinton made a point of explicitly criticizing Souljah. At the time, this was interpreted by the pundits (and pitched by the Clinton campaign) as a sign of Clinton's willingness to stand up to the more extreme members in one's party. The political analysis then and now was wrong: Clinton's "Sister Souljah moment" was actually an act of immense cynicism and political cowardice playing to the stereotypes of African Americans perpetrated by conservatives. But nonetheless, the Sister Souljah moment became something to which politicians were supposed to aspire. Ever since, candidates have tried to manufacture opportunities where they take a shot at an extreme figure in their party to prove their mainstream appeal.[10]

Either way, there has never been an easier or more obvious

---

10 It's a pretty simplistic and stupid element of political commentary, but much of political commentary is simplistic and stupid.

opportunity to attempt Clinton's trick than Donald Trump's birther crusade in 2011. In an effort to promote his reality TV show—*The Celebrity Apprentice*—Trump was all over the airwaves promoting the absurd conspiracy theory that Obama was an illegitimate president because he was secretly born in Kenya.[11] Trump quickly realized that spouting this racist dreck got him more press attention[12] and the undying affection of a segment (i.e., majority) of the Republican Party.[13] Certainly, some people believed Trump—polls repeatedly show that a dangerous number of Republicans still think Obama wasn't born in the United States—but many were just as excited that someone was unabashedly giving it to Obama.

Inside the White House at the time, we kept waiting for the Republicans to "Sister Souljah" Trump. It was such obvious low-hanging fruit. Trump wasn't some revered Republican figure; he was a clown. A man famous for being famous whose primary job was selling schlocky goods and starring in an absurd reality show where he would reward a B-list[14] celebrity with a fake job. You literally couldn't ask for an easier opportunity to show the broader electorate that your party wasn't defined by the racist buffoon with the comb-over.

But the Sister Souljah moment never came. No one said anything. The Republican leadership refused to take on Trump. They never stood up to Trump. They never stood up to the parts of the base that continued to push the racist conspiracy theories about Obama. They clearly made a decision that being seen as racist was better politics than condemning racism.

Obama eventually gave into the absurd demands of the moment and released his birth certificate. Trump was literally laughed off

---

11 He wasn't.
12 Which is his oxygen.
13 We'll call them the racist brigade.
14 "B-list" is super generous.

the national stage as he became the butt of every joke at the White House Correspondents' Association dinner that year. At the time, Trump was contemplating a run for the Republican nomination and was leading in early polls. Obama's counterpunch knocked him out of the race and off the political scene. But Trump wasn't gone for long.

There is an alternative universe where the Republicans speak out against birtherism and declare that there is no place in the Republican Party for the purveyors of racist conspiracy theories. Trump is shunned by the party and shunted off to the sidelines of American politics. In this timeline, the Republican Party bets on selling tolerance instead of weaponizing intolerance.

Alas, that wasn't to be. Within a few months of Trump's public humiliation, every Republican presidential candidate made a perverse pilgrimage to Trump Tower to beg for his endorsement. In a pattern that is now sadly familiar to the country, Trump turned the whole thing into a reality show.[15]

Mitt Romney eventually won the racist rose in this sordid episode of political *Bachelor*. The Republican front-runner flew to Las Vegas to receive Trump's endorsement among much fanfare. A patrician Republican from Massachusetts embracing[16] Trump sent an unmistakable message that would echo for years—the most extreme views were welcome within the Republican Party, and there was no penalty for spouting racist conspiracy theories.

The truth that no Republican wants to admit is that Trump's racist birther crusade made his endorsement in the primary more valuable, not less.

---

15 It's pretty telling that the endorsement of a racist reality TV star who regularly went on Howard Stern's show to detail his sexual and extramarital exploits was seen as a boost among Republican voters.

16 They didn't actually embrace, because Trump is a germophobe and Romney is very awkward.

WHY-TE

The history of the modern Republican Party is clear. Trump didn't make the Republican Party comfortable with racism. The Republican Party's comfort with racism made them comfortable with Trump.

None of this is to say that all or even most Republican voters are racist. A shocking number of Trump supporters voted for Obama twice. The reasons why people choose a particular candidate are incredibly complicated and personal. Maybe this is naivete on my part, but I think a lot of people voted for Trump despite his racist statements. But it's also true that choosing a racist despite their racism is the deranged epitome of white privilege.

But Trump's ascension to the presidency has represented a change in strategy for the Republican Party. The racist rhetoric went from subtext to urtext. There were more Republican politicians and commentators willing to openly embrace a white nationalist message. Anti-immigration policies became the central issue for the party. None of these things is an accident. There is an underlying political logic to this approach.

The electorate is getting less white every year, which means that the Republican Party's success depends on getting a higher and higher percentage of the white vote—specifically white men without a college degree. And those white voters are getting more conservative—driven by the fear of a "changing" America that barely resembles the country that they grew up in. This fear has been fueled by the racism-for-profit operation at Fox News.

During the 2008 campaign, there was much consternation both inside and outside the Obama campaign over the electability of an African American president. A lot of the questions about Obama's electability were implicitly about the fundamental question of whether a black man—not to mention one with the middle name Hussein with a father from Kenya—could win enough support from white voters in an electorate where three of four voters were white. Since the first forty-three presidents were all white men, the election of an African American was an untested proposition. Pundits speculated endlessly about what would happen when people went into the voting booth. There were thousands of stories about the "Bradley effect." In the 1982 election for the governor of California, Tom Bradley—the African American mayor of Los Angeles—was leading in the polls against a white Republican.

Despite the polls, Bradley lost because he did less well with white voters than the polls indicated. Analysts hypothesized that some number of white voters told pollsters they would support Bradley to be politically correct even though they had no intention of voting for him. The Bradley effect is likely bullshit and the result of the usual margin of error in polling, but in 2008 it was still a central point of discussion whenever an African American candidate was on the ballot.

The concern permeated our campaign to the point that some advisor argued that it would be a mistake for Obama to reference Martin Luther King in his address to the Democratic National Convention, even though he would be delivering it on the anniversary of King's "I Have a Dream" speech.[17]

An irrational fear of the Bradley effect kept me up at night in the final weeks of that campaign. On Election Day 2008, I was in the "boiler room," which is the room where the campaign leadership sits on Election Day to monitor voter turnout, look out for voting problems, and mostly just freak out about what is happening. Every few hours, we would get turnout reports across the country. Election observers would track the number of people voting in blue and red precincts to see if we were meeting our goals in the right places. In the first report of the morning,

---

17 Obama wisely dismissed this advice after Jon Favreau almost threw his laptop at said advisors for suggesting something so stupid.

things were going well everywhere—except the must-win state of Pennsylvania.

I muttered "fuck" a little too loudly when the report came in. David Plouffe, our campaign manager, and others in the room glared at me. I might have said it, but I knew they were thinking it. All of us were immediately concerned that the Bradley effect that had haunted our dreams was real. Pennsylvania, where I lived for a while as a kid, seemed ripe for a white backlash to a black candidate. Urban population centers with a diverse electorate surrounded by vast rural and exurban areas that were lily-white. If it was going to happen anywhere, Pennsylvania would be it.

As it turns out, it was simply a data error, and Obama was doing just fine in Pennsylvania. He went on to win the state, and there was no "Bradley effect."

According to exit polls, Barack Obama actually did better with white voters than John Kerry,[18] the Democratic nominee, did four years prior.

Four years later, after massive economic tumult, the passage of an important but controversial health-care law, and a ton of racial demagoguery, Obama was reelected by a large margin, but the numbers looked very different. Only 39 percent of white voters supported Obama—two points worse than Kerry did in 2004. Obama still won a huge electoral victory, because the percent of overall voters that were white dropped from 77 percent in 2004 to 72 percent in 2012. Five percent doesn't sound like a lot, but it is a massive shift when you consider that African Americans are voting for Democrats at a rate of nine to one, and Latinos and Asian Americans vote for Democrats at about a two-to-one margin.

There was a particular group that had moved against Obama—

---

18 Who is in fact white.

whites without a college degree. Obama received only 34 percent of the vote from this group, which was notable because he was running against a plutocratic private-equity executive who had proclaimed on the campaign trail that he "liked firing people." Romney looked, acted, and talked like the embodiment of everything that was wrong with the American economy.

The results of the 2012 election gave the Republicans two paths to reclaiming the White House.

Option one: broaden their appeal to nonwhite voters and young voters. This path would help in the short and long term. A Republican strategy to improve their standing with Hispanic voters would open up more paths to the 270 votes required to win the White House. States like Colorado, Nevada, and New Mexico are suddenly in play, and the Republicans would no longer need to run the table in the industrial Midwest to win. This approach would also prevent Democrats from turning Texas blue, which would be Electoral College checkmate.

Option two: double down on white voters by making more explicit racial appeals because non-college-educated white voters are overrepresented in congressional elections where gerrymandered House districts dilute the political power of people of color, and in the Senate where sparsely populated, rural, mostly white states like Idaho have as much power as populous, diverse states like California.

After Obama was reelected, I thought the Republicans were headed down the first path. Republican Speaker John Boehner quickly announced that "Obamacare was now the law of the land." This was important because Republican support for repealing the Affordable Care Act was one of the more potent attacks that helped drive Latino voters to overwhelmingly support Obama's reelection. Republicans from Rupert Murdoch to Marco Rubio to Lindsey Graham came out in favor of comprehensive immigration reform. Republican National

Committee chair Reince Priebus[19] conducted an autopsy report on the 2012 election results that argued that the best path for the party was to broaden their appeal to people of color, women, and young people. Not long after, the Senate passed an immigration bill with the support of sixty-eight senators. It seemed like the race-based Obama Wars could be coming to an end. The Republicans had learned their lesson.

Nope.

Four years later, Donald Trump became president by sweeping the "Rust Belt" Midwest, flipping the states of Wisconsin, Ohio, Pennsylvania, Iowa, and Michigan. All of which Obama had won twice with some measure of ease. Trump didn't improve on Romney's margin with Latinos and African Americans, but he did jack up turnout among white voters in rural and exurban areas. This was not a landslide by any stretch of the imagination: Trump lost the popular vote by three million votes and won the Electoral College by fewer than eighty thousand votes spread over three states. In many ways, Trump is an accidental president. He was aided by Russian hacking, poor Democratic cybersecurity, James Comey's infatuation with his own reputation, Republican voter suppression, cable television's thirst for ratings, Facebook's general terribleness, and Hillary Clinton's aversion to visiting Wisconsin in the fall.[20]

But his victory shocked the nation and the political system, and it made the Republican Party the party of white voters.

A lot of people in the GOP—the Never Trumpers who advocated a more inclusive path—hoped that Trump's loss would knock some sense into the rest of the party. A third consecutive loss would be the evidence they needed to push the party toward

---

19 Priebus would go on to become Trump's chief of staff until he was fired by tweet.

20 Just to name a few extenuating circumstances. Also, Hillary Clinton not visiting Wisconsin is not why she lost.

a more inclusive, future-oriented path. Trump's victory settled the debate. They would become a white nationalist party.

In 2019, Texas Republican senator John Cornyn tweeted an article from the *Texas Tribune* about new census data. Cornyn pulled out the part of the article that he found most compelling: "Texas gained almost nine Hispanic residents for every additional white resident last year."

There was zero subtlety about this tweet. Cornyn's message was clear: white people should be very scared about a changing America. He isn't some fringe Republican like Steve King. Cornyn is a party leader who would be on the short list to replace Mitch McConnell, were the current majority leader to ever retire or be exposed to sunlight for too long. The tweet was rightly decried as racist. Cornyn didn't even bother to defend himself—protecting white Americans from scary nonwhite people was now the explicit message of the Republican Party.

It is, however, important to understand Cornyn's tweet as more than a message to fire up the base in a coming election. It is the Rosetta stone to understanding the Republican Party strategy of the last decade. For the foreseeable future, the Republican strategy will be to win elections by appealing to white voters and white voters only.

This is a scary proposition. Every year, the American electorate is getting more diverse, which means that Republicans need to get more and more votes from a dwindling white base. This means the rhetoric is going to get more inflammatory. The appeals are going to be more explicit. This will threaten to tear apart the moral fabric of the country, ripping American democracy apart at the seams.

CHAPTER 4

THE REPUBLICAN PLOT AGAINST AMERICA

While the rest of us have been fretting about Trump's tweets, reading the latest tell-all from disgruntled C-list White House staffers, and arguing about whether Trump is a dictator or just a dick, the Republicans have been systematically rigging American democracy. They have been diluting the power of the majority of Americans and trying to install minority rule in this country. More than Jim Comey, or even Russia, this is why Trump won.

It's happening right before our eyes, but per usual in politics in the twenty-first century, the media, the pundits, and a disturbing number of Democratic politicians are all focused on the wrong things.

The first step to fixing our democracy is understanding the steps that Republicans have taken in Congress and in the states to hold on to power long after their voters become a distinct political minority. You can't win the game if you don't know how the game is rigged. Here is the Republican plan for minority rule.

STEP ONE: STOP PEOPLE FROM VOTING

Heading into Election Day 2008, the Republicans knew they were probably going to lose. We had heard reports that some of the staff on the McCain-Palin campaign were spending the last weeks of the race updating their résumés and leaving early to go to happy hour.

While the fact of Obama's victory wasn't surprising,[1] the size of the victory shocked the Republican Party. Obama crushed McCain all across the country and especially in the so-called battleground states that decide presidential elections: Obama won Wisconsin by fourteen points, Iowa by nine points, Pennsylvania by eleven points, and Michigan by a whopping sixteen points. He flipped Ohio and Florida, which were the states that delivered the election to Bush four years prior. But the scariest part for the Republicans was that Obama won previously deep-red states like Virginia, Indiana, and North Carolina that no one thought a Democrat could compete in, let alone win.

Many of these battleground states allowed what is called "early voting," where voters are allowed to come to a designated location to cast their vote well in advance of Election Day.

Voting is hard. It takes time. And a lot of Americans don't do it because they are simply too busy with work and family.[2] Early voting policies are a pretty commonsense, theoretically noncontroversial solution to the problem of low turnout. The Obama campaign saw an opportunity in these policies. Our victory depended on getting large numbers of new and less-frequent voters to the polls. Typically, campaigns have one day to bug the shit out of people to vote. There is a high margin for error

1 It should have been. Obama just a few years removed from the Illinois State Senate beating the one-time most popular politician in America is an upset for the ages.

2 And too many politicians don't give them a reason to. Or pass laws preventing them from doing it.

when you have maybe twelve hours to remind someone to vote, tell them where to vote, and make sure they know how to get there. It's much easier and more effective to have weeks to accomplish the same task. The Obama campaign would organize rallies within walking distance of early voting sites. After Obama was done speaking, the campaign staff would march the attendees over to vote early. Our campaign research told us that the more people heard about early voting, the more likely they were to do it. So, we talked about it all the time. I was the communications director on that campaign, and we developed a strategy to pitch as many stories as possible about our early voting strategy. Ohio, Florida, and some other states had a tradition known as "Souls to the Polls." On the final Sunday of early voting, African American churches would organize an effort to get people to go directly from church to the polls. "Souls to the Polls" Sunday is often the day with the highest turnout among African American voters. Maximizing turnout on these days was a huge priority for the campaign.

This strategy was remarkably effective. According to a study by the Pew Foundation, early voting in 2008 increased by 14 percent over the previous election. There was a particular increase in African American voting. According to the ACLU, 70 percent of African American voters in North Carolina voted early as part of an overall increase in African American turnout of more than 6 percent.

Beyond using early voting to increase turnout among existing voters, registering new voters was another key to victory. From the very early days of the campaign when we were plotting how Barack Obama could possibly win, we came to one very sobering conclusion. If the same people who voted in 2004 voted in 2008, we would almost certainly lose. The only way to win was to increase the size of the electorate. This sounds obvious, but it was an audacious idea at the time. Registering voters is hard, expensive, and inefficient. This is why most campaigns spend most of their time fighting over the limited pool of certain voters.[3] But Barack Obama didn't have a choice.

Guess what?

Getting as many people to vote as possible is a great strategy for winning elections.[4] In the wake of this "revelation," the Republicans had four years to figure out how to do the same thing—register new Republican voters and use early voting to turn out more existing Republican voters.

Did they do that?[5] Obviously not.

Instead of trying to figure out how to get more Republicans to vote, the Republicans decided to figure out how to get fewer Democrats to vote.

In 2008, Michigan, Iowa, Pennsylvania, Ohio, and Wisconsin had Democratic governors. In 2010, all of those Democrats were replaced by Republicans. The new Republican governors immediately passed a series of laws to make it harder to vote. While Republicans cut or eliminated early voting and made it harder to register people to vote, voter identification laws were the centerpiece of their strategy to wrest power from the public.

On its face, voter ID laws seem harmless—you need to show an ID to get in a bar and to buy cold medicine. The evil genius of these laws is that they sound so harmless that too many Democrats are afraid to make the argument[6] against them. They are not harmless. They are quite effective at keeping the people most likely to vote Democratic from voting.

---

3 In other words, older, white voters.
4 Reminder: politics is not that complicated, and it's in the economic interest of the pundits and consultants to make you believe you need a guru on an expensive retainer to understand it.
5 If you have made it this far in the book, you know it's a rhetorical question.
6 To paraphrase Wayne Gretzky via Kobe Bryant: you lose 100 percent of the arguments you don't make.

Here are some facts:[7]

- A Loyola Law School study found only thirty-one credible allegations of in-person voter fraud—the "problem" voter ID is supposed to address—from 2000 to 2014 out of more than one billion votes cast.[8]
- According to the Brennan Center for Justice, 25 percent of African Americans don't have a government-issued ID. Only 8 percent of whites don't have an ID.
- Getting an identification card is prohibitively expensive for a lot of voters. One study cited by the ACLU found that obtaining an ID can cost between $75 and $175.

If you aren't persuaded by facts, the Republican architects of these laws are more than happy to admit the truth. *Washington Post* reporter Aaron Blake very helpfully collected a number of these examples in a 2016 article:[9]

- Republican congressman Glenn Grothman argued that a Republican would be able to win Wisconsin in 2016 because "now we have photo ID, and I think photo ID is going to make a little bit of a difference as well."
- In 2012, the Republican leader of the Pennsylvania State House listed a newly passed voter ID law among his accomplishments by saying, "Voter ID, which is going to allow Governor Romney to win the state of Pennsylvania."[10]
- The chair of the Pennsylvania Republican Party specifically credited their law with improving Republicans' election perfor-

---

7 That is, talking points to use with your racist, MAGA-loving uncle.
8 Yes, that's "billion" with a "b."
9 In part because they are honestly too dumb to know why they shouldn't. These yahoos have probably ruined every surprise party they have ever been invited to.
10 It didn't, but the state was closer because of it.

> mance by saying, "We probably had a better election. Think about this: We cut Obama by 5 percent, which was big. A lot of people lost sight of that. He beat McCain by 10 percent; he only beat Romney by 5 percent. And I think that probably photo ID helped a bit in that."

And here's an amazing fact that reveals the truth about these laws. The state of Texas, which generally has the same affection for democracy as North Korea, accepts concealed carry permits for voting, but not student IDs. Hmm, I wonder which party that policy helps?

If the Republicans can't win your vote, they will take your vote. This effort followed in the tradition of the Jim Crow policies put in place after Reconstruction to prevent newly freed slaves from having any political power.[11]

These laws are costing Democrats elections and helping Republicans maintain power despite appealing to fewer and fewer voters. According to one study, Wisconsin's voter ID law potentially suppressed 200,000 votes.

Donald Trump won that state by 22,700 votes.

Seems like a problem.

STEP TWO: GERRYMANDER

Here's a little riddle:

The Republicans won the popular vote in the 2010 elections for the House of Representatives by about seven points and picked up sixty-three House seats.

If in 2018 the Democrats won the popular vote by eight points, how many seats did they pick up?

---

11 What's old is new (and racist) again.

More than sixty-three, right? More votes should mean more seats, right? Seems like a pretty basic principle of democracy.

Nope. The Democrats picked up only forty seats.

This is not some freak accident. It's by devious design. It's a direct result of the Republican Party using the redistricting process to hold on to more power with fewer votes.

A quick briefing on redistricting:

Not all elections have equal results. Every ten years, congressional and state legislative districts are redrawn based on the results of the most recent census. States have different ways of accomplishing this task, but many of them allow the politicians in power at the time to draw the district lines as they see fit. The politicians who happen to have this power also happen to frequently draw the districts in ways that help deliver more political power to the party they happen to be a member of. Redrawing the districts in absurd ways to favor one political party is known as gerrymandering.[12]

In 2011, the Republicans used the power they had to gerrymander the hell out of the congressional map, locking in a congressional majority. The Republicans saw their opportunity and seized it—the Republican committee that elects state legislators outspent its Democratic counterpart three to one in 2010.

It worked like a charm—in 2012, the Democrats won more votes in House races but only picked up a meager eight seats.

The state of Wisconsin has been ground zero in all of the Republicans' antidemocratic efforts, from voter suppression to gerrymandering to union busting to outright power grabs. The Democrats won every statewide election in 2018—some by wide margins—yet the Republicans still won sixty-three of

12 It's a long story about a Massachusetts governor and a salamander, but that's what Wikipedia is for.

ninety-nine state assembly seats and eleven of seventeen state senate seats. The goal of gerrymandering to this degree is not just to make your vote count less; it's to make you know your vote doesn't count in the hope that you won't vote again. Because why put in the effort if it doesn't matter anyway? Cynicism is the ally of conservatism.

In North Carolina, the Republicans just happened to draw a district line right through the middle of North Carolina A&T, the state's largest historically black university. In public and in court, the Republicans argued that their plans had nothing to do with race. This claim was absurd on its face but was eventually proven to be a bald-faced lie. In North Carolina and elsewhere, the Republican Party was advised by Thomas Hofeller, a Republican operative known as the "master of the modern gerrymander."[13] After Mr. Hofeller's death, his estate became ensnared in a legal battle. Throughout the course of that case, seventy thousand files from his computer were made public and painted a vivid picture of Republican efforts to rig democracy.

Hofeller had conducted intense studies of the racial makeup of college students in North Carolina. The files also revealed that Hofeller may have illegally helped Florida Republicans redraw their district lines. He was also the brains behind the failed Trump administration effort to add a citizenship question to the 2020 census because it would "be advantageous to Republicans and non-Hispanic whites."

The Hofeller files should forever put to rest the notion that the Republican gerrymandering efforts are about anything other than taking political power from people of color to help Republicans win elections.

Democrats had some success over the years challenging the constitutionality of these gerrymandering schemes in courts. Since the

---

13 Seems like a flag.

1960s, the Supreme Court had upheld the standard of "one person, one vote," which held that representation had to be proportional. Overly partisan districts were periodically struck down. The antidemocratic wing of the Republican Party found this annoying, so they fixed it. In 2019, the conservative Supreme Court decided that democracy wasn't that important. In a five-to-four decision, the Supreme Court discarded the "one person, one vote" standard and ruled that gerrymandering was an issue for voters to decide, not the courts. In other words, the Supreme Court said if you don't like gerrymandering, vote out the people doing the gerrymandering—except you can't vote them out because of (yes, you guessed it) gerrymandering. Apparently, Harvard Law doesn't require a course in common sense for a law degree.

Heads, Republicans win; tails, Democrats lose.

What a country!

STEP THREE: PUTTING A FOR SALE SIGN ON DEMOCRACY

One day in January 2010, I was sitting in the Roosevelt Room in the White House in one of a series of interminable meetings about the upcoming State of the Union speech. Lauren, my assistant, came in to hand me a note.

"Go to the counsel's office."

Generally, this is a note that you don't want to receive. Nothing good ever happens in the counsel's office, but I wasn't worried. My schedule in the White House would often be twelve hours of straight meetings, and Lauren would sometimes come spring me from meetings so I could actually get some work done.[14] I presumed that's what this was.

---

14 She would also spring me from meetings so that I would eat, because I become an even bigger pain in the ass when hungry. This is a trait I

I walked out of the meeting and across the hall to the suite of offices[15] where I worked and sat down at my desk to plow through the backlog of emails. After a while, Lauren returned to her desk.

"What are you doing here?" she asked.

"What do you mean 'What am I doing here?'" I replied without looking up from my computer.

"You're supposed to be in Bauer's office," she said with more than a hint of exasperation, referring to Bob Bauer, the White House counsel.

"Oh shit." I gathered my stuff and ran to Bob's office upstairs. I walked in midmeeting. Gathered around the wood-paneled office[16] were David Axelrod, Obama's senior advisor and political strategist; Jim Messina, the deputy chief of staff and campaign manager in waiting; and Patrick Gaspard, the White House political director. It looked more like a funeral than a meeting.

"What's up, guys? Everything okay?" I asked.

"The Supreme Court ruled for the plaintiffs in the *Citizens United* case," Bauer said.

"That's the case people said we couldn't lose, right?[17] What does this mean?"

"It means we're fucked,"[18] muttered one of the attendees.

Bauer went on to explain that corporations and other groups were now going to be able to spend unlimited amounts of

---

share with my wife. I tell people that if anyone ever finds us dead together, check the contents of our stomachs. If they are empty, you can assume it was a murder-suicide situation.

15 "Suite of offices" greatly overstates the case for where I worked. More like a "coterie of closets with desks," but I digress. The White House is glamorous, and I am not complaining.

16 The counsel's office in the West Wing looks like every office in every commercial for a personal injury attorney on cable television.

17 Never believe anything anyone tells you "can't happen." A lesson I wish I had learned before the 2016 election.

18 This turned out to be quite the understatement.

money on campaigns. Democrats, who generally didn't have the support of corporations or most ultra-wealthy people, were going to get massively outspent in the upcoming congressional election.

The group arrayed around the office had decades of experience running campaigns and were all doing the math in their heads.

Obama's reelection was about to get much harder...and much more expensive.

The prediction that we would be fucked turned out to be accurate. The *Citizens United* ruling caused a flood of political spending from moneyed interests. According to the Center for Responsive Politics, outside groups spent approximately $70 million during the last midterm election before the *Citizens United* decision. In 2010, the first midterm election since the decision, outside spending increased to more than $300 million. Democratic candidates were washed away in a wave of money. The outside spending allowed the Republicans to put a lot more races in play, and the Democrats were simply unable to keep up. *Citizens United* helped turn a tough election for Democrats into a historic ass whipping.

In 2012, Republicans outspent the Obama reelection campaign. Obama was able to raise more money than Romney, but the Republican-affiliated groups unleashed by the new law outspent their Democratic counterparts $418 million to $130 million.

Thanks to *Citizens United*, the problem of money in politics is getting much worse. More than $90 million was spent by outside groups in the 2018 Florida senate race, which helped the Republicans flip a senate seat in an otherwise Democratic year. Florida is a big state, but that is an absurd amount of money.

Thanks to *Citizens United*, the Republican Party is a wholly owned subsidiary of the Koch brothers—the Kansas-based oil executives and billionaires who spend hundreds of millions of dollars every election to elect Republicans up and down the ballot. If you have ever wondered why Republicans pretend to believe climate change isn't real, it's because they live in fear that the Koch brothers—who profit off opposition to climate change—will drop a million bucks on behalf of a primary opponent more willing to walk the company line. The voices of millions of voters are being drowned out by a new Republican-supported campaign finance system that makes candidates dependent on billionaires to get their message out. But it's also bad for Democrats: there are simply more Republican billionaires willing to spend more of their billions to win elections. It takes a hundred thousand Democrats donating $10 to match one Republican writing one $1 million check.[19]

Advantage Republicans.

STEP FOUR: RIGGING THE COURTS

The Republicans have taken steps to prevent you from voting, worked to make your vote count less if you do vote, and empowered billionaires to buy elections. But what if all those things fail and Democrats still win?[20]

Don't worry—the Republicans have a plan for that.

The courts.

Conservative control of the Supreme Court is the Republican break-glass plan so that they can block progressive policies no matter what the voters want.

Imagine this scenario: A Democratic House and Senate pass a

19 MATH!

20 Don't forget Democrats were less than a hundred thousand votes from winning the White House in 2016.

new Voting Rights Act that protects against voter suppression and gerrymandering. A newly elected Democratic president signs that bill hailing a return to more representative democracy in America. A Republican governor sues, and the case winds its way through the court system, landing in the Supreme Court. The Supreme Court strikes down the law in a five-to-four opinion authored by Justice Brett Kavanaugh.

Ouch. Democrats do everything right and still lose.

Republicans in general and Mitch McConnell in particular have always known that there is nothing more important than shaping the courts. It's why they have gone to unprecedented extremes to get their judges confirmed and to prevent Democratic appointed judges from being confirmed.

This strategy has already borne an unbelievable amount of conservative fruit that has consolidated Republican power. The court has

- struck down the Voting Rights Act, allowing for more voter suppression and gerrymandering;[21]
- gutted campaign finance laws, paving the way for greater spending by Republican-aligned special interests;
- eliminated portions of the Affordable Care Act, denying life-saving health care to millions and making it easier for Republicans to run against the law; and
- overturned some of Obama's efforts to deal with immigration, climate change, clean air, corporate greed, and Wall Street excess—all of which just happen to be a boon to the corporations that fund the Republican Party.

The courts are a real problem for progressives that has gotten ex-

21 Gutting the VRA is one of the most underrated, fucked-up things that has happened this century.

ponentially worse during the Trump era. The Republican plan to hijack the courts is a long time in the making.

The Republicans built a farm system of right-wing lawyers who are groomed for the bench starting as early as law school. This is basically the East German athletics model but for right-wing judges.

The Federalist Society is an organization of conservative lawyers that was founded in the early '80s. Its origin story is filled with a who's who of destructive conservative figures. Two of the Federalist Society's first advisors were Robert Bork and Antonin Scalia.[22] The Koch brothers provided some of the early money. The whole effort was about more than creating a safe space for right-wing lawyers to swap theories of originalism over scotch; it was about pushing conservative[23] legal philosophy at every opportunity and moving the entire legal system to the right.

Membership in the Federalist Society became table stakes for any aspiring Republican attorney with eyes on a prestigious clerkship, a job at the Department of Justice, or a conservative law firm. When one of these conservative whippersnappers gained notice as a potential star, the Federalist Society sprung into action. The network helped these young Scalias-in-training work their way up the conservative legal ladder to ensure they had the necessary experience and credentials at a young age to be considered for the bench. Getting people ready for the bench at a young age was a crucial part of the strategy, since federal judicial appointments are lifetime appointments. With every passing year, the Federalist Society got more powerful.

When George W. Bush was president, every single judicial appointment was either a member of the Federalist Society or

---

22 Was Roger Ailes busy?
23 Republican.

approved by the Federalist Society. When Trump was running for president in 2016, he assuaged conservative concerns about his judicial appointments by releasing a list of people he would consider for the Supreme Court. He basically cut and pasted a list sent to him by the Federalist Society. Once Trump won the White House, he outsourced the process for picking and confirming judges—including two Supreme Court justices—to the Federalist Society.

The second part of the plan is to make sure Democratic presidents get to confirm as few judges as possible. When Obama was president, Mitch McConnell and the Senate Republicans did everything in their power to gum up the works and slow down judicial confirmations. In Obama's first term, Republicans used legislative maneuvers to slow down the confirmation of Obama's appointments. The Republicans would filibuster even non-controversial nominations, which would demand sixty votes, and extend the amount of time spent on each confirmation. The delay process was very effective because the Senate works on a schedule that sloths would consider lazy.

The Republicans also abused something called the "blue slip" procedure, which gives senators an informal veto on judicial nominations for seats in their state. The idea behind this archaic concept of legislative etiquette is that senators may know the most about a nominee from their state and therefore their voice should be worth more than 1/100th of the total voters. For decades, senators mostly played by the rules and only failed to return blue slips in extenuating circumstances. This behavioral norm changed—as these things seem to do—when Barack Obama became president. Republican abuse of the blue slip process meant numerous nominations were stuck in perpetual limbo.

In 2013, the Senate Democrats, fed up with unprecedented levels of Republican obstruction, made the wise decision to eliminate the filibuster for judicial appointment. For a brief period, Obama was able to get judges confirmed, including several key appointments to the DC Circuit Court of Appeals, which is the second most important court in the land. However, this return to constitutional governance was brief. The Republicans won the Senate in 2014 and ground the process to a halt. Thanks to McConnell's norm-shattering approach, Obama left office with more than one hundred vacancies, including a Supreme Court seat that, if filled, would have tipped the court in a liberal direction.

EMBRACE THE FEAR

If I just scared the shit out of you, good. That was the point. We should be very scared about the situation in which we find ourselves.

While Democrats spend our time passing the best policy regardless of politics, the Republicans have spent years rigging the game to hold on to political power. If there is one thing I took away from my time working in the White House, it is that winning the next presidential election is not enough. Don't get me wrong—presidents have tremendous power,[24] and there is no better place to positively impact people's lives than the White House. But presidencies are term limited, and therefore their impact is time limited.

For all the justified harrumphing about Trump's authoritarian leanings, the challenges to our democracy began long before he showed up and will be around long after he leaves. American democracy, which has never been perfect, is now being corrupted. Our politics have been rigged in favor of conservative billion-

---

24 Probably too much power.

aires. Democrats won't be able to advance their agenda until we recognize that fact and start doing something about it.

The next Democratic president will be governing with one hand tied behind his or her back if the party does not engage in an aggressive, comprehensive strategy to unrig the game and "Make America a democracy again."

But all of this is moot, if we don't win in 2020.

PART TWO

HOW TO UN-TRUMP AMERICA

CHAPTER 5

OPERATION 2020

To: The Democratic Nominee
From: Me
Re: Unsolicited Advice

Congratulations on your hard-fought victory. You came out on top in the largest, most talented field in Democratic primary history. It's quite an achievement. You should be proud.

Great. Now get to work.

During the seemingly endless 2008 primary campaign, someone told me that winning the nomination in a presidential campaign was like winning a pie-eating contest and being rewarded with more pie. If you think you are tired now, wait till the general. The only people who get to sleep on presidential campaigns are the people who lose presidential campaigns.

First, the bad news.

This campaign is going to be really hard:

- Incumbent presidents rarely lose. It's happened three times since 1972, and there were somewhat extenuating circumstances in all those cases.
- Trump has a massive head start. While you were eating pork

tenderloins in Iowa and ice-cream cones in New Hampshire, the Trump campaign spent enough money on Facebook ads to buy Mark Zuckerberg several seats on Elon Musk's space plane.

- Every Republican billionaire is going to be highly motivated to spend money to protect their tax cuts. Every super PAC will have more money than they need. It's certain that you will be massively[1] outspent.
- Trump and the Republicans will fight dirty as hell. Voter suppression, voter intimidation, politicized criminal investigations, weaponization of the entire federal government, and another round of Russian hacking.[2]

So, it's not going to be easy. And not to put too much pressure on you, but the fate of American democracy and the health of the planet are on the line.[3]

Presidential campaigns take place on the shifting sands of real-time events of which you have no control. In 2004, Osama bin Laden released an audiotape threatening America the weekend before the election, perhaps tipping the election to Bush. Barack Obama's 2008 campaign was upended six weeks before the election by the collapse of the American financial sector. In 2016, Hillary Clinton suffered through a series of "October surprises," not the least of which included the FBI director kinda, sorta, but not really reopening a criminal investigation into her email protocol. The point is not to scare you (although I hope you're scared) but to say that there will be a lot of things out of your

1 *Massively* is a grand understatement. Think Yankees and Tampa Bay.
2 Trump already committed multiple impeachable offenses to try to get Ukraine to interfere in the election, and those are the only ones we know about...
3 Think of this like the movie *Space Jam*: One game is going to decide the fate of the world, and we picked you to play—so channel your inner MJ, not your Shawn Bradley (he was in the movie... I swear).

control. The best campaigns focus on the things they can control. They get the basic building blocks right so that they have the best chance to navigate the gauntlet of unforeseen events looming before them.

With that caveat in mind, here are my recommendations to maximize your chances of defeating Trump. These strategies are based on what went right (and wrong) in 2008 and 2012 and what went wrong (and right) in 2016.[4]

Before we get into the specific strategic recommendations, there is one piece of advice that is more important than all others:

Don't get hacked.

Seriously.

Don't.

Say it with me now—two-factor authentication.

CHANGE THE GAME

Campaigns have certainly changed in the last decade or so—sophisticated data and analytics, souped-up digital departments, a focus on social media, etc. However, these innovations have been tacked on to the same old campaign structure that has existed far longer than my two decades in Democratic politics.

Television ads, phone calls, and mail are still the primary strategies for persuading voters. This is a massive error. If you don't believe me, assemble everyone on your campaign staff under the age of thirty-five.[5] Ask them the following questions:

- When was the last time you watched a commercial on TV?

---

4 Despite what the media would have you believe, winning campaigns don't do everything right, and losing campaigns don't do everything wrong.

5 If that's not 80 percent of the campaign staff, you're fucked.

- When was the last time you answered the phone from an unknown number?
- When was the last time you checked your mail?

Crickets.

In a rapidly changing world where Democrats depend on high turnout among young voters to win, why would campaigns continue to use tools that have no chance of success with those voters?

Poverty of ambition, risk aversion, and a compensation structure that creates perverse incentives for political consultants to hang on to the sinking ship of old media are just a few reasons. In too many campaigns, the chief strategist is the same person who makes the TV ads and takes a cut from the ad buy. Therefore, it is always in the interest of the strategist to argue for a strategy that spends more money on TV ads and less on digital and field.

I once worked on a campaign where the chief strategist was the TV consultant and the person responsible for all spending decisions was a partner in the chief strategist's firm. Every strategy decision was polluted with the perception of profiteering.

That campaign lost.

The world has changed, but campaigns haven't changed (enough). Because Trump was a pretty dim reality TV star who was unable to hire traditional political operatives to staff his campaign, he stumbled into innovation. Because most Republican donors thought Trump was too embarrassing to be associated with, his campaign didn't have the money to build the traditional structures or run the same television ads of previous campaigns. He was forced to do things differently, and he won because of it.[6]

---

6 With an assist from the Russians and Jim Comey, so let's not induct him into the Candidate Hall of Fame just yet.

To beat Trump, your campaign needs to be different. But what does different mean?

Democrats need to once again revolutionize how campaigns are run. Break down the model and build it from the ground up.

Question every assumption. Break every tradition. Hire people who came up questioning how politics is practiced as opposed to experts in the old ways. Find the smartest people under the age of twenty-five on your campaign and listen to them. They are unburdened by tradition and blessed by a fresh perspective.

A few points on what that means:

- Your campaign needs to be digital first. Digital is not a department within your campaign. It's a mentality. It's 2020; everything is digital[7]—advertising, communicating, organizing, and fundraising.
- Polling should be done to know how you are doing in the race, never to determine what you should say or believe.
- Most campaigns are top-down, hierarchical structures. A different campaign is bottom-up, pushes responsibility down to the grassroots, and trusts your volunteers and organizers to win the race for you.
- Don't rely on the mainstream media to get your message out. You need to build an alternative media ecosystem that tells your story on your terms.

HIT TRUMP WHERE HE IS STRONG

A primary tenet of modern political strategy is to find your opponent's secret weakness, expose it to the world, and then ruthlessly exploit it.

---

7 Except voting—more on that later.

In 2008, John McCain's biggest weakness was his strong support for the policies of the incredibly unpopular Bush administration—particularly the war in Iraq. Nearly every ad we ran used footage of McCain hugging Bush at the 2004 convention or McCain puttering around in a golf cart driven by Bush at his family estate in Kennebunkport. In 2012, Mitt Romney's biggest weakness was that he was a plutocrat with a policy platform designed to help his fellow plutocrats.

Trump is a very different politician.[8] As we know from 2016, the strategies that worked on (more) typical politicians like McCain and Romney don't work as well on Trump. Some of the unofficial autopsies of 2016 attribute that to a failure of execution. The Democratic Party's effort to disqualify Trump in the minds of voters was far from perfect. But the same strategy executed perfectly would have led to the same result. I think the problem was something bigger.

Trump's weaknesses are not some secret to be revealed with great opposition research and a killer ad. Trump's flaws are on display for the world to see. Expectations for Trump are so low that voters find almost nothing shocking. Less than a month before the 2016 election, a tape leaked with Trump bragging about sexual assault in the most heinous way, and numerous women came forward to accuse him of sexual misconduct. This would have ended any other candidate in any other race. Not Trump.

Yet, too many Democrats wake up every morning, turn on their phones, and fire up the *New York Times* app, hoping to find the end of Trump. Every new revelation of historic misconduct brings fresh hopes for Trump's support to collapse. But it never happens: An exhaustively reported *New York Times* story that proved beyond the shadow of a doubt that Trump engaged in tax fraud had no impact. Neither did the Mueller report or

---

8 This is the kind of top-notch observation that you are (not) paying me for.

Trump being named an unindicted coconspirator in a case to defraud the public by paying hush money to a woman with whom he had an affair.

There are undoubtedly private investigators being paid by liberal billionaires to scour Eastern Europe for the famous "pee tape."[9] And if that ever surfaces, once we all stop laughing, we will look at the polls and see no change.

My advice would be to hit Trump where he is strong. Instead of trying to exploit Trump's many and very manifest weaknesses, erode his strengths. Immigration and trade are Trump's two best issues—they fire up his base and persuade just enough swing voters. They were key to his victory in 2016, but he is also vulnerable on those issues, if your campaign makes a strong, sustained argument.

There are three components to winning the immigration argument against Trump.

First, call out his failures. Trump spends most mornings tweeting about hordes of invaders marching toward the southern border. He rants about a crisis in the system and Salvadoran gang members threatening white people all across the country. None of this is true, but Trump has painted a persuasive picture of immigration in America. Just enough Americans believe Trump because he taps into long-standing racial fears, which are exacerbated by a growing fear of a changing country. Trump, with the help of Fox, has done a very good job of making some white Americans feel like the country they knew is under assault.

Here's the part Trump doesn't say. He has been in charge of the immigration system for the last three years. Trump stood on the stage at the Republican convention and said, "I alone can fix it." He hasn't, and we know this because he tells us every day.

Trump's political imperative to fire up his base with racist

---

9 Something if found we will never unsee.

fearmongering is in direct conflict with his message of "promises kept." Exploit that conflict by laying the blame for it at his feet.

Second, not only has Trump failed to fix the system, but he profits off its brokenness. Mr. Tough on Immigration has used undocumented laborers at many of his businesses. He even staffed one of his golf clubs with an entire village of undocumented workers from Guatemala according to one of those workers.

The final component to winning the argument is the most important. Too many Democrats end up playing Trump's game. They get into a bidding war about who is tougher and smarter on immigration. In doing so, they play right into his trap by inadvertently buying the premise of Trump's argument. Don't play Trump's game. Call out his game. Tell people why Trump is trying to scare them. Something like this may work:

> President Trump is lying to you about immigration. He is trying to scare you, and he is trying to distract you. He doesn't want you to know that he pays for his tax cut for the wealthy and Wall Street by cutting Medicare and making your health care more expensive. He doesn't want you to know that he is letting corporations pollute your air and water and make your food and your kids' toys less safe. And he is doing all of this while using his office to help his friends, punish his enemies, and enrich himself.

Trump's success in the Republican primary can be attributed to a number of things,[10] but trade may have played the biggest role. For years, there has been a growing gap between the free-trade policies of Republican elites and the populism and isolationism of the Republican base. Trump broke with the party's

---

10 His sixteen opponents running sixteen of the worst campaigns in modern American history didn't hurt.

position on free trade. This split with his fellow Republicans is what made a Manhattan billionaire[11] with a gold toilet[12] credible to working-class voters. Taking down Trump's approval rating on trade by a few points may be the most effective way to flip states like Michigan, Pennsylvania, and Wisconsin.

Here are some messages on trade to use against Trump:

- Trump talks tough on China, but much of the Trump-branded products including his hideous ties are made there.
- President Trump launched an incompetent trade war with China that cost American farmers and consumers billions. When he started losing, he tried to help farmers. But he screwed that up, too. Most of the money went to big corporations instead of family farms. The money for Trump's corporate farm bailout was borrowed from—yes, you guessed it—China.

REMEMBER IT'S BOTH/AND, NOT EITHER/OR

Ever since Trump won, Democrats have engaged in a never-ending, emphatically stupid, ill-informed debate about whether the party should appeal to a growing base or try to court more moderate "swing" voters. This is a false choice—up until the moment the Electoral College is abolished.[13] The only way a Democrat can piece together the 270 votes necessary to win the White House is to do both. Your campaign needs to turn out first-time and periodic voters AND win over independent voters, particularly in the exurban and rural counties that turned Florida,

---

11 So he claims.
12 This is where he sent all those tweets, probably wearing a monogrammed robe. I will not apologize for painting that picture.
13 If you continue reading, you will see that is also part of the plan.

Ohio, Michigan, Wisconsin, and Pennsylvania from Obama blue to Trump red.

This is the task, and as daunting as it seems, it is very doable. Obama did it twice without twisting himself into an ideological pretzel. And dozens of Democrats did it in 2018.

Many in the media—whose brains have been broken by Twitter[14]—treat the Democratic base and swing voters as warring factions with insoluble differences. They think every base voter you attract repels more than one swing voter and vice versa. That's wrong and demonstrates a truly one-dimensional view of politics.

The truth is that the same message can work on both groups. You don't have to tack right or swerve left. They share concerns about an economy that is rigged in favor of the wealthy. They both believe health care is a right and that the Affordable Care Act should not be repealed. They are both concerned about the rampant corruption in Trump's Washington.

You can say the same thing in Philly and Scranton and win voters in both places. You just have to go to both places and offer a message that speaks to the shared concerns of all Americans. A unifying message can seem naive in the polarized dystopia that is politics in the Trump age, but it's actually your best path to victory.

MAKE IT A CHOICE, NOT A REFERENDUM

Conventional wisdom is that the best way to unseat the incumbent is to make the race a referendum on the incumbent as opposed to a choice between two candidates. But in politics, *conventional wisdom* is often a synonym for *wrong*.

In 2012, the Romney campaign tried to make the election all about Obama's stewardship of a struggling economy. In doing

---

14 Who among us...

so, Romney focused all of his campaign energy on tearing down Obama and none on building himself up. In a different circumstance, the 2016 Clinton campaign made a similar mistake because they believed impressions of Hillary Clinton were set in stone, so the best way to move voters was to focus on Trump. Neither strategy worked.[15]

No matter what you do, this election will be a choice between you and Trump, and you have to spend a lot of time, energy, and resources making the case for yourself. The case against Trump is self-evident—he is a racist, corrupt buffoon who is an embarrassment to the country. Everyone knows the argument. They knew this in 2016 and enough people chose him anyway. Your campaign must argue why the country should choose you instead of Trump. Why are you the better choice? How will people's lives improve if you are president? What about your story makes you the one individual out of three hundred million to lead our nation at this moment?

Trump's deficiencies as a president and a human are priced into the baseline. His supporters are not dumb. They voted for Trump with eyes wide open to his flaws and the risks involved. Some were, of course, racist and appreciated Trump's racism. Others were partisan Republicans who would vote for a mayonnaise sandwich[16] if it had an *R* next to it. And finally, a lot of voters decided that their frustration with politics as usual was sufficient to justify a big gamble. It's your job to show those voters (a) why that gamble didn't pay off, and (b) why you are worthy of another gamble only four years later.

You have spent the last eighteen months campaigning all over the country. You have done approximately eight hundred town halls. You have been on *Rachel Maddow* thirty times and *Pod*

---

15 Spoiler alert.
16 Disgusting.

Save America more times than you can count.[17] Yet the voters who will decide this election know almost nothing about you. It's a weird feature[18] of American politics that the people who end up deciding the election are the ones that pay the least attention to politics. The pundits would have you believe that this group is a bunch of fickle, white working-class voters with undiagnosed economic anxiety in Ohio and Wisconsin. They are wrong.[19] Too often we think of undecided voters—the "soccer moms" and "NASCAR dads" of elections past—as "swing voters" choosing between two candidates. But the biggest group of undecided voters is the people simply deciding whether to vote.

Therefore, your campaign needs to spend a lot of time, energy, and resources introducing you, your vision, and your platform to these voters. Of course, you should make the case against Trump, but not at the expense of making the case for yourself.

RUN TO WIN, NOT TO NOT LOSE

Here's some hard truth: you will probably lose. It's nothing personal and it's not a comment on you as a campaigner. It's just a fact. Incumbents usually win, and they almost always win in a strong economy. The odds are not in your favor.[20]

You can win, but you have to run to win. You can't run the political equivalent of the prevent defense. This means having a high-risk tolerance in your campaign. Barack Obama won in 2008 in part because he had nothing to lose. We knew the odds were long, so we were willing to push the envelope strategically. We

---

17 This is why you won the nomination, FYI.
18 More of a bug, actually.
19 There is a theme here.
20 *Hunger Games* political metaphors are only slightly more tired than *Game of Thrones* metaphors, which are slightly less tired than Marvel Comics metaphors. We need more *The Wire* metaphors.

didn't take risks for risk's sake, but we tolerated a lot of risk if we thought there was a real strategic reward if the bet paid off. Risk aversion is the natural state of being for most politicians, but it's a great way to lose a presidential campaign, especially when challenging an incumbent.

David Plouffe, Obama's campaign manager, would remind us—Obama included—that we were at our best when we were on what he called the "high wire." The risk made us a better campaign and Obama a better candidate. The willingness to take risks allowed us to experiment. It's why we had Obama deliver his convention speech in a football stadium in front of eighty thousand people[21] instead of in a convention hall in front of a few thousand political insiders. It's why Obama subjected himself to the tough questioning of Tim Russert on *Meet the Press*[22] the Sunday before the Iowa caucus even though he was leading in the polls. And it's why Obama went on an overseas campaign swing in the middle of the race when one mistake could have sunk the whole campaign by validating concerns about his lack of traditional political experience.[23]

We tried to keep our foot on the gas. Sometimes that meant we crashed and burned, but running a traditionally cautious campaign was a guaranteed loss for a nontraditional candidate. In your case, it is also a guaranteed loss to run a traditional campaign against a nontraditional[24] candidate like Trump.

It's easier to be bold in the primary, but now that you are the nominee, you will have every elected official, party leader,

---

21 The risks were empty seats or a midspeech thunderstorm that derailed what would be Obama's biggest audience of the campaign.

22 This was back in the days when Sunday shows were the biggest deal. I know it's hard to believe.

23 The other benefit to Obama's foreign trip is that four years later, Mitt Romney would feel compelled to go on his own foreign trip. Let's just say it was Griswoldesque—if the Family Truckster were a Bentley with its own elevator.

24 *Nontraditional* is doing a lot of work in this sentence.

and washed-up consultant[25] whispering in your ear and second-guessing your every move—usually through the media. It's super annoying and can lead to caution and risk aversion since every decision elicits criticism from someone.

There is only one option—tune them out. If there are good ideas, take them, but you have to run your race and run to win it.[26]

WIN THE ECONOMIC BATTLE

Trump has made the economy the centerpiece of his reelection campaign. He spends most mornings giving himself a pat on the back via Twitter for creating the "greatest economy ever!"[27] Trump is his own "Hype Man."

Now, we know this is all bullshit. Trump didn't create the economy, and it's not as great as he says—unless you are someone like Trump.[28] All the data shows that Trump is taking credit for all the work that Obama did to put the economy back on track. Trump's only real accomplishment was a tax cut that did nothing to help the economy but did make the rich a lot richer and add a trillion to the deficit.

Even when there is bad economic news, Trump pretends it didn't happen, yells, "Fake news!" or blames the Fed chair that he appointed.

Nonetheless, the economy is Trump's best answer to every question.

---

25 And some podcasters.

26 It helps to visualize walking off the podium after your inauguration, grabbing one of these leaders who anonymously shat on your campaign for a celebratory hug, and then whispering in their ear, "I know it was you." The Mafia "kiss of death" is up to you.

27 Trump has ruined the exclamation point for a generation.

28 Rich, not a racist asshole.

He uses it to push back on questions about his competence. He uses it to ease concerns about his corruption. And the economy is his best argument against changing horses midrace.

Despite this, you must take on the economic debate and win it.

Step one: use the success of the Trump economy against him. The traditional markers of the economy are good—unemployment is historically low. The stock market is up since Trump came into office. You don't want to have to depend on economic downturn to win.[29] Therefore, you need to reframe the question from "How good is the economy?" to "How fair is the economy?"

Make it a debate about values. Who you are fighting for and who Trump is fighting for. Most of the gains have gone to the wealthiest Americans, Wall Street, and the big tech companies, and that is by design. Trump believes that the rich and powerful should get the benefits, not the working and middle class.

Here's a proposed message:

> Corporate profits are up, corporate taxes are down, wages are basically flat, the cost of food, college, gas, and health care are up. If Trump is reelected, this will get worse. The rich will get even richer, and you will pay the bill. If you want an economy that works for you, vote for a Democrat.

Step two: hammer the Trump tax cut. A plan to give massive tax cuts to billionaires, companies that ship jobs overseas, and Wall Street banks and pay for it by cutting Medicare and jacking up health insurance premiums is an A+ answer to the question, How would a candidate commit political suicide most efficiently? Yet this is the signature legislative accomplishment of the Trump presidency.

---

29 Although, we are seemingly always one tweet away from tomorrow being the wrong day to need to access your 401(k) or 529.

Trump ran for president as a populist—a blue-collar billionaire who would fight for working-class voters and raise taxes on the wealthy. But he has governed as a plutocrat. Trump (with the help of Paul Ryan) has given Democrats the political gift of a lifetime. Take advantage of it. Use the tax plan to tell a story about who Trump is fighting for and how he thinks the economy works. Here are a couple of examples:

- Thanks in part to Trump's plan, many huge multinational corporations pay ZERO dollars in federal taxes. **Americans pay more for their Amazon Prime subscription than Amazon pays in federal taxes. If you think that is right, vote for Trump. If you think corporations should pay their fair share, vote for a Democrat.**
- Trump promised to protect Medicare, but he wants to pay for his corporate tax cut with hundreds of billions of dollars in cuts to Medicare, Medicaid, and Social Security.

Step three: you need policies, but not for policies' sake. You can't beat something with nothing. It's not enough to just criticize Trump's policies; you have to offer an alternative economic path for the country.

You are a self-described wonk.[30] You may not love all the debates and cable news interviews.[31] You are probably so bored of giving the same stump speech at every event. But the policy . . . that's the part that gets your blood going. Everything else is the price you pay to get to office, so you can work on policy.

You are not alone. Late in his second term, I asked Barack Obama if he had any desire to be president for more than eight years.

---

30 Every politician, or at least every Democratic politician is a wannabe wonk. On the other side, stupid sells.

31 The podcast interviews are awesome, right . . . ?

"The thing I will miss most is working on complicated problems with really smart people. If I could cut a deal where I could just get beamed into meetings from the beach in Hawaii to focus on the issues and someone else did the rest of the job, I would definitely consider it."[32]

Elections are not policy debates. He or she with the most white papers is not the de facto winner. The problem is that most voters are too busy to read the well-thought policy on your website (honestly, most are too busy to go to your website), so your policy ideas must have a compelling elevator pitch, and in this era, the elevator ride is at most 280 characters long.

While most voters know they aren't experts on the intricacies of a specific policy, they do know people. And that's how they often make a decision. Therefore, your policy ideas need to tell your story—who you are, where you came from, and who you are fighting for. If they don't tell people something about your values and character, they aren't worth spending time on in the campaign—no matter how good an idea they are.

DON'T CHASE TRUMP DOWN RABBIT HOLES

In the run-up to the 2018 election, Democrats across the country had been running on a very specific and effective message—Republicans want to take away your health care and cut your Medicare to pay for a tax cut for corporations and billionaires.[33] Trump, whose approach to politics is more instinctual than intellectual, sensed that this was a problem. He decided to change the subject.

Out of nowhere he started tweeting about an "invasion" of

32 I bet we all wish he could be doing that right now.
33 Or "people of means," as person of means Howard Schultz calls them.

MS-13 members and terrorists marching toward the southern border. Like all Trump lies, there was just enough of a kernel of truth buried deep in there to give Fox News and the rest of the propaganda operation permission to run with it. It was true that there were a large number of Central Americans fleeing violence who were coming to the United States seeking political asylum. The group was largely children and thousands of miles from the border when Trump began tweeting. To protect against this invasion (invented in his own demented racist cortex), Trump even sent US troops to the border.

Democrats refused to fall into Trump's trap. Instead of responding to his absurdities and changing the subject from health care (which excites our voters) to immigration (which excites his voters), Democrats stayed on message and won.

This approach was a lesson learned from 2016.

In 2016, the Democrats chased Trump down nearly every rabbit hole and responded to his every tweet, outrage, and scandal. This machine-gun-spray message strategy meant that voters were exposed to a lot of information about Trump—but it was never woven into a coherent narrative. There was no message repetition to drive home the information. It was just ephemeral—one day Trump was racist, another day he was a misogynist, and on a third day he was a crooked businessman.

The lesson is clear. Trump's political superpower is turning the political conversation to the topics that help Republicans and hurt Democrats. Winning requires the discipline to tell a coherent story about why you should run the country and why Trump shouldn't, without getting distracted by all the shiny objects Trump throws in your path.

This is harder than it sounds, and it is much harder to ignore Trump when you are running against him than against a random Republican member of Congress. All of the incentives of our totally broken media ecosystem will push you toward the rabbit hole.

Want retweets? Deliver a sick burn to Trump's latest tweet.

Want coverage on cable TV? Talk about whatever Trump is talking about.

Unless you are a Kardashian or Trump,[34] all PR is not good PR.

The question isn't how much coverage you got. It's how did that coverage advance your strategy? What did you communicate to your target voters to help persuade a plurality of them in the states that add up to 270?

Nothing else matters.

JUST BE YOU

My closing piece of advice is the most annoying advice possible. Whenever Barack Obama would hit some turbulent political seas, there would be some meeting with some outside advisors: old friends, former staff, or seasoned Washington types. The purpose of this meeting was to get outside the unavoidable bubble of working/living in the West Wing. The president wanted to talk to people with fresh perspective.

The same thing would happen in every meeting. At some point, one of the attendees would affix their gaze on the president and, with a Smithersesque obsequiousness, say, "My recommendation is that your staff needs to let Barack be Barack."[35]

Every time, this suggestion made me go briefly blind with rage. It implied that his advisors were trying to change him or bend him to our will. That was insulting to Obama and his advisors. It was also apple-polishing pablum. A way to kiss up to the president without

---

34 Kinda, sorta the same thing, except Kim is good at business.

35 This phenomenon was brilliantly spoofed on *Veep* with the character Karen Collins. I would like to believe a lot of people in Washington knew they were being ridiculed. Unfortunately, one of the essential traits of being a Karen Collins is not knowing you are a Karen Collins.

actually offering a specific suggestion that could be judged on its merits. No one can disagree—"No, sir, I disagree; you shouldn't be Barack" wouldn't go over well.

My former colleagues are going to kill me for this, but...

Just be you. It's either going to be enough or isn't. Trying to be someone else definitely won't work.

Voters have an amazing BS detector. They will know if you are trying to change who you are in order to win their votes. In a weird way, Trump won because he allowed the true essence of his insecurity-driven assholery to shine through.

The best campaigns are the most authentic ones. Run as your best self, but run as yourself.

Good luck. We are all counting on you.

Don't fuck it up.

What You Can Do to Help

- Support the Democratic nominee, no matter who it is, because they are approximately one trillion times better than Trump.
- If you live in a contested state, VOLUNTEER for the Democratic nominee. Canvass, phone bank, host meetings, drop food off at the campaign office, or if you have an extra bedroom, consider housing a campaign staffer.
- If you don't live in a contested state, go to a contested state to knock on doors for the campaign and the Democratic Party.
- If you don't live in a contested state and can't go to one, reach out to the campaign to see how you can

volunteer from afar to make phone calls, send texts, and send postcards.

- If you can give money, any amount will help.
- Make sure all your friends are registered to vote. Annoy the shit out of them if you have to. If Trump wins again, losing a friend or two will be the least of your problems.

CHAPTER 6

THE DEMOCRACY PARTY

I have been a Democrat my entire life. One of my first memories is my mom on the verge of tears when Reagan won. I met Joe Biden at a fair when I was seven. He shook my hand and put a sticker on my shirt that I wouldn't let my parents take off for weeks. I almost got in a fight with a kid in my neighborhood who told me that Democrats killed babies.[1]

I played Michael Dukakis in a middle school mock debate.[2] I went to Georgetown University in part because that is where Bill Clinton went.[3] I have worked for a president, a vice president, several senators, and Democratic governors.

I am a proud Democrat because of what we believe in and who we fight for. The Democratic Party has made America stronger, more tolerant, and more just. Democratic presidents led the way on ending Jim Crow,[4] passing Social Security, Medicare, the Affordable Care Act, and legalizing marriage equality.

---

1 I would have lost that fight.
2 I did lose that fight.
3 I came for Clinton but stayed for Allen Iverson.
4 A lot of Democrats were on the wrong side of the civil rights battles of the 1960s, but it was the Democrats who pushed forward and the Republican Party that welcomed the angry segregationists with open arms.

Democrats are the ones who saved the country during the Great Depression, World War II, and the Great Recession.

Whenever the country faced a critical juncture, it was the Democratic Party that stepped up, made the tough decisions, and saved America.

We are in one of those moments right now. What happens in the next few years is going to decide the fate of the country for generations. Will our politics look like Obama's—a democratic, inclusive, and tolerant country working to bend the arc of this nation toward justice? Or will America become Trumpian—an authoritarian, white nationalist, plutocratic dystopia where a chosen few succeed and the rest suffer?

We have a two-party system. We know the Republicans are the problem, so it's up to the Democrats to be the solution. That's why it is so important that as Democrats, we are willing to look at ourselves in the mirror. For me, that starts with trying to answer a question that hangs over the Obama years.

THE OBAMA GAP

These two things are somehow true at the same time:

Barack Obama is the greatest politician of his generation. He won states that no Democrat had won in decades and is the first president since Eisenhower to win 51 percent of the vote twice.[5] Every time he has reemerged on the national stage during the Trump era, Obama reminds us of his tremendous oratorical gifts and innate decency.

But it is also true that the Democratic Party collapsed during Obama's presidency. During his eight years in office, Democrats lost twelve governors' mansions, more than sixty House seats,

---

5 Reagan didn't achieve this, and Clinton never got a majority of the country once.

eleven Senate seats, and nearly one thousand state legislative seats. Not to mention the fact that Hillary Clinton lost the presidency to a scandal-plagued doofus with zero experience.

I have spent a lot of time since Election Day 2016 trying to reconcile these two ideas. I have been around a lot of politicians in my life, and I have zero questions about Obama's political talent. The results in his campaigns speak for themselves. In basketball, the analytics nerds often use a stat called "on/off," which evaluates a player's value based on a comparison of the team's performance when the player is on the court and when he or she is off the court. Obama's on/off differential is massive.

When Obama was on the ballot in 2008 and 2012, Democrats gained a total of

> 29 House seats;
> 10 Senate seats.

When Obama was off the ballot in 2010 and 2014, Democrats lost

> 76 House seats;
> 15 Senate seats.

Understanding the "Obama gap" helps explain how Democrats got in this mess and how we can strengthen our party to fix it.

EXPLAINING AND LEARNING FROM THE LOSSES

Before you indict Obama[6] and his team for the political failures that occurred on our watch, I feel compelled to point out some

6 JK—you can't indict a sitting president. More on that later.

mitigating circumstances. Presidents almost always lose seats in their first midterm election. Only George W. Bush succeeded in bucking this trend, and he needed to politicize the tragedy of 9/11 in the most disgusting way possible to do so. Obama was also a victim of his own success. The magnitude of his losses in 2010 is a direct result of his successes in 2008, which were a historical anomaly. Not only did Obama have the best coattails of any candidate in history in 2008, but he did so after a Democratic wave election in 2006. In other words, there were a lot of Democrats sitting in seats in pretty Republican districts. They rode a historically large wave into Washington, and as soon as the tide receded, they were going to be left stranded. And boy, did the tide recede.

Obama would have lost a lot of seats in 2010 and 2014 even under the best circumstances. Historical trends and unfavorable maps guaranteed it, but Obama didn't face the best circumstances. The 2010 election occurred in the midst of the worst economic crisis since the Great Depression. Unemployment was near 10 percent; the housing market was a disaster; and Congress had passed a massive bailout for the very Wall Street banks that precipitated the crisis. It was a perfect storm of terrible politics.

In 2014, Democrats were defending a bunch of Senate seats that we might have lost in 2008 if Obama hadn't been on the ballot. The House map was terrible because the Republicans had used their newfound political power to gerrymander the crap out of the country. That election also occurred amid a media panic about an Ebola outbreak in Africa and the rise of the Islamic State in Syria and Iraq.[7]

---

7 CNN and others fanning the flames of paranoia for ratings is not something that looks great in hindsight and will be hard to explain in the near future when cable news as we know it has gone the way of the CD player.

However, in the simplest of terms, Obama won when he was on the ballot because a core group of voters turned out, and those same voters stayed home when he wasn't. And this is about more than the fact that Democrats generally have better turnout in presidential elections. The Obama gap is also partially responsible for the trauma that is 2016.

It is historically very hard for a party to win three presidential elections in a row. Usually, the two-term incumbent limps into the twilight of their term. George W. Bush left office so unpopular that when a hurricane forced the Republicans to cancel his speech to the Republican convention, everyone breathed a sigh of relief and no one tried to reschedule it. Bill Clinton had a high approval rating but was so marred with scandal that Al Gore was unwilling to campaign with him. Obama, on the other hand, left office with high approval ratings and a strong economy. He was in demand on the campaign trail. Without a doubt, Hillary Clinton had a unique set of challenges as a nominee. As a general rule, running for president with the looming specter of an FBI investigation is not ideal—even when that investigation is a bunch of trumped-up bad-faith bullshit.[8] But ultimately, Clinton's fate was sealed when four million people who voted for Obama in 2012 didn't vote in 2016 perhaps because Obama was "off the court."[9]

There is a core truth about politics that the consultants, pundits, and political reporters don't want you to know: it's the big things—the economy, demography, gas prices, and world events—that dictate what happens in an election. Almost all of it is outside the control of the candidates and the campaigns. What campaigns do and say really only affects things on the margins. In a close

---

8 We know this because when Jared Kushner and Ivanka were also discovered to be using private email servers, no one in the Republican Party or the media gave two shits for more than two minutes.

9 Voter suppression undoubtedly also played a big role in this gap.

race, the margins matter. But the best candidate with the best campaign can't overcome the gravitational pull of history.

The preceding argues against the idea that there was some obvious thing or set of things that Team Obama could have done to reverse these trends. He ended his presidency scandal-free, substantively successful, and politically popular. To this day, his approval rating among Democrats is north of 90 percent. But the president is the leader of the party, and all of us who worked for him need to try to figure out why the Obama coalition hasn't yet turned into the Democratic coalition. We are living with the consequences of that failure every single day. It's not just Trump, his cruelty, and conservative judges. Republican majorities at the state level are denying people health care, restricting their right to vote, and banning abortion.

As President Obama said in an interview on NPR after the election, "I am a proud Democrat, but I do think that we have a bias towards national issues and international issues, and as a consequence I think we've ceded too much territory. And I take some responsibility for that."

A plan to reform and reinvigorate the Democratic Party for battle against Trumpism begins with understanding where we came up short in the Obama era. Some of the critiques are dumb, others are bad-faith bs, but some are quite fair. There is no question we could have done a better job:

- improving the party infrastructure;
- converting Obama voters and volunteers into Democratic Party voters and volunteers;
- focusing on down-ballot races.

I'm sure others will find additional shortcomings, but these are the ones that I think could have minimized some of the losses and better prepared us for the battles to come.

We can't go back in time and undo those mistakes (as appealing as that would be),[10] but we can learn from them. They inform my view of how to fix and modernize the party machinery.

WHAT IS THE DEMOCRATIC PARTY?

This sounds like a rhetorical question at the start of a Sean Hannity rant, but it really is a question worth answering in the modern era of politics. Too often people confuse the Democratic National Committee (DNC) with the Democratic Party. Whenever anything goes wrong, they blame the DNC. When someone has an idea, they say, "Call the DNC." I think a lot of Democrats around the country imagine a Justice League–style building where all the party players have an office and there is a conference room where Nancy Pelosi, Chuck Schumer, the presidential candidates, and all your favorite Blue Check Marks on Twitter get together to make strategic decisions. The conference room looks like the command center in *Apollo 13* or the Situation Room (the one in the White House, not the one on CNN).[11]

Bad news. No such place exists.

The Democratic Party is a coalition of different groups with different and sometimes conflicting interests. The Democratic National Committee is the umbrella organization for the fifty state parties and the four hundred–plus DNC members who are local and national elected officials who choose the DNC chair. The Democratic Congressional Campaign Committee, or DCCC, is charged with electing Democrats to the House. It is chaired by a member of Congress chosen by the Democrats in

---

10 If time travel were real, I would use it to go back in time and ask Fred Trump to hug his son.

11 Any plane the president is on is automatically called Air Force One, and any room Wolf Blitzer is in is automatically called the "Situation Room."

the House. The Democratic Senatorial Campaign Committee, or DSCC, does the same thing for the Senate. There are also Democratic committees dedicated to electing governors, state legislatiors, and attorneys general. Super PACs, longtime progressive organizations like Planned Parenthood, EMILY's List, labor unions, and the NAACP as well as think tanks like the Center for American Progress and the Brookings Institution are part of the party. And there are new insurgent grassroots organizations like Swing Left, Run for Something, and Indivisible that formed after the 2016 election to address the failings of the aforementioned groups.

It's a broad, diverse coalition that agrees on little more than Trump's general terribleness. Their individual interests often conflict. In 2018, for example, Nancy Pelosi and the DCCC were focused on defeating Republican incumbents in blue and purple districts that Trump lost. This strategy depended on drawing sharp contrasts with the Republicans. Chuck Schumer and the DSCC were defending Democratic incumbents in red states that Trump won, which sometimes called for blurring distinctions with Trump. The left hand and the other left hand were sometimes moving in opposite directions.

To make matters worse, the post–*Citizens United* campaign finance laws dramatically reduced the influence of the traditional party organizations. Under current law, an individual can give a maximum of $35,500 a year to the DNC. This is far from a paltry sum, but it pales in comparison to the unlimited amounts super PACs and political nonprofits can raise from individuals and corporations. The outside groups have exponentially more resources than the inside groups with little of the accountability to the public or traditional political stakeholders.

The Democratic Party has never been particularly hierarchical or orderly—especially when we are out of power. No one has the power to convene all the players, and everyone has the power to veto any sort of collective action. The whole process tends to work (a little?) better when there is a Democrat in the White House. When Obama was president, his team helped convene a weekly meeting among all the progressive stakeholders under the banner of something called the Common Purpose Project. It was an opportunity for the White House to brief the groups on our agenda and strategy and plot out plans to enact and defend our shared agenda. It didn't always work. We didn't always agree, but getting around a table together was ultimately invaluable. The passage of the Affordable Care Act and the defeat of GOP budget cuts to education, food stamps, and Medicare wouldn't have happened without it. That level of coordination is much harder when Democrats aren't in the White House, which is a cruel twist of fate because it's when we need it the most.

In other words, the whole thing is a large, cacophonous mess.

Before you put this book down, pack your bags, and move to Denmark,[12] keep in mind that the Republican Party was an epic shit show when Obama was in office and very well may still be. Nothing like winning to hide all the warts. The primary function of the Republican National Committee is to employ Trump's flunkies, pay the legal bills of other Trump flunkies, and hold fundraising events at Trump properties, thereby funneling money from Republican campaigns into the pockets of Trump and his dilettante children. The Republican chair is Ronna Romney McDaniel—Mitt's niece and someone with so little dignity that when President Trump told her to stop going by Romney because of his distaste for Mitt, she agreed.

But...before you relax and soothe your nerves with Trump's idiocy and endless grift, the Republicans are better organized

---

12 Where you can enjoy a Danish and some sweet Bernie-style Democratic Socialism.

and much better funded. They have an easier task come election time—they simply need to turn out a group of mostly homogenous[13] very reliable voters. The Democrats have to turn out a larger, more diverse group of people who vote less reliably. We have to overcome voter suppression laws, while getting massively outspent by the other side.

Defeating Trumpism requires reimagining and reforming the Democratic Party. Here is a nonexhaustive list of ideas to do so offered with the humility of someone who would have bet their life on Hillary Clinton being president right now and Donald Trump being the sixth member of *The Five* on Fox News.[14]

Become the Defenders of Democracy

Fixing democracy needs to become the primary purpose of the Democratic Party. I know this sounds cheesy, but nothing else happens if we don't pursue aggressive steps to fix our democracy. There will be no Medicare for All, no Medicare for some,[15] no Green New Deal, no $15 minimum wage, and no new gun safety laws.

The party platform needs to lead with aggressive reforms—many of which I will lay out in coming chapters. Leaders need to use their platforms to raise the alarm. Democracy needs to be the central message.

This can't be a campaign trail hobby that gets forgotten once the election season is over. Democratic elected officials from the White House to the statehouse need to work every day to make our

---

13 Read: old white people.

14 *The Five* is the single worst show on television. It is so bad that it should be good, but it isn't. It is also a museum-worthy exhibit of the lack of talent, humor, and intellectual rigor in conservative media personalities.

15 There may be no Medicare at all if people like Paul Ryan have their way.

democracy work better. They need to pull every lever and leave no stone unturned. There is nothing more important.

Democratic voters and activists have a critical role to play here. They need to hold Democratic politicians accountable once they are in office. If a Democratic governor is not expanding access to voting, they should be called to the carpet. If someone runs as a reformer but starts palling around with big donors, they should be protested. If they don't respond to the pressure, they should face a primary challenge.

The stakes couldn't be higher. Democracy is under relentless assault from the Republican Party and their special interest supporters. Democrats must launch an aggressive counterattack designed to establish majority rule in the country. If we don't, nothing else matters.

End Our Obsession with the Presidency

This is going to sound weird coming from a former White House staffer who worked on multiple presidential campaigns and cohosts a podcast that spends an inordinate amount of time covering Trump and the Democrats trying to beat him. But...the Democratic Party is too obsessed with the White House.

Don't get me wrong—the presidency is incredibly important. To repurpose an old Obama saying, the president can do a lot with their pen and phone.[16] Without Congress even showing up to work,[17] the next Democratic president can reenter the Paris climate agreement, strengthen the Affordable Care Act, enforce civil and reproductive rights, put back in place regulations that make

---

16 Nothing made Republicans angrier in the Obama years than Obama talking about his executive authority—those same Republicans are notably silent now that the "authoritarian curious" Trump is in office.

17 Not a bad bet.

our air and water cleaner, and repeal Trump's ban on transgender troops serving in the military. The next Democratic president could fill up most of their first term signing executive orders undoing the bad shit Trump has done to America.

However, the Democratic Party's focus on winning the White House has come at the expense of everything else. Democrats have controlled the House of Representatives for only six of the last twenty-five years and the Senate for about nine of the last twenty-five. We have done worse in governorships and lost nearly one thousand state legislative seats during Obama's presidency. The consequences of not controlling Congress are well-known and painfully obvious every time the Supreme Court hands down some right-wing ruling that seems like it came directly off a whiteboard in McConnell's office or Koch HQ.[18]

But in an era where Congress can't agree on naming a post office,[19] statehouses are where policy is made. States manage elections; they can expand or infringe upon reproductive and civil rights. States can make guns easier or more difficult to buy. Most important, state governments draw the congressional and legislative district lines. Traditionally, Democrats have't cared as much about these down-ballot races. This isn't just the fault of the Democratic Party leadership. Democratic donors (big and small) give less money in nonpresidential years. The further you go down the ballot, the less money is raised. The Democratic gubernatorial and state legislative campaign arms usually raise a lot less money than the congressional committees, even though you can argue that those offices have a greater impact on the lives of more people. Voter turnout drops precipitously for Democrats when it's not a presidential election. This dropout explains Democratic

---

18 These are the same thing.

19 And by *can't agree*, I mean Republicans won't let Democrats name post offices.

losses in 2010 and 2014, which are the losses that allowed the Republicans to gerrymander much of the country and control the Supreme Court for decades. Democratic candidates seem much more interested in running for Congress than state legislatures, which means until recently the Democratic bench looked as shallow as the Warriors bench in the 2019 finals.[20]

Republicans, on the other hand, have spent decades and millions of dollars investing in running and winning state elections. To be fair, Republicans have two advantages (and one of them isn't that they are smarter). First, Republican voters are older, more reliable voters who vote in every election regardless of who is running. Therefore, they don't have the same drop-off in midterms that Democrats do. Second, the Republican donor network invests in politics up and down the ballot. They pay to train candidates. They understand that $50,000 may be a drop in the ocean of a presidential campaign, but it can tip a state legislative race. They know that today's school board candidate is tomorrow's congressional candidate.

We have to win the next presidential race, but a lonely victory at the top of the ballot will not be enough. The Republican response to the last Democratic president was to use every weapon at their disposal to nullify the results of the elections. That will happen again.

Without the Senate, the next Democrat will have a limited impact at best on the federal courts. Democrats need to be prepared for the fact that if a Supreme Court justice retired in the middle of the next Democratic president's inaugural address, McConnell would hold the seat open for four years.

If there is a progressive in the White House and conservatives control the statehouses, most of America will never feel the full

---

20 The Warriors bench was very thin due to injuries and other reasons. Even Jon Lovett should have been able to figure this out from context clues.

impact of progressive policies. The Affordable Care Act included what was essentially free money for states to expand Medicaid to insure their citizens. States with Democratic governors leapt at the opportunity to take care of their citizens without affecting their already tight budgets. Many Republican governors became the first politicians in recorded history to turn down free money and forced their citizens to go without lifesaving health care. There was no argument about fiscal responsibility or small government. The whole point was to fuck with Obama's policy. The less successful the policy, the better the chances of defeating Obama in 2012 or another Democrat in 2016. I don't want to be overdramatic about this, but a lot of people died because Republican politicians cared more about hurting Obama than helping their fellow human beings.

Elected officials, party leaders, and even podcasters need to use their platforms to focus attention on the importance of winning down-ballot races. We need to convince donors and political operatives to invest their money and time in these races. We need to talk about the policy consequences and opportunities that come from political power at the state and local level. For example, one of the best ways to protect a woman's right to choose is to elect governors and legislatures who can pass laws to protect their citizens from an adverse Supreme Court ruling.[21]

There is good news on this front. In 2017 and in 2019, Democrats made huge gains in the Virginia assembly, picking up seats in districts Republicans had held for decades by contesting even the most Republican of seats. In 2018, the turnout among Democratic voters was so high that it was on par with recent presidential elections, which helped the Democrats take control of the House of Representatives and rip the gavel from Paul Ryan's cold,

---

21 *Adverse Supreme Court ruling* is sadly redundant phrasing these days.

emotionally dead hand. Democrats also flipped seven governors' offices from red to blue.

Without a doubt, this burst in activity was a response to the racist, authoritarian criminal "working" in the White House. The wind was at our back. But the historic turnout of 2018 was also the product of a wave of activism that started right after Trump was elected. The work of everyday citizens who want to make America better was supercharged by new, innovative, tech-savvy groups like Run for Something, Swing Left, Sister District, Indivisible, and others. These groups are the future of the party. We cannot turn our backs on them once the specter of Trump has been exorcised.

It's easy to be distracted by the presidential election. But we can't afford to let that happen again. The extraordinary results of '17, '18, and '19 need to become ordinary. That's the only path to progressive success.

The Campaign Never Stops

On the first day I walked into the White House, I thought to myself, "The campaign is over. It's time to govern." I had spent my entire career as an itinerant campaign operative. Sure, I had worked in government, but those posts were just way stations to the next campaign. I always felt the most comfortable in a campaign office wearing jeans[22] and being part of a team working around the clock and putting everything on the line. I never loved working on Capitol Hill—the pace was slow, the results few and far between, and besides, I don't like to play softball, which is the primary nonwork activity of Hill staffers.[23]

22 Suits and ties are inherently stupid and impractical as daily work attire, particularly in a city built on a swamp.

23 I'm also terrible at softball.

For a while at least, I loved the political combat of campaign season. I was pretty good at making myself hate the opponent—no matter who they were.[24] But ultimately, I was doing those campaigns because I wanted a shot at working in the White House. That was the ultimate goal. Now that I finally had that opportunity, I wanted to remind myself to govern, not campaign. My mentality at the time was consistent with how Democrats think. There is a time for campaigning and a time for governing. Campaigning is dirty work. Governing is important, and rarely, if ever, shall the two meet. Don't get me wrong—every job in the White House is inherently political, and we thought a lot about how our governing decisions affected Obama's political standing. However, we worked hard to avoid being overtly political.

Despite being in a very politically precarious position heading into the reelection campaign, Obama didn't raise a single dollar for his own race until the spring of 2011—less than eighteen months before the election. And even then, we were very nervous about opening the reelection campaign office.

"What message would it send to voters that Obama wanted their vote?" was in hindsight a really stupid thing to worry about, but worry we did. To be fair, it wasn't just us. The decision to form the reelection campaign in April 2011 was mildly controversial within the hothouse of stupidity that is DC punditry. The right-wing noise machine came after us for launching earlier than any other candidate in recent memory. We announced one whole month earlier in our term than George W. Bush did in his. In the eyes of some, pulling the political calendar forward by one month was a greater sin than invading the wrong country after 9/11.[25]

---

24 I STILL hate Mitt Romney despite his plaintive tweets about Trump and tremendous thirst to be the Never Trump poster child.

25 Note to the very talented and detail-oriented fact-checkers: This is an overstatement for effect.

Donald Trump, a man not known for caring about norms or criticism,[26] didn't wait until April of the year before the election to start running for reelection. He filed for reelection five hours after he was inaugurated. Most of his staff hadn't located the bathrooms in the White House by the time Trump was running for reelection. Trump's campaign immediately started raising money and holding rallies where they could sign up volunteers and identify voters. Some of the money was used to pay the legal bills of the crooks on his staff and in his family and hush money to fired White House staff who had seen a little too much during their brief tenures. But the rest of the money was used to build campaign infrastructure, accumulate data, and run ads. All of this activity gives him a massive head start in the 2020 election while the Democratic candidates fight with each other.

Trump did receive some criticism for the early start to the campaign. I am sure I was one of the people who did the criticizing, but Trump was right.[27] The demands of politics in the age of social media and Wild West–esque campaign finance laws mean this is the era of the permanent campaign.

The DNC, the super PACs, the campaigns, and even the voters can no longer take the odd years off. The Far Right and the Koch organization don't take time off. They are out there every day working to enact their agenda of racial grievance and tax cuts for rich people paid for by taking health care away from poor people. Fox News and the rest of the right-wing propaganda machine relentlessly push their message—savaging progressive politicians and ideas and shifting the political conversation to the right. Democrats are not just outgunned; we keep our guns in the holster. Our political groups don't have the funding to sustain activity

---

26 Fact check: not true. Trump cares more about criticism than anyone; he is just too dumb to know which things lead to criticism and too narcissistic to wonder why he is being criticized.

27 That was as painful for me to type as it was for you to read.

in the off years. We don't have a propaganda network and therefore rely on the mainstream media to carry the message without the air cover of political advertising. In the Obama years, we constantly found ourselves on the defensive with little to no ability to respond. The Republicans were running fully funded campaigns, and we were responding with press releases and the occasional tweet. It wasn't a fair fight.

By starting his campaign so early, Trump has pressed this advantage. He is governing with the force of the White House bully pulpit unburdened by norms or laws, and spending millions on campaign ads to push his agenda.

There needs to be a 24-7-365 Democratic campaign operation that is registering new voters, reaching out to "swing" voters, and running ads pushing the progressive message and defining Republican politicians and policies. This needs to happen when Trump is in office, and it needs to happen when (if) there is a Democrat in office.

This means that campaigns can't wind down after Election Day. It means that political operatives don't get to spend their non-campaign time consulting for corporations, trade associations, or sketchy politicians in the far reaches of the world. Defending democracy is a full-time job.

This all sounds good in principle. But how would it work?

To answer the question, let's use the hypothetical of a Democrat in the White House.[28] President Oprah Winfrey[29] has just been sworn in. Her first legislative priority is passage of a package of gun safety laws, which she announces in a nationally televised address. Her campaign, which never shut down and never stopped raising money,[30] runs digital ads on Facebook, Instagram, Twitter,

---

28 Sometimes the glass can be half-full—I swear.

29 I'm as surprised as you are. Let's just say it was a very eventful Democratic convention.

30 I would hope that her message would be, "You don't get a gun. You don't get a gun. You don't get a gun."

and Google encouraging people to watch the speech. Her campaign staff and volunteers, who, after a short and well-deserved postelection vacation, organize watch parties for supporters to see the speech. After President Winfrey announces her proposals, her campaign runs digital ads telling people what is in the proposals instead of relying on the media to characterize the proposals accurately or fairly. When the legislative push begins, her campaign targets Republican members with ads and grassroots organizing—blowing up their phones and filling up their email inboxes. When the NRA, Fox, et al., demagogue her proposals, the campaign apparatus responds on the ground and on the air. No attack goes unanswered. After the legislation passes, the campaign runs more ads telling the story of what passed long after the media has moved on to the next clickbait crisis du jour.

Our government would function better if there were distinct seasons for campaigning and governing like I hoped for when I first walked into the White House. In the long run, the system can and should be reformed to make governing easier—getting big money out of politics would be a great start. But in the meantime, we need to campaign like our future depends on it—because it does.

America Has More than Twenty States

When former Vermont governor Howard Dean ran to be the DNC chair in 2005, he promised to enact a fifty-state strategy to fund every state Democratic Party and build political organizations in even the reddest parts of the political map. Dean's promise was both an insightful understanding of a flawed Democratic strategy to write off, like, 60 percent of the country and a very clever way to appeal to the state party officials that pick the DNC chair. Dean was certainly sincere in his efforts and tried to implement the fifty-state strategy. But when push came to shove, the time, energy, and resources went to the twenty or so battleground states. Every person who has ever contemplated becoming DNC chair since Dean has also called for a fifty-state strategy. Everyone talks about it, but no one does it.

Why?

There are a couple of reasons. The first and biggest reason is money.

There is not enough money to go around, which leads to short-termism. Investing in Wisconsin may win an election right now while investing in Utah may help win elections many years from now. The people making the spending decisions in politics—like a lot of general managers in sports—know they won't be around when the long-term investment pays off, but they will be held accountable for what happens in the short term. Today matters; tomorrow is someone else's problem.

The other factor is that the DNC is essentially an adjunct of the presidential campaign. By tradition, the Democratic nominee takes over the operations of the DNC at the outset of the general election. When Obama won the nomination in 2008, he dispatched Paul Tewes, the mastermind of his victory in the Iowa caucus, and Brad Woodhouse, a famously aggressive communicator I had worked with in the past, to run the DNC. Most of the original staff stayed, but the decisions were made by Team Obama. Therefore, the strategic filter applied to each decision was "How does it help Obama win now?" not "How does this help the Democratic Party grow years from now?" The same thing happened in 2012, in 2016, and will certainly happen in 2020.

If Democrats really want a fifty-state strategy, we need to break this cycle of symbiotic short-term dependence and replace it with a sustainable strategy to win now and win more later. Walking and chewing gum is possible—you just have to have a plan to do so.

Step one: Take the DNC out of the middle of the process and create a program where donors big and small adopt state parties in the nonbattleground states. Imagine a subscription or recurring donation program where donors give a small (or large) monthly amount to a state party to help them grow.

Step two: DNC chairs should serve eight-year terms as opposed to the current four-year cycles. They need to be responsive to the party writ large as opposed to the Democratic nominee in the year they are up for reelection.

Step three: Democratic presidential candidates must use their platforms and fundraising bases to help grow the party outside of the battleground states. The DNC controls the voter file—the repository of information on voters across the country. To gain access, Democratic campaigns currently must write a big check to or raise money for the DNC. A better idea would make access to the voter file contingent on candidates raising money for three red-state Democratic Parties chosen by the DNC. They could use their email fundraising lists or agree to attend a fund-raiser for the state party in either the state itself or the candidate's home state.

Step four: Don't depend on the DNC to do all the work. The DNC is just one part of the Democratic Party. The DCCC and DSCC have some of the same short-term incentive problems. If all the party committees could put aside their differences and work together on building infrastructure across the country, it would make a huge difference. The question is how to make that happen.

I generally hate working groups because they are often organizational oxymorons,[31] but we need a working group that includes representatives of the House, Senate, gover-

31 Because they often don't "work." Get it?

norships, state legislatures, and so on. It should be chaired by someone with the power to convene everyone and shouldn't have a vested interest in the elections right before us. Perhaps someone like Barack Obama or Hillary Clinton.[32] We could call it the Fifty-State Committee, and maybe item one on the agenda could be a better name. Anyway, you get the point.

End the Consultant Culture

After the 2000 election, I was back in DC, unemployed, and living on a rotating series of couches while I looked for a job. Bush was about to take office, and approximately ten thousand Democrats who worked in the Clinton administration were about to be fired. Every job listing had a ton of applicants, and every time I was lucky enough to land an interview, I would walk in and see the same group of people (many older and more qualified) waiting in the lobby.

Through a friend of a friend, I got an opportunity for some temporary work helping Terry McAuliffe's campaign for DNC chair. McAuliffe, who would go on to be a very successful governor of Virginia, was a top fund-raiser and close friend to the Clintons. He was running as their de facto choice to run the party in their absence. The campaign was essentially a fait accompli—McAuliffe had the support of the entire Democratic establishment in DC, and most of the state party chairs were handpicked by the Clintons.

I took on the gig because I had a very large personal cell phone bill from working for Vice President Gore during the Florida

32 President Obama is going to be annoyed that I volunteered him for this task.

recount.[33] I also hoped to do some networking to find a more stable stream of income.

This was also my first true look at the machinery of the Democratic Party—a culture of political consultants with lucrative retainers for little work. I heard a story about how Jimmy Carter's daughter's babysitters had been put on the DNC payroll in the '70s and stayed there for decades. This story is possibly and even likely apocryphal, but it spoke to a larger truth. The Democratic Party is a cash cow for a lot of professional Democrats. Tom Perez, the current chair, has done a lot to reform how the DNC works to make it more efficient and responsive to the needs of our candidates and state parties, but this problem is bigger than one DNC chair.

Much of the Democratic Party is in the thrall of a class of political consultants who have failed up and gotten rich doing so. In my twenty-plus years in and around the Democratic Party, there has been shocking little turnover in which consulting firms do the bulk of the work for the party and its top politicians. This is, in part, why we keep making the same mistakes over and over again. It is the financial interest of the consultants to adhere to the way things have been done, as opposed to the way things should be done. A modern, more effective and progressive Democratic Party depends on ending the consultant culture that dominates the party.

While there are plenty of exceptions, the economic model for political consulting is to work to elect Democrats in even years and work for the corporations that often oppose Democrats in odd years. This is more than an appearance of a conflict of interest. It sows distrust with the grassroots of the party. It's hard to be a party that advocates for universal health care when the people

33 Back in those days, the campaign gave us a choice of a pager or a cell phone; I chose a pager because it seemed more useful. I am old.

advising the party have homes at the shore paid for by the health insurance industry.

Many of these consultants are my friends and former colleagues. They are talented, good people, and they have every right to make a living however they want. And they are going to be pissed at me for this, but they don't have a right to work for the Democratic Party.

The DNC and all the other wings of the party should enact a rule that says, "If you want to work for the Democratic Party, you have to give up your corporate clients for a period of two years." This is not a radical idea. It's how most presidential campaigns operate, and it's how the party should operate. Trumpism and the Republican Party are funded by corporations and Wall Street banks that are willing to tolerate racism for tax cuts and fewer regulations. Democrats have to take on these bad actors, and we can't do it when our best operatives are on the same payroll as our Republican opponents.

Stop Triangulating

The 2016 election did real damage to the brand of the party among the supporters of Bernie Sanders and people who don't like losing to Trump.[34] But long before that, the Republicans spent decades and untold amounts of money demonizing the Democratic Party. Heck, they have an entire television network dedicated to the project. The media loves nothing more than stories about Democratic infighting, so much so that the idea of "Dems in disarray" has become an internet meme.

However, the worst criticism of the Democratic Party too often comes from inside our own house. Bill Clinton's "triangulation"

---

34 So, basically everyone.

strategy is the root of this problem. It should come as no surprise that it was developed by Dick Morris, a Republican strategist who worked for Clinton, and Mark Penn,[35] a former Democratic pollster turned private-equity investor and Trump defender.

By painting Democrats as too liberal, Clinton accepted the premise of the Republican argument and advanced it.

In 2008, Obama campaigned against triangulation. The line "We have had enough of triangulation and poll-driven politics" was a staple of the stump speech. Obama's wins in 2008 and 2012 were supposed to be the death of triangulation in Democratic Party politics. And then 2016 happened.

One of the major narratives that emerged from that election ascribes Clinton's loss to Democrats being too liberal and too focused on issues like LGBTQ rights, police violence against African Americans, and immigration and therefore failing to appeal to "real Americans" in the Midwest. This narrative was roundly rejected by most in the party and those that looked at the data, but it took hold in a lot of "official" Washington.

It is true that Trump received critical votes from moderate Obama supporters in rural counties, but it is also true that four million people that voted for Obama in 2012 didn't show up in 2016. Nevertheless, there is a wing of Democrats echoing Republican talking points and calling Democrats too liberal for the Rust Belt, Midwest, or whatever euphemism for white people that you want to use.

The early 2020 presidential primary debates were filled with arguments about whether Democrats were too liberal, elite, or out of touch that could easily have been confused with something heard on the set of *Fox & Friends*. Maryland congressman

---

35 Mark Penn was also Hillary Clinton's chief strategist in 2008. He proposed a racist, xenophobic strategy to defeat Obama, claiming that Obama "didn't have American roots." Clinton rejected the strategy. She should have also fired him on the spot.

John Delaney seemed to be running for the sole purpose of attacking other Democrats with vaguely Republican-sounding talking points. In the Congress, there is a bipartisan group of members called the Problem Solvers Caucus whose purpose is to cause problems for the Democratic Party. It is, not coincidentally, run by New Jersey congressman Josh Gottheimer, a protégé of Mark Penn. Triangulation also helps explain how some Democrats have approached "the Squad"—the quartet of progressive women of color elected in 2018. Some in the party seem as intent on articulating their differences with Representative Alexandria Ocasio-Cortez as they are with Mitch McConnell.

Democrats have to stop running against the Democratic Party. Even Obama, who explicitly rejected triangulation, could have done more early in his presidency to talk about what it meant to be a Democrat. Our 2008 electoral coalition involved Republicans and independents, and we were too often too reticent to proudly link "Obamaism" with the Democratic Party. This got better over time as we realized that Obama's political prospects and agenda rose and fell with those of the Democratic Party—which is ultimately the lesson going forward. If we want to convince voters of all stripes to vote for Democrats, we have to stop triangulating and start talking proudly about the Democratic Party—who we are, what we stand for, and who we are fighting for. There is room for good-faith intraparty debates, but let's put to rest the resurgent triangulation politics of the 1990s.

America has only two parties, and one of them is a morally bankrupt, intellectually dishonest collection of elected racists and grifters, so if we have any hope at all of getting out of this moment, we need a reenergized, reformed, and smarter Democratic Party. Democrats are the last hope for democracy.

Let's act like it.

What You Can Do to Help

- Adopt a down-ballot race—volunteer, donate, and see if you have a skill that the campaign is in need of. The more local the race, the smaller the staff. If you can help with writing, coding, graphic design—the list goes on—the campaign could oftentimes use the help.
- Run for office (seriously, do it).
- If you don't run (you should), donate to Run for Something to support candidates up and down the ballot.
- Check out Sister District—they connect Democratic volunteers with red districts to help flip them.
- Support the Democratic Legislative Campaign Committee.
- Get involved with your local Democratic Party.

CHAPTER 7

THE ART OF INFORMATION WARFARE

But most importantly, @CNN is bad for the USA. Their International Division spews bad information & Fake News all over the globe. This is why foreign leaders are always asking me, "Why does the Media hate the U.S. sooo much?" It is a fraudulent shame, & all comes from the top!

—@realDonaldTrump, September 9, 2019

If it weren't for the never ending Fake News about me, and with all that I have done (more than any other President in the first 2 1/2 years!), I would be leading the "Partners" of the LameStream Media by 20 points. Sorry, but true!

—@realDonaldTrump, September 11, 2019[1]

Here we go with the Fake Polls. Just like what happened with the Election against Crooked Hillary Clinton. ABC, NBC, CNN, @nytimes, @washingtonpost, they all got it wrong, on purpose. Suppression Polls so early? They will never learn!

—@realDonaldTrump, July 15, 2019

---

1 Yes, the president tweeted this absurdity on the eighteenth anniversary of 9/11.

> The Mainstream Media has NEVER been more dishonest than it is now. NBC and MSNBC are going Crazy. They report stories, purposely, the exact opposite of the facts. They are truly the Opposition Party working with the Dems. May even be worse than Fake News CNN, if that is possible!
>
> —@realDonaldTrump, January 9, 2019

In addition to being exhibits A through D in a very compelling Twenty-Fifth Amendment hearing, these tweets are just a small sampling of the hundreds of times the president has used his Twitter account to complain about the press. If you were to believe Trump, his supporters, and his advisors at Fox, you would think that the media was engaged in a well-coordinated effort to take down the president of the United States.

There is a rich irony to these Trumpian Twitter tantrums: the media that he loves to beat up might just be helping him.

Most reporters are personally liberal. Most of their editors are personally liberal. The executives who run the tech companies that distribute the news written and edited by liberals are also mostly liberal.

Yet somehow, despite the overwhelming number of liberals who make and share the news, the media deck is stacked against Democrats.

This hard truth is counterintuitive and uncomfortable for a lot of Democrats. It's our party that romanticizes the role of the media. I would wager that 90 percent of the audience for the films *The Post* and *Spotlight* were Democrats. It's our party that believes in rules and norms. We want to live in a world with fact-checkers who can call out the lies and referees who can penalize the liars. As Donald Trump has puppeted authoritarians and called the media the "enemy of the people," it's Democrats who have rushed to their defense and subscribed in solidarity to the *New York Times* and *Washington Post*.

Democratic politicians and political operatives are friends with reporters. We drink, eat, and socialize together. They attend our weddings and baby showers, and we attend theirs.[2] Ultimately, we believe in the media's mythology about themselves—it's a mythology born of Watergate when reporters were the ones that brought down a corrupt president. That's a huge mistake. That story wasn't true then, and it certainly isn't true now. There is no modern-day Bob Woodward about to walk through those doors and save us from Trump.[3]

Let me be clear: Democrats are right to value the role the media plays in public life and defend the press from Trump's dangerous attacks. Subscribing to the *Times* and *Post* is a good idea—they put out great products.[4]

However, this affection for the old-world media has blinded Democrats to the way the landscape has changed and prevented us from adopting the policies and strategies necessary to communicate in the modern age.

The change happened slowly and then suddenly. An aggressive right-wing propaganda machine, the corporate consolidation of media, and the emergence of social media as a primary distributor of news have amplified right-wing voices and drowned out left ones.

None of this is to say that the members of the media are themselves conservative. They aren't. I'm not arguing that they want the Republicans to win. They don't. I am arguing that cultural and technological trends, institutional biases, and the economic

---

2 Despite Trump's rhetoric, Republican politicians and operatives also hang out with reporters, but they don't like to admit it publicly. It's sort of a "camp friendship" in that way.

3 We know this because Bob Woodward wrote a pretty devastating book about Trump, and the president didn't immediately resign.

4 Don't get me wrong: I will spontaneously combust if I read one more profile of a bar/diner/bowling alley in Pennsylvania where all the people wear MAGA hats.

incentives of the modern media advantage the Republicans. Trump's election is proof positive of this phenomenon.

Democrats started losing the messaging battles in the latter years of the Obama administration,[5] got clobbered in 2016, and have yet to adjust to the new reality. As long as we cling to a nostalgia for a world that no longer exists,[6] Trumpism will continue to prevail.

FACEBOOK + FOX = FUCKED.

I remember the moment I realized that the ground had shifted. It was 2013, a year plagued by a series of political problems and bad luck that made me often wonder if Barack Obama had wished for reelection on W. W. Jacobs's monkey's paw.[7]

Washington was kicking the crap out of Obama on a daily basis. The cable channels were overflowing with asinine conventional wisdom about the fate of Obama's presidency. The pundits were calling for a shake-up of the president's staff.[8]

We were buffeted by events beyond our control on a near daily basis. It was impossible to get a message out, and every time we got a little momentum, there would be some problem that originated in a backwater office of some government agency that would knock us off message.

To top it all off, we were staring down the barrel of an absolutely brutal midterm where Senate Democrats were defending seats in very Republican states.

---

5 Although, Obama and his White House staff did a phenomenal job in the years after I left and wrote the playbook for what must come next.

6 Like the idea that a couple of *Washington Post* reporters that look like Redford and Hoffman could bring down a president.

7 TLDR: you get a wish, but it destroys your life.

8 My name in particular was being bandied about as a potential sacrifice on the altar of conventional wisdom.

Not great.

Through this period, I comforted myself with my long-held belief that there was a chasm between the things DC obsessed over and the things voters cared about. During Obama's first term, there would be an endless series of political conflagrations that would lead to an endless series of cable segments, stories in *Politico*, and hand-wringing from political observers. Yet whenever we would conduct a poll or focus group to check in on the electorate, they would have no knowledge about any of the brouhaha du jour in DC.

This opinion research consistently helped us separate the signal from the noise and understand the difference between what voters cared about and what politicos (and *Politico*) cared about. It was a cudgel we used to argue with reporters about the political ramifications (or lack thereof) of various picayune obsessions.

The quintessential faux scandal of the Obama era centered around allegations that the Cincinnati office of the Internal Revenue Service had scrutinized conservative groups applying for tax-exempt status. This became a massive story right away. It had echoes of Watergate—when Nixon weaponized the IRS and every journalist of a certain generation looks in the mirror and sees Bob Woodward.[9] The media was in a feeding frenzy—was this another example of a president using the IRS to punish their political opponents? Now, of course, there was no evidence of any connections or communications between Obama and the perpetrators, and the idea that Obama was running a political vengeance scheme through career bureaucrats working out of the third-largest city in Ohio is implausible, to say the least.

The story broke on a Friday and for a variety of reasons, based on my guidance, Obama didn't address the press about it. My

9 The Robert Redford version from *All the President's Men*, not the current one from the *Morning Joe* roundtable.

main rationale was we didn't know anything, and I generally believe that it doesn't make sense for a president to address the press about something that has little to do with them when none of the facts are in.[10] And what the heck is the president supposed to do about a group of people in Ohio that he didn't hire, has never met, and couldn't really fire if he wanted to?

The Republicans and conservative media fanned the flames into a media inferno. Because no new information emerged over the weekend, the story turned—as it often does—to the optics of Obama's response.

Why didn't he address the media? Was he too aloof? Out of touch? Was this a political gaffe? Et cetera, et cetera, et cetera.

The *Morning Joe* roundtable was frothing at the mouth. Panicky Democrats on Capitol Hill were going on cable to complain about the White House response.

This was one of the first big political messes of the second term. There had been an exodus after the reelect, and we had a lot of new folks sitting around the table in the chief of staff's office for the morning senior staff meeting. People were a little shaken up after we all got our asses kicked for a few days. I was the senior political person in the room. I had been there for all the other near-death experiences, so I wanted to reassure people that this would all be fine.

"Look, this sucks. It's our time to be in the barrel. But this isn't the kind of thing that is going to matter to voters. I would be shocked if any 'real people' have any idea about all this."

I was wrong. A few days later, the Democratic National Committee conducted their regular round of focus groups. Lo and behold, the voters were very well aware of this particular Beltway scandal. They were essentially reading back the Republican talking points to the moderators.

---

10 This turned out to be logical but very bad advice.

I told myself that maybe this one was different because of the echoes of previous scandals.[11]

Early the next year, there were shocking reports of problems at the Department of Veterans Affairs. Same result. It kept happening over and over again. The controversies that dominated Washington that were fanned by conservative media were all of a sudden breaking through to the populace at large. They weren't just aware of the story. They were hearing about and understanding the story through the chosen frame of Obama's opponents.

When the focus-group moderators asked the group where they got this information, they got the same answer every time—Facebook.

It was a point of pride in the Obama land that we understood the media landscape better than most. We were ahead of the curve when it came to using the internet and social media to communicate with voters. Long before Trump was starting wars and offending countries with his Twitter account, Obama was using Twitter to go around the filter of the media and communicate directly with the public. Obama was the first president to appear on late-night TV, YouTube, and Medium.

But somewhere, somehow, the ground shifted under our feet. We were now at a decided disadvantage.

Seven years later, most Democrats are still playing from behind. Just rerunning the same old plays and wondering why they aren't working.

There are three factors pushing the media environment in the decidedly wrong direction:

The first is conservative propaganda as a viable business model and a successful Republican Party strategy. Much has been written about the rise and pernicious role of Fox News.[12]

---

11 And likely future ones.
12 I even wrote some of it.

I will also state this for the ten thousandth time. Fox doesn't do "journalism." It is a pure partisan propaganda outlet that employs a handful of journalists that don't do journalism as it is commonly understood. They stand in front of cameras and attend press conferences, but they aren't seeking out the truth. The Fox reporters are doing journalistic cosplay. They are propaganda beards. It is a party organ. There is no equivalent on the Democratic side. Not. Even. Close.

It was a burr in Obama's saddle,[13] but in the Trump era, Fox has become state television akin to something you would see in North Korea or Russia.[14] Its reach and influence have grown as it becomes the primary information source of the president of the United States. Republican politicians who want the support of the president don't meet with the White House political director.[15] They go on Fox News as often as possible in the hopes that the president will see them in the many, many hours he isn't working. Trump has been known to dial Lou Dobbs and Jeanine Pirro into policy meetings in the Oval Office. He has considered *Fox & Friends* host Pete Hegseth for multiple cabinet positions and Laura Ingraham for press secretary. Trump even hired Bill Shine, the former president of Fox News, for my old job in the White House. In addition to having zero qualifications for the post, Shine had been fired from Fox News for spending years covering up a wide array of sexual misconduct and other illegal activities.

Tucker Carlson, who has replaced his whale belt with one featuring Pepe the Frog, overruled the president's national security team and stopped a military strike against Iran while the planes were reportedly in the air.

---

13 A really sharp, racist burr.
14 It's not an accident that these are Trump's favorite world leaders. I think we call this "dictator envy."
15 Whoever that sad, soon-to-be-incarcerated soul may be.

Fox is no longer alone. In its shadow, digital upstarts like Breitbart, the Daily Caller, and the Gateway Pundit have grown in size and influence. One America News Network is a media outlet that was created on the premise that Fox News isn't insane enough. The most dangerous example of Republican propaganda may be the effort by Sinclair Broadcast Group to bring Fox-style propaganda to local television. Sinclair is a conservative media company that owns more local TV stations than anyone else—nearly two hundred, reaching 39 percent of the population. Sinclair forces all of their stations to run a national political message that is always pro-Trump or anti someone who is anti-Trump. They forced their anchors to parrot White House talking points about "fake news." They hired Boris Epshteyn, who was fired from the Trump White House, to direct their political coverage. Sinclair has huge expansion plans—they tried to buy Tribune Broadcasting, which would have given them nearly three-fourths of the national broadcast market. That deal was scuttled by Trump's own FCC after reports of improper contacts between the FCC chairman and Sinclair but will almost certainly be revived in the future. They are also buying up regional sports networks and other outlets to increase their reach in the coming years.

Sinclair is so dangerous because a lot of the right-wing propaganda is something you have to opt into. You turn on Fox or Rush Limbaugh or click on Breitbart with at least an inkling of what you are signing up for. Local news is a passive activity. It's been the most trusted news source for decades. A study by political science professors at Emory University found that Sinclair is already having an impact. According to the authors of the study, "Stations bought by Sinclair reduce coverage of local politics, increase national coverage, and move the ideological tone of coverage in a conservative direction relative to other stations operating in the same market."

All across America, people are sitting down to find out what's happening in their community, check out the weather, or get some local sports highlights, and pro-Trump propaganda is being beamed into their brains.

Propaganda is here to stay as a Republican Party strategy. It's something they have always believed in and tried to utilize. It was just done on the sly. Republican political consultants and campaigns are now creating fake media outlets to house and propagate pro-Republican and anti-Democratic messaging. Definers, a leading Republican consulting firm run by former aides to George W. Bush and Mitt Romney, created its own news site that they populated with opposition research and articles written by their employees to promote the agenda of their clients. Republican congressman Devin Nunes created his own "alternative" news site to push his propaganda. We are going to see more and more of this in the coming years.

The second problem is Facebook. The social media platform isn't new. It has been around for nearly fifteen years at this point. Facebook was a key organizing tool for college students that wanted to support Obama in 2008. Obama's reelection campaign spent millions on Facebook ads targeting voters. But something had changed by Obama's second term; Facebook had reached a tipping point where it was becoming a primary vehicle for news distribution. It was exposing voters to political information that they otherwise would not have sought out. In theory, that's a good thing. We want a more informed citizenry. However, the public wasn't seeing objective reporting. This wasn't *PBS NewsHour* on speed. Facebook was pushing partisan propaganda and willful misinformation. Much has been written about how Cambridge Analytica, Russian government trolls, and money-hungry Albanian teenagers abused Facebook's naive utopianism to affect the election. Those problems are (theoretically) fixable.[16] Facebook

---

16 Whether Facebook is willing or able to do so is a different question.

can change the rules, impose better security, and develop better technology.

The bigger problem for democracy and Democrats is that the algorithm that powers the biggest media company in the world promotes conservative content more than progressive content.

Wait—how is that possible? Trump and Republican politicians have been screaming about the big tech companies being biased against conservatives. They claim they are being censored and "shadow banned." This is—per usual—bad-faith bullshit. Yes, of course it's true that Mark Zuckerberg, Sheryl Sandberg, and just about everyone else in Silicon Valley is a Democrat. Yes, it's true that most of the people who work in tech are Democrats. But their products are playing a key role in shifting the political conversation to the right.

People are being bombarded with something more like what comes on Fox News at 9:00 p.m. than what comes on the local news at 6:00 p.m.[17]

The most rudimentary explanation of the process is that you only see some of what your "friends" post on Facebook. Because Facebook's goal is to keep you on the site for as long as possible so that they can show you as many ads as possible, Facebook surfaces the posts that they think you are most likely to engage with. Therefore, the Facebook algorithm, which is a black box,[18] promotes the posts that receive the most engagement. Facebook usually defines engagement as the sum total of comments, likes, and shares. As it turns out, the content that drives outrage leads to the most engagement. And it also turns out that outrage is the language of the Right.

As *New York Times* columnist Charlie Warzel wrote, "Just as television favored a new brand of well-coiffed, charismatic,

---

17 Non-Sinclair local news.
18 And the closest thing we have to Skynet.

and dynamic political figures, Facebook offers a disproportionate advantage to those most likely to stoke negative emotions."

Sound like anyone you know?

Facebook is the answer to an important riddle. For all the talk about the influence of Fox News, the network's audience is relatively miniscule. Sean Hannity's show is the most watched on the network, and it only reaches about three million people. This makes it the most-watched show on cable—a dwindling medium. But it's a fraction of the overall populace.[19] Yet what is said on Fox News is believed by a portion of the Republican electorate that is exponentially larger than a couple of million people. The virus is spreading, and Facebook is the carrier.

Fox News and digital upstarts like Breitbart, Ben Shapiro's the Daily Wire, and the Daily Caller quickly realized the opportunity that Facebook presented them. They gamed the algorithm by writing outrageous stories with even more outrageous headlines that would generate online controversy—headlines like these:

"Birth Control Makes Women Unattractive and Crazy"
"Gabby Giffords: The Gun Control Movement's Human Shield"[20]

There would be thousands of comments. Never-ending angry debates in the comments section. Each comment meant more and more people would see the post. Each controversy would build a larger online audience for the publication. Rinse. Repeat.

Because outrage fuels the algorithm and outrage is the language of Republicans not Democrats, we are at a decided disadvantage. For all the media's obsession with Twitter, Facebook is where the conversation happens, and it's a conversation defined

---

19 *Pod Save America* episodes have reached more people.
20 These are real headlines from Breitbart. I don't have the perverse creativity necessary to make this shit up.

by conservative voices. In the run-up to the 2020 election, Facebook's actions raised questions about whether they were casting their lot with the Republicans. Facebook made the incredibly controversial decision to allow politicians to run ads that contain provable lies on their platform, which certainly advantages Trump. Mark Zuckerberg couched this decision as a defense of free speech, but free speech and paid speech are not the same thing. Facebook is doing more than letting politicians say what they want. Facebook is allowing politicians to pay them to target lies at the voters that Facebook's data says are most susceptible to believing those lies. It's disinformation for profit.

As more and more Democrats come out for breaking up Facebook, some are left to wonder whether Facebook—like other giant corporations—feels that its interests are better served by Republican control of Washington.

The third problem is also Facebook. Well, sort of. Facebook helped destroy the business model of traditional journalism.[21] Most media outlets depend either largely or entirely on digital ads to keep the lights on. This creates a strong financial incentive to engage in journalism that drives traffic to their articles. The more traffic, the more money. There is nothing inherently wrong with this approach, for all of our deification of the media—journalism is first and foremost a business. Great journalism or writing that no one sees and advertisers won't advertise with ultimately serves no purpose. The problem is that the pressure for clicks is pushing media outlets down a Trumpian rabbit hole. Facebook delivers a lot of the traffic to articles. Therefore, media outlets are prisoners of the perversions of the Facebook algorithm.

Trumpian outrage fuels Facebook, which sends traffic to

---

21 Google helped. As did the internet more generally, combined with some really dumb business decisions from media outlets that decided to give the product away for free.

articles about Trump, which means the media writes more articles about Trump. Lo and behold, Trump now functions more as the nation's assignment editor than its commander in chief. Trump influences what the press writes about, broadcasts, and tweets about. When he doesn't like the direction the conversation is going, he skillfully changes the topic by tweeting something outrageous, offensive, or both.

The mainstream media is not "pro-Trump." Far from it. He calls them the "enemy of the people." He accused the *New York Times* of treason—a crime punishable by death.[22] His rhetoric puts their lives at risk. In 2018, a Trump supporter—taking his cues from the president's tweets—mailed pipe bombs to CNN. Yet the bulk of the coverage happens on Trump's terms. Even if the tenor of the coverage is often not great for Trump. We are still talking about what Trump wants us to talk about. The issues that matter to Democratic voters, the ones that help us win elections—health care, economic inequality, and civil rights—will never get their due in the current media environment. They aren't outrageous enough.

Democrats may win an election or two under these conditions, but we will never defeat Trumpism or move the country in a truly progressive direction. Despite all the disadvantages, Democrats can win the message war.

PREPARE FOR WAR

The biggest takeaway from this change in the media environment is that political communications is no longer public relations; it is modern information warfare.

22 Trump seems to do this a lot, which is what psychologists call "projection."

When I started in politics, you won or lost the media cycle on the quantity and quality of your news coverage. Republicans and Democrats were competing to see who could do a better job spinning the same reporters. Speeches, press releases, and sit-down interviews were the tools of the trade.

Campaigns are now modern information warfare. We are dealing with a massive state-adjacent propaganda operation, Twitter bots fueling outrage and driving coverage, Facebook pages running out of the former Soviet republics that reach more people than the *New York Times*, and foreign countries like Russia trying to actively intervene in the election.

To compete in this new and terrifying environment, Democrats need to abandon our old strategies and nostalgia for bygone days and get on a war footing. Here are seven commandments for winning the information war.

1: CHANGE OR DIE

My first job in political communications was twenty years ago. When I started, we faxed press releases to reporters. If they weren't in the office, they didn't get them. We would reach out to reporters via a pager. On the night before a big story was supposed to be in the *Washington Post*, I would go to the loading dock outside the *Post*'s headquarters to get a copy of the paper after it came off the presses but before it was loaded into the trucks to be taken to newsstands all over the city. This was the only way to know what was going to be in the paper until some kid tossed it on your doorstep the next morning. To the extent that you got emails from reporters, they were sent more like letters—with the acknowledgment that you may not see them for hours and, in some cases, days. The campaign staff that tracked the opponent would videotape every speech (with a camera) and then mail the tapes (in an envelope) back to the headquarters, where we would watch them days later to see what our opponent said. Rapid response wasn't so rapid.

The evening news was the most dominant event of the day—the staff usually gathered around to watch it to see how we did in terms of getting our message out.

Obviously a lot has changed in two decades.[23] The news cycle is 24-7. No one reads an actual paper.[24] The news is beamed into our phones, and no one is ever more than an email, text, or tweet away. Facebook, Twitter, and Instagram have fundamentally changed how people—and politicians—communicate. The mainstream media of today is unrecognizable compared to twenty years ago. A lot of outlets have gone the way of the dinosaurs. What used to be paramount is now peripheral.

Yet despite a massive technological, economic, and cultural transformation, the basic model for how Democratic politicians communicate has barely changed. After Obama won the White House, I joined the presidential transition team that was helping Obama staff the government that he was about to take over. My task was to develop the staffing structure for the communications operation. On my first day, I was provided with the organizational charts for every White House from Jimmy Carter to George W. Bush. I was curious to see how things had changed in the White House as the media had changed. I was shocked by what I found—the way the White House did communications had barely changed in thirty years. Team Obama had big thoughts about how to modernize White House communications. But, while our initial approach was certainly different—and more digital friendly—it was still uncomfortably close to the way things had been done.

---

23 Just typing that sentence made me feel so damn old.
24 Besides my parents.

The theory of communications that has undergirded politics for decades is as follows:

Politician says something → press covers it → public reads or watches the press's account of what the politician said.

The fundamental idea is that other than paid television ads that are used in campaigns, the primary way get the message out is through the media. It's the job of the politicians to get the message to the media, and then it's the media's job to get the message to the public. Back in the days when Americans got all their information from the newspapers delivered to their doors and the news that aired on the small number of channels on their TVs, this strategy made sense. This strategy is doomed to fail in the era of Trump and Twitter.

Blowing up the old model is so far overdue. The task of the modern communications department is not about getting "coverage"; it's about influencing the conversation. It's about using every tool available to persuade people—the traditional media is just one tool in the box, and it ain't the main tool.

2: THE *NEW YORK TIMES* IS NOT GOING TO SAVE US

Democrats love reporters. We romanticize the media. Trump's authoritarian tantrums against the media have actually reinforced our crush on journalism. To be anti-Trump in this era is to be pro-media. Subscribing to the *New York Times* and watching CNN is an act of resistance.

It's time to fall out of love.

I deeply respect the work that journalists do. I don't believe the media "elected" Trump. We are living in a golden age of accountability journalism. Democrats should speak out loudly and often against Trump's antipress rhetoric. The next Democratic president should reinstate the daily White House briefing that Sarah Sanders killed.

However, it's time we realized that journalists are not on our side. We have vastly different agendas and competing interests. It's not their job to convince voters that Trump is bad. They are not the guardians of democracy[25] or arbiters of truth. The media as it is commonly understood is no longer the primary conduit of information about public affairs and world events. They reach fewer people, and their stories have less impact. As I mentioned previously, the *New York Times* ran a story in 2018 that assiduously documented that Trump was guilty of tax fraud (which is a crime), and no one cared. It's not that people don't care whether the president commits crimes;[26] it's that the power of one story in one paper to drive the conversation is greatly diminished in the rapid-fire world of Twitter, Netflix, YouTube, and smartphones.

Traditional media powers are now just one voice in a cacophonous, chaotic information ecosystem where anyone with a smartphone in the right place at the right time can be as influential and impactful as—if not more than—the entire White House press corps.

It's time to adopt a more holistic communications strategy that includes but is not limited to the traditional media.

3: BECOME YOUR OWN MEDIA OUTLET

The definition of what is a media outlet has grown incredibly elastic in the internet age. The New York Times is a media company, in addition to the newspaper—they have podcasts, a website, newsletters, and even a TV series—but so is Crooked Media, the parent company of *Pod Save America*. We also have podcasts,

---

25 Despite ad campaigns to the contrary.

26 Although polling does show that most Republicans don't care if a Republican president commits crimes.

newsletters, and a television series.[27] What the Times and Crooked Media have in common with each other and with BuzzFeed, the Ringer, TMZ, and ESPN is that we are all in the content business. Communication in the modern age is about creating and distributing content to people who may be interested in that content. Campaigns need to become their own content factories. When you pass your message through the press to the public, you are passing it through a filter that dilutes the power of your message. The media outlets that cover politics are often marketing specifically to a group of politically obsessed consumers as opposed to the public at large. This has always been true to an extent, but the problem has gotten much worse in the Trump era. Obsession with the never-ending horror show set in the White House has been a stimulus package for the struggling media. Subscriptions are way up, and people are tuning into cable at levels much higher than one would expect in nonelection years. Instead of covering plane crashes nonstop, CNN and MSNBC cover and debate politics 24-7.[28] This means that every issue the press covers is put through a sometimes cynical political filter: How does this help their campaign? How does Candidate A's criminal justice policy affect African American turnout? How will Trump voters respond to a wealth tax?

That filter reinforces all the worst impressions about politics. It's particularly damaging for Democrats whose only path to victory depends on convincing nonvoters to become voters. The solution is to go above, around, and through the filter. Every day the campaign needs to wake up thinking not about their press strategy, but about what content they are going to create to tell their own story. The idea of campaigns creating their own videos,

---

27 Crooked doesn't have a newspaper, because the idea of printing news on a dead tree is really dumb.

28 Except when MSNBC pivots to its very odd block of prison documentaries, in which many Trump officials may make a cameo.

memes, and tweets has been around for years. Many politicians do it. Some even do it well.[29] But it is always a secondary strategy, since the communications director still spends the overwhelming majority of their time planning the press strategy—what interview the candidate should do, which media outlet to leak an announcement to, how to spin the talking heads on cable. That's all important stuff on a campaign, but it's not the most important—not even close. The focus needs to be on how to tell the candidate's/president's/political party's story, not how to get the press to tell the story. This means following the model of Beto O'Rourke's Senate campaign where he told his story directly to the voters without relying on the mainstream media. His campaign livestreamed him at events, driving in the car, skateboarding in the Whataburger parking lot, and even making breakfast with his kids. He told his story on his terms. This strategy allowed him to navigate the media environment and talk about the issues that he wanted to talk about, not the issues the press (and his opponent, Ted Cruz) wanted him to talk about (which were usually the issues Trump tweeted about). The traditional media still has an important role to play, but it's a role, not THE role.

To truly accomplish this strategy, we need to blow up the staffing structure that has existed in campaigns for decades. Replace the communications director with a chief content officer who builds an overall strategy for persuading the public via all available means—advertising, digital content, social media, and the press. The old way isn't working. We got clobbered in 2010, 2014, and 2016. We will again and again if we don't update our strategies to reflect changes in the media.

29 Most are a walking dad joke of an internet strategy.

4: PROGRESSIVE MEDIA IS THE FUTURE

One of the by-products (and causes) of the diminishing influence of the mainstream media is the rising influence of the conservative media. When the mainstream media was more powerful, it drove the political conversation, while the right-wing stuff existed on the fringes of talk radio and the dark corners of the internet. In this environment, the loudest, most outrageous voices rule the day, especially when the president uses the bully pulpit of the White House as a turbocharger. Every day, social media is flooded with conservative content from Fox, Breitbart, and Trump's Twitter account. Nothing is more important in the long-term effort to defeat Trumpism than to build an aggressive, compelling media infrastructure that can be a countervailing force. We need to speak directly to progressives across the country. There have been some really good efforts to do this since 2016. I am very proud of *Pod Save America* and Crooked Media's role in those efforts, but there is so much more work to do. We need so many more progressive media outlets generating compelling content and pushing it into the social media ecosystem to shift the national conversation leftward. There are more progressives than conservatives, yet they have a fraction of the media options that conservatives do. Progressives dominate the eighteen-to-forty-nine-year-old cohort that advertisers and politicians covet. Yet there has been a limited willingness by the traditional players to invest in truly progressive media. There is as of yet no liberal Rupert Murdoch who wants to push their political agenda and build a successful business.[30]

A lot of the Democratic response to the rise of conservative media has been to bolster traditional media. Amazon founder Jeff Bezos bought the *Washington Post*, billionaire Democratic donor Laurene Powell Jobs bought the *Atlantic*, and Obama fund-raiser and

---

30 If you are a potential liberal Rupert Murdoch, my DMs are open.

Salesforce CEO Marc Benioff bought *Time* magazine. Philanthropists are investing in nonpartisan investigative journalism. All of these efforts are worthwhile, but they come at the expense of an investment in new and existing outlets that can amplify a strong progressive message. It's easy to see why this is important with Trump in the White House—*Pod Save America, The Intercept,* and others serve as Radio Free America while Trump occupies the White House. But a robust progressive media will be necessary for the next Democratic president[31] to advance any sort of agenda. Unless changes happen very quickly, the next Democratic president will be hamstrung trying to communicate with a diminished bully pulpit and through a mainstream media that will savage him or her to prove to Trump supporters that they aren't "biased."

5: IT TAKES AN ARMY

My wife, Howli, is a political organizer at heart. She helped Obama win North Carolina in 2008. Every election, she puts on her walking shoes and heads out to canvass for the nearest campaign of note. She brings me along even though down deep she considers me to be a subpar canvasser who slows her down.[32] In 2016, we went to Las Vegas to knock on doors for Hillary Clinton and Catherine Cortez Masto, who ran for Senate. In 2018, we drove a couple of hours to Modesto to volunteer for Josh Harder, who was running for the House in a Republican district.[33] We brought our then five-month-old daughter with us.[34] This sort of

31

32 Who am I kidding? It's not down that deep.

33 Technically, Howli is undefeated.

34 Taking an infant for hours of walking seems insane on its face, but she was pretty good and certainly cute enough to maybe swing some votes.

field organizing has been the lifeblood of Democratic campaigns for decades. Research shows that the best way to persuade a voter is a face-to-face conversation. This is why campaigns spend so much time hiring field organizers and recruiting volunteers to go door-to-door.

In the modern information age, this model doesn't reflect the speed and reach of communication today. To be clear, I am not arguing that we should abandon traditional field organizing, and not just because I would like to stay married. Traditional field organizing is critical and effective and must continue, but it's not sufficient. Democrats need to build tools and strategies to take the wildly successful grassroots organizing that is the heart and soul of the party and move it online as a communication strategy.

Nearly every American is walking around with a supercomputer in their pocket that lets them communicate easily with anyone in the world. The average Facebook user has 338 friends. The average Instagram user has more than 100 followers. Everyone has a growing list of contacts in their phone. Imagine a world where campaigns built tools that told you which of your contacts were undecided or unregistered. What if the campaigns had a hub where you could access memes, graphs, or videos to persuade your friends to support a candidate? What if every person who supported a candidate could be asked to echo the message of the day—to take the short clip from the speech or the boffo news article and share it with their friends? What if there were tools that made it easy for you to respond with factual information when you saw your uncle or high school gym teacher sharing false information on Facebook or somewhere else on the internet?

I wonder sometimes if we would have been able to stop birtherism (and maybe Trump) in its tracks in 2008 if these sorts of tools and technologies had been available back then. People could have been flooding Facebook with copies of Obama's birth certificate or reaching out directly to their contacts with other evidence to rebut the conspiracy theories that the Right uses to "other-ize" Democrats.

The good news is that much of this technology has been built. It just needs to be updated, incorporated, and utilized.

A communications effort that mobilizes millions to amplify the message is the single best way to push back against the flood of right-wing propaganda coming out of Fox News and through Facebook.

6: ACTIVISM WORKS

Corporate America wants to have it both ways. They celebrate Pride Month with rainbow-colored social media posts and floats in parades. They have progressive diversity policies and syrupy commercials that celebrate the contributions of immigrants to America. But then their ads run on Fox News right after a racist rant by a millionaire white nationalist TV personality. If corporations want to decry racism and court racists at the same time, it's important to call them out. And here's the thing. It can work as a strategy.

In 2016, Breitbart was the leading edge of the pro-Trump propaganda machine. It is the preeminent white nationalist site on the internet and pumps out a shocking amount of racist, misogynistic, and homophobic content.[35]

After the election, Matt Rivitz and Nandini Jammi decided to do something about Breitbart. Rivitz and Jammi are not political operatives by profession. They both work in advertising in the Bay Area, which gave them an inside view of how companies make decisions about where to advertise. They started Sleeping Giants, an anonymous Twitter account that asked the public to

35 It's a place so racist and absurd that Ben Shapiro left.

take screenshots of company ads appearing on Breitbart. Sleeping Giants would use that screenshot to pressure the company to remove their ad. A large portion of digital advertising happens through ad networks, and the entity placing the ad often doesn't know where the ad is placed. Many of these companies were shocked to find their ads on Breitbart and immediately removed them. This strategy was phenomenally successful.

Steve Bannon, the former head of Breitbart and former Trump senior advisor, was quoted in the documentary *The Brink* as saying that because of Sleeping Giants Breitbart's ad revenue "dropped like 90 percent." Sleeping Giants has turned their focus to Fox News—pushing companies to stop advertising during Fox's prime-time hours when Sean Hannity, Laura Ingraham, and Tucker Carlson pollute the airwaves.[36] In 2019, they were making real progress especially during Tucker Carlson's show. A number of major advertisers fled, and Fox was forced to run ads for other Fox programs during otherwise lucrative commercial slots. The efforts of Sleeping Giants and others were having a real financial impact on the network. They were struggling with the stink of being a platform of, by, and for racists when all of a sudden an unlikely savior swooped in.

Bernie Sanders.

Yes, that Bernie Sanders[37]—the Democratic Socialist from Vermont. As part of his campaign for president, Sanders agreed to do a town hall broadcast on Fox News. Sanders, to his credit, crushed it. He made Bret Baier, the moderator, look foolish and got the crowd to go wild for single-payer health care.[38] Somewhere in the eleventh circle of hell, Roger Ailes's head exploded.

Sanders's success caused a mad rush of Democrats to schedule

---

36 And influence a president.
37 Sanders made what was the best decision for his campaign.
38 A historic moment in TV history.

Fox town halls. Mayor Pete Buttigieg also had a boffo, campaign-boosting performance in his Fox town hall. Senators Gillibrand and Klobuchar were next, and it went on and on. It got to the point where Fox, which is often scraping the bottom of the barrel for a Democrat to go on air, was turning away Democrats. All of this activity—while good for each of the individual campaigns—undid a lot of work to expose Fox's racism and propaganda to the public and advertisers.

This burst of Democratic enthusiasm happened right around the upfronts, which is the annual gathering when TV networks make their pitch to advertisers. Fox was able to go into those meetings and use Bernie Sanders, Pete Buttigieg, and others as validators. One could argue, these town halls helped keep Tucker Carlson on the air.[39]

I believe the Democratic Party should, as a policy, support the work of Sleeping Giants and others who are pressuring advertisers to square the circle between their company policies and what is said on Fox every day. There should be no Democratic town halls, debates, or other forums on Fox News. No Democrat would post on the white supremacist site 8chan. The degrees of difference between 8chan and a lot of what is said on Fox are fewer than most Democrats want to admit.

Conservatives, of course, scream "censorship" at the top of their lungs. But this isn't censorship. It's activism, and it works.

7: A PICTURE IS WORTH MORE THAN 280 CHARACTERS

For decades political strategists spent their time trying to figure out how to condense complex policies and nuanced messages into

---

39 And before all of you tweet at me about Obama doing a Super Bowl interview with notorious sexual harasser and then Fox host Bill O'Reilly: That was a mistake. We shouldn't have done it. Lesson learned.

thirty-second sound bites. In those days, television news was the primary vehicle for communicating with the public. If you wanted your message to get out, you needed to condense it into a bite-size increment that could be shown on the news. In recent years, the 280-character tweet has replaced the thirty-second sound bite as the maximum length for a message. If it can't be tweeted, it's too complex or confusing to break through.

Trump reminds us every day why Twitter is a problematic choice for the arena of political discourse. The measure of a successful message on Twitter is the retweet. The more RTs, the better. The problem with this approach is that Twitter is a bubble filled with activists, reporters, and white supremacists. It is not exactly a great proxy for the American public. What works on Twitter doesn't necessarily work in real life.[40]

The search for approbation from the Twitterverse can send politicians in strange directions. Hillary Clinton's most "successful" tweet in 2016 was replying to a Trump tweet with "Delete your account." This sick Twitter burn was retweeted a half million times.

Seems like a huge victory, right?

Maybe.

But what strategic goal did this tweet accomplish? Did it make anyone more likely to vote for her? Did it tell potential voters about her policies, character, or personal story?

This tweet isn't why Hillary lost.[41] It says more about Twitter than it does about Hillary the Twitterer.[42] While retweets for the sake of retweets is not an effective way to communicate a winning political message, it does speak to one key truth about communicating in the social media age. The only way to get your message

---

40 Or we should at least hope that is the case.

41 Although it is an example of how Trump forces everyone to play his childish games.

42 Tweeter?

out is to make it compelling enough that people want to share it on social media. The consumer is not only the end user; they are also a potential multiplier.

The most shareable messages are pictures, memes, and videos. People want to share them. They pause on them when they are scrolling through Facebook or Twitter while standing in line at the coffee shop. And they can be used on mildly less terrible social media platforms like Instagram.

Barack Obama is a historically talented orator who told his story better than any politician in memory. He was a wonk with well-thought-out, compelling policies. He had tremendously creative digital staff and ad makers. Yet the most compelling piece of content in his reelection campaign was not a speech, white paper, digital video, or television ad.

It was a simple chart.

We called it the jobs chart, and better than anything else, it showed the economic progress made since Obama took office. It was amazingly simple. People got it right away, and most important, our supporters loved sharing it on social media.

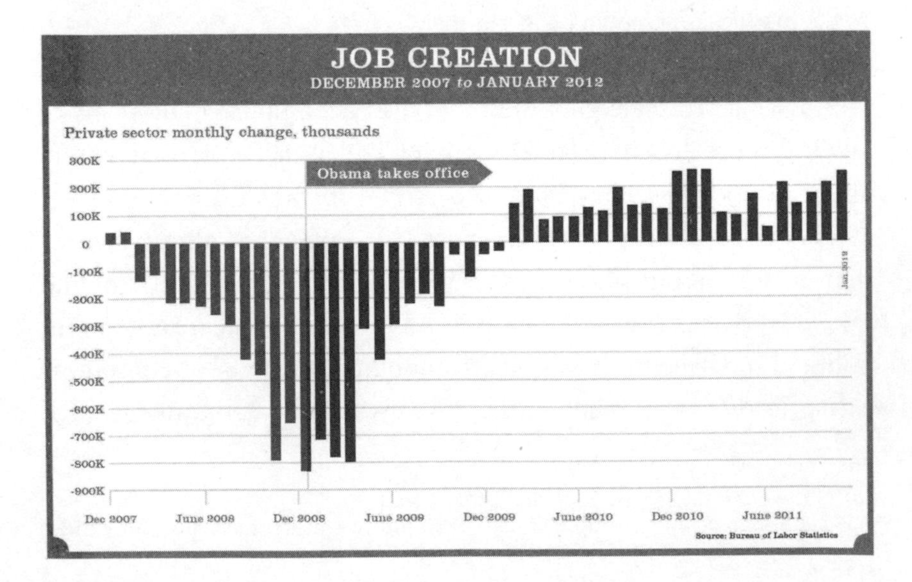

The Democratic Party needs a "jobs chart" for the Trump era, to cut to the heart of Trump's populist hypocrisy. We need memes that communicate his corruption and criminality.

Maybe it's tough to admit that the American attention span has been so diminished that we need to use pictures to tell a story, but that's where we are.

A WINNABLE WAR

Every meeting with politicians or their donors invariably becomes a discussion about "message." They believe that "message" is the answer to all of our problems. If we only look hard enough and long enough, we will find a message that will take down Trump and right all the world's wrongs. They want to find the Democratic version of "Make America Great Again."[43]

This holy grail–esque search is ultimately a distraction. There is no perfect phrase or killer slogan that will turn an election. The truth is that the efficacy of a message has a lot more to do with the messenger than the message itself—is it delivered in an authentic way by someone who inspires trust?

The Democratic Party would be so much better off if we took the time and energy spent on what the message is and spent it on developing tools and strategies that ensure people hear what we have to say.

On this measure, Democrats have fallen far behind. We have the better story, the more popular policies, and the best argument—making sure people know that is the key to winning more elections and passing progressive policies like universal health care and the Green New Deal.

---

43 A low point in Democratic messaging was Democratic leaders trying to turn "Make America decent again" into a thing.

Trump is a moron, but he is a masterful communicator who understands our dystopic media environment. We will not beat him if we don't get better at the basic task of telling our story.

What You Can Do to Help

- Support progressive media outlets like *Mother Jones*, the *American Prospect*, *The Intercept*, and others.[44]
- Subscribe to your local paper (if it still exists).
- Share stories and information that push the progressive message on social media. We have to tip the conversation away from your racist uncle.
- Pay for good journalism, including the *New York Times*.[45]
- Boycott the businesses that support Fox News.
- Support the work of Sleeping Giants.
- Donate to Acronym, a progressive nonprofit that is helping change how we communicate.

---

44 Also *Pod Save America* and all the other amazing offerings from Crooked Media.

45 You don't have to read Bret Stephens. Life is just more enjoyable if you can make yourself forget that he exists.

CHAPTER 8

(IMAGINARY) SUPER PAC SPENDING SPREE

It's important to have a hobby. Some people golf; others collect stamps.[1] My hobby—these days, at least—is super PAC cosplay. I spend more time than I should thinking about how I would use well-funded super PAC help to defeat Trump. I turned it into a recurring bit on *Pod Save America*—"Dan Pfeiffer's Imaginary Super PAC"—where I throw out ideas about how I would spend millions of imaginary dollars on ads and other things designed to drive down Trump's approval rating. This bit is equal parts thought exercise and unsubtle plea to some billionaire to hand me their checkbook. Trump is eminently beatable, but I stay up at night worrying about whether Trump will win the race long before we have a nominee, so I spend my time screaming into the void and/or tilting at windmills.[2]

The origin of my super PAC fascination dates back years.[3]

Nearly two years before Obama's reelection, Karl Rove's super PAC was poised to spend tens of millions of dollars to take down Obama long before our campaign would be up and running. To

---

1 Weird.

2 My super PAC fantasies are also an acknowledgment that I probably miss campaign work more than I am generally willing to admit.

3 It's still weird, but not as weird as you probably think.

say that this announcement scared the shit out of us would be an understatement. I remember an early campaign strategy meeting at David Axelrod's Washington, DC, apartment where David Plouffe laid out how he would spend Rove's millions. His ideas were frighteningly devious—ads targeted at college students attacking Obama for not doing enough to deal with climate change; ads targeted to Latinx voters in Colorado, Florida, and Nevada to detail Obama's failure to pass immigration reform in the first year, and so on.

Each idea was scarier than the next. They would have driven a wedge between Obama and the voters we needed to win, and since Rove had more money than we did, there was nothing we could do to stop it. I woke up every day wondering when the inevitable assault would start.

It never did.

Rove flushed millions of dollars down the toilet with poorly crafted, overly expensive TV ads.[4]

When Trump won, I harkened back to that meeting at Axelrod's apartment. What if someone—anyone—had Rove money but used it the way we feared Rove would? I made the rounds of the Democratic billionaires with my pitch but found no takers. Folks either thought it was too early or they were too burned by what happened in 2016 to invest in an e-only advertising campaign. Many pledged to invest heavily in an anti-Trump effort once the midterm elections were behind us.[5] A year after the midterms and a year before Trump's election, no such effort has started.

I don't have billions (or millions), but I do have ideas.[6] Here's how I would spend the millions that no one will give me:

The news people need: One of the weird ironies of our 24-7

---

4 Turns out Rove's moniker as "Bush's Brain" said more about Bush than Rove.

5 The effort started in late 2019. Better late than never.

6 If you have billions (or millions) and like my ideas, we should talk.

Trump obsession is that voters actually know very little about Trump. This is not an accident. Trump has a real ability to dominate the conversation in a way that blots out the sun, which means that a lot of really important stories never break through.

Here are some news stories that in a different media environment would have been game changers but went unnoticed:

"Trump Hotel in Washington Charged Secret Service $200,000 between 2016 and 2018," NBC News, June 27, 2019

"EXCLUSIVE: Trump vineyard also hired undocumented workers," *Univision*, May 2, 2019

"Deficit Tops $1 Trillion," *Wall Street Journal*, September 12, 2019

"Trump Pledged to Protect Medicare and Medicaid, but His 2020 Budget Calls for Major Spending Cuts," *CNBC*, March 12, 2019

"Trump Outpaces Obama, Bush in Naming Ex-Lobbyists to Cabinet," *Associated Press*, September 17, 2019

They came and went without notice or fostering debates on cable news or Facebook. They were rarely discussed on Twitter or at the watercooler at work. Therefore, they might as well never have happened.

In 2019, Crooked Media conducted a series of polls of battleground states that showed that when swing voters[7] learned the

---

7 Crooked Media defines swing voters as people trying to decide who to vote for and people who are trying to decide whether to vote.

information in the aforementioned stories, they were 25 to 40 percent less likely to support Trump. The lesson is clear. There is plenty of information that would cause all but Trump's MAGA base to break with him, but none of that information is getting to those voters organically.

Therefore, the very first project of my "imaginary super PAC" would be a rapid-response ad campaign that took new stories and used ads on Facebook to make sure that voters saw the information. The idea is to supercharge these important stories so that voters see them. We cannot rely on the press to do this job for us.

Project Two Corinthians:[8] Trump famously (infamously) went to Liberty University and fumbled the name of his "favorite" book in the Bible by calling Second Corinthians "Two Corinthians." Now, I am not sure that any sentient human actually believes that Trump is a practicing Christian let alone a biblical scholar.[9] But the incident does point out a real mystery in American politics: Donald Trump is a profane, thrice-married adulterer, but he won the support of 80 percent of white evangelicals in the 2016 election. Evangelicals gave him the nomination and the presidency. Even a small drop in their support could cost Trump the election. Many Democrats have assumed that Trump's evangelical support is unshakeable and not worth fighting for.

I'm not sure I agree with that premise and would be willing to spend some imaginary money to test the proposition by investing in an ad campaign to dampen Trump's evangelical support. I would run ads on Christian radio that included a supercut of Trump repeatedly taking the Lord's name in vain. There have been

---

8 I will be in big trouble if I don't mention that this is an idea my wife has been very focused on since early 2017.

9 Trump also famously doesn't read books. Think about that for one second—the president doesn't read books. And before you call me an elitist, there is nothing elitist about wanting a president with intellectual curiosity and attention.

numerous reports that his tendency to do so is problematic for some of his supporters, and evangelical leaders have repeatedly urged him to stop.

Trump has a long history of saying horribly profane and misogynistic things. He was a regular guest on Howard Stern's radio show for years. In those appearances, he often bragged about his sexual escapades. I would fund a television, radio, and digital campaign that reminds voters who they elected president. Here are examples of some of Trump's greatest hits that I would put in my ad campaign:

Donald Trump Talking . . . :

Trump: My daughter, Ivanka. She's six feet tall; she's got the best body. She made a lot of money as a model—a tremendous amount.

Howard Stern: By the way, your daughter...

Trump: —she's beautiful.

Stern: Can I say this? A piece of ass.

Trump: Yeah.

Donald Trump discussing dressing rooms full of teenagers:

"You know they're standing there with no clothes. Is everybody OK? And you see these incredible-looking women. And so I sort of get away with things like that."

I don't believe evangelical voters are naive about who Trump is, but I would want to make it as hard as possible to forget who they are putting in the Oval Office.

Audience of one: I am generally anti–television ads. They are often an outdated, inefficient means of reaching voters. I get particularly annoyed by the bipartisan consultant grift of convincing wealthy interests and well-funded advocacy organizations to spend a bunch of money on television ads that run in the

DC market to "influence policy makers." But there is one major exception to my anti–TV ad rule: commercials with an audience of one.

Trump's poll numbers generally go from bad to middling when the political conversation is focused on something other than Trump, and his numbers go back down to historically terrible whenever he has one of his weeklong Twitter tantrums. My super PAC would ask some of America's most interesting filmmakers—think Jordan Peele, Adam McKay, and Greta Gerwig—to create commercials specifically designed to trigger Trump.[10] These ads would be aired on Fox during Trump's favorite shows. The ad buys would be built around the president's schedule—a big focus on the morning show he watches during "executive time" and the nightly opinion shows he watches to fill the bottomless hole in his heart.

One ad could be a series of disaffected Trump voters speaking directly to Trump, expressing their regrets for voting for him.

Script: "Regrets"

Open with: "A Message to President Trump from MAGA Nation."

Voter 1: Mr. President, you promised to fight for workers like me, but instead you are helping the elites on Wall Street.

Voter 2: Sir, you promised to drain the swamp; instead, you became just like every politician in Washington.

Voter 3: I thought you were going to save my job, but you failed.

Voter 4: Why are you always tweeting instead of working?

Each voter would be wearing a MAGA cap and would take it off after they deliver their missive.

---

10 Richard Linklater made some incredible anti–Ted Cruz ads in 2018, which are the model for this project.

Another ad would pick at Trump's massive insecurity complex when it comes to Barack Obama. The ad would open with a comparison of their inauguration crowds and then go on to detail how Obama's legislative and economic records were superior to Trump's, and how Obama won the popular vote twice and was better received on the world stage. The coup de grace would be the closing scene of Obama accepting his Nobel Prize.

A third ad could sow dissent in the Republican Party by running ads that included all of the terrible things that Trump's cabinet members and congressional allies said about him. For example, Mick Mulvaney, who Trump hired as his acting chief of staff, once wrote, "What he said in the audiotape is disgusting and indefensible. My guess is that he has probably said even worse ...I've decided that I don't particularly like Donald Trump as a person." There are so many quotes like this from Republicans who serve Trump.

Trump can beat himself. He just needs our help. Time and attention are finite resources, and every Trump Twitter tantrum is another day he isn't making a case to the voters he needs to win the election.

Nonvoters → voters: Too much of our political discourse is centered on persuading swing voters to vote for Democrats, and not enough is focused on persuading nonvoters to become voters. This would be a central focus of my imaginary super PAC. Trump is president in large part because four million people who voted for Obama in 2012 didn't vote in 2016. An effort to find those voters and get their asses off the sidelines needs to be a priority. This is one of the many places where former president Obama can play a huge role in the 2020 election. I would try to convince him to tape a series of pleas to voters to register and vote that would talk about what was on the line in 2020. Let's just say recording ads and other direct-to-camera videos was never his favorite activity.[11] But in this imaginary scenario, he would agree to sit for hours so that we could record dozens of videos that were specific to the issues people cared about (Obamacare is on the line), the state people lived in (Wisconsin, it's up to you), and circumstance (Florida, your registration deadline is October 5, 2020). I would do the same thing with a wide array of celebrities like LeBron James, Beyoncé, Jennifer Lopez, Chance the Rapper, and the casts of *Game of Thrones*, *Avengers*, and *Star Wars*.[12]

All of these videos would be used in ads and also available in a library that people could access to share them with their potentially nonvoting friends.[13] Celebrity endorsements are often mocked for good reason—but they can be very useful for reminding people to vote. When the famously (infamously) nonpolitical Taylor Swift[14] posted on Instagram reminding people to register to vote in her home state of Tennessee, there was a huge spike in registrations. Creating lots of potentially viral content from influencers with loyal followings and huge platforms could make a real turnout difference in an election that will be decided by a few votes in a handful of states.

Whether it's these ideas or other, better ones, beating Donald Trump (and the next Trump) is going to require an all-hands-on-deck, innovative, creative ad campaign. The same old TV ads won't work. Waiting till voters "tune in" won't work. Fighting back against Republicans is a 24-7-365 effort. There is no time like the present.

As I said, I don't have billions (or millions), but if you have billions (or millions) and you like these ideas, my DMs are open.

---

11 Despite being so good at it, he was called "one take" Obama.

12 I thought hard about putting the cast of *Succession* on this list, but it might send the wrong message.

13 Get better friends.

14 I was Team Kim Kardashian until Kanye went all MAGA and Kim started hanging out with Jared Kushner.

PART THREE

HOW TO MAKE AMERICA A DEMOCRACY AGAIN[1]

1 America's democracy has always been far from perfect, and technically the United States is a republic, but this is a play on Trump's slogan—work with me, people.

CHAPTER 9

VOTE SAVE AMERICA

One consequence of a long career in politics and a briefer, more recent career in podcasting[1] is that I have met a lot of politicians. To be honest, most fit the stereotype of mediocre white men with too much ambition and not enough ability. But some truly stand out as the best and brightest our country has to offer. Patriotic public servants with tremendous abilities who put those talents to use in the service of making people's lives better. People like Barack Obama, John Lewis, Nancy Pelosi, and Hillary Clinton, to name just a few. But there is another name that belongs on that list.

Stacey Abrams.

Stacey Abrams is one of the most talented, smartest, and most charismatic politicians I have ever met. She was the minority leader of the Georgia State House. She's been a business owner. A civil rights activist. A voting rights activist. A nonprofit leader. She has a master's degree from the University of Texas. A law degree from Yale. She went from a typist to the speechwriter on a congressional campaign when she was in high school because her

---

1 I guess this is my job now. Podcaster. It sounds less cool when you put it like that.

edits were so impressive. She wrote a series of popular romance novels under a pseudonym just because.

And she did all of this before the age of forty-five.

Stacey Abrams was a guest at a *Pod Save America* show in Atlanta in 2018 right after she won the Georgia Democratic gubernatorial primary. None of us had met her before. We didn't really know what to expect. In general, politicians—particularly those standing for election—are often our worst guests. Too much caution, not enough charisma.

Not Stacey Abrams.

She was a rock star. The crowd went insane for her. After years of disappointments with milquetoast moderates, Georgia Democrats had finally found a candidate they could get excited about.

Jon, Jon, Tommy, and I were blown away. When we walked off the stage after the show, we looked at each other and all thought the same thing.

"Stacey Abrams isn't just the future of the Democratic Party. She's the future of the country, and fuck, she better win."

She didn't win.

She got more votes than any Democrat—including Barack Obama and Bill Clinton—in Georgia history.

Yet, despite all of her talent, charisma, and broad appeal, Stacey Abrams is not governor of Georgia. This was a huge loss for the state of Georgia, the Democratic Party, and the country. She would have been the first African American woman governor in American history, and it would have happened in the heart of the new South. What a powerful symbol.

But in truth, she didn't lose the election. It was stolen from her. Electoral larceny. Her opponent, Brian Kemp, just happened to be the Georgia secretary of state who just happened to be the person in charge of the election. And boy did he take advantage of that fact.

Several months before the election, he purged tens of thousands of voters off the rolls—a group that was overwhelmingly African American and most likely supporters of Abrams. This purge came on top of nearly seven hundred thousand voters who were purged in 2017. This effort was about making it harder for a Democrat to win.

What happened in Georgia is not an aberration; it's both a story about what has happened to Democrats and a warning about how much worse it's going to get. As Republicans become more of an electoral minority, their efforts to suppress the majority from voting are only going to get worse.

Fighting voter suppression efforts in the courts is important but ultimately not sufficient. The right response to Republican voter suppression is an aggressive, deliberate strategy of voter expansion that combines new laws to make voting easier, with a political strategy to make Republicans pay a steep political price for stealing elections.

EXPAND THE VOTE

The Republican approach to elections is un-American, immoral, often unconstitutional, and devastatingly effective.

A theme of this book is that Democrats don't have to emulate the Republicans to win, but on this issue, we need to take a page out of their book and flip the script. The first priority for every Democrat elected at every level must be an aggressive expansion of voting rights. It starts with repealing the voter ID laws that Republicans passed to explicitly reduce voting by people of color and college students, but we don't stop there. Their strategy is voter suppression; ours needs to be voter expansion.

For too long, Democrats have been too scared of the politics of getting more people to vote. We've been afraid of the optics of looking like we are putting our thumb on the scale in favor of measures that benefit Democrats at the ballot box.

Voting is good.

More people voting is likely (but not necessarily) to help Democrats, but that is beside the point. Everyone should want every eligible voter to get a chance to exercise their right. It's up to the political parties to have agendas that appeal to a majority of those voters.

Pushing to make voting easier and more accessible is the morally right and politically smart thing to do, but too often Democrats don't push the envelope.

The best/worst example of Democratic reticence about voter expansion happened when I was working in the White House. The National Voter Registration Act, or "motor voter law," passed in 1993 and requires agencies that provide public assistance from the department of motor vehicles to the health department to offer opportunities for people to register to vote. The motor voter law was a very smart, effective law from the days when BOTH parties saw declining voter participation as a problem.

Healthcare.gov—the once glitchy website that was the portal where people went to look for health plans under the Affordable Care Act—was required under that law to provide people with information and opportunities to register to vote. The Obama administration could have aggressively used the site to register people to vote, but we didn't.

While there was a link buried on the site that was a pitiful attempt to comply with the law, we made a specific decision to downplay the voting information on the site. Well over a million people a day visited the website at its peak. This is the exact group of people we most need to get more engaged in our democracy.

Why did the Obama administration pass on an opportunity to register voters?

Fear.

Fear of the politics of being political, and fear of a right-wing noise machine. We were afraid that asking people to vote on the Obamacare website would look "too political." That it would incite the GOP base to hate the law even more. The worst part about this decision is that it didn't come after a bunch of heated debates. There wasn't much of a debate at all. The folks involved—myself included—thought the Affordable Care Act had to be viewed as apolitical as possible. We didn't do the right thing; we did the safe thing.

This, more than anything, is indicative of the Democratic mentality that has led to conservatives dominating the levers of power in American politics. Republicans are destroying democracy, and Democrats are afraid to fight for it, because of what Republicans might say about us if we do.

The Republicans have a tried-and-true playbook. First, they drum up fears about nonexistent voter fraud to justify making it harder to vote. Second, they attack any proposal to make voting more accessible as a Democratic plot to steal elections by making it so undocumented immigrants, dead people, and other scary groups can vote.

This strategy has too often cowed Democrats from doing the right thing for democracy (and the Democratic Party).

WINNING ELECTIONS = WINNING MORE ELECTIONS

Elections are run by state governments—not the federal government—which means that we have a patchwork of laws and processes and a sliding scale of democracy based on where you live. If you live in California, your government wants you to vote. If you live in almost any state in the Deep South, not so much.

This makes close to zero sense, given how far we have come from being thirteen separate colonies. But thanks in part to a Supreme Court that gutted the Voting Rights Act, we are stuck with an antiquated system of electoral federalism, which means the best way to fix our elections[2] is to win more elections at the state and local levels.

These down-ballot races have too often been ignored by too many in the Democratic Party and donor community. Organizations like EMILY's List and the Democratic Legislative Campaign Committee have been the exception, not the rule. Republicans have spent years recruiting, training, and funding candidates to run and win at the state and local levels. But that is starting to change, thanks to groups like Swing Left, Run for Something, and the Arena that sprung up in the wake of Trump's victory.[3]

It begins with winning those races, but it doesn't end there. Expanding the vote must be the top priority for these newly elected Democrats.

Every Democrat up and down the ballot should sign onto a voting expansion agenda that includes a series of long-discussed, widely accepted, but rarely implemented ideas to make voting easier, including

- automatic voter registration;
- same-day registration;
- vote by mail;
- expanding early voting;
- restoring voting rights to ex-felons who have paid their debt to society;
- making it easier for college students to vote.

---

2 Fix as in repair, not rig (that's what Republicans do).
3 The Democratic Legislative Campaign Committee has been doing yeoman's work in this area for years, but they are finally getting some help.

All of these ideas are proven to increase turnout, and there is no reason they shouldn't be done. There is good news on this front—most of the states run by Democrats have instituted automatic voter registration and other elements of a voter expansion agenda. In 2018, voters in Florida passed an amendment to restore voting rights to felons.[4]

California has put in place a model for how to make voting easier that every state should emulate.

Traditionally, your voting location is based on where you live. This location, which is often a school gym, church, or firehouse, is the only place you can vote. Your voting location can change every election. If you show up at the wrong location, you can be turned away. Making someone vote near their house instead of their job when Election Day is a workday is painfully stupid.

A few years ago, California passed a law giving counties the option to eliminate neighborhood polling places in exchange for voting centers where anyone could vote, drop off a mail ballot, register to vote, and get a replacement ballot. The voting centers are open seven days a week and convenient for people to visit before and after work. Five counties experimented with the new law in 2018, and guess what?

Are you sitting down? It turns out if you make voting easier, more people vote.[5]

For too long, Republicans have defined the conversation around voting. They screamed about fraud, and we whispered about suppression. A 2016 *Washington Post* / ABC poll found that 46 percent of voters believe voter fraud happens "very or somewhat often." Voter fraud is a myth. A 2014 study also published

---

4 The Republicans in the state legislature are undermining it by instituting a Jim Crow–era poll tax, which is another reminder that Republicans hate democracy.

5 No shit.

in the *Washington Post* found that between 2000 and 2014, there were thirty-one incidents of voter fraud out of *more than one billion ballots cast*. Donald Trump repeatedly blamed his popular-vote loss to Hillary Clinton on baseless claims of "massive voter fraud." With much fanfare, he appointed a commission to look into these allegations. He staffed the commission with some of the worst partisan hacks.

That commission eventually disbanded without finding any evidence of voter fraud—which hasn't stopped Trump from continuing to blame his popular vote loss on voter fraud.[6]

Republicans loudly made their case in the public arena, and we quietly fought back in the courts. This was a strategic choice. Democrats looked at the polling around issues like requiring an identification to vote and decided we couldn't win the argument. Democrats believed (with reason) that talking about how hard it is to vote would discourage some people from voting. So we stayed silent, and Republicans were able to disenfranchise millions of their own constituents without paying a political price.

The reason that Democrats haven't won the argument on voting is that Democrats haven't made the argument. That has to change. Democrats need to make a consistent and aggressive case to voters about why Republicans don't want them to vote. The best political arguments (and all arguments) have a who, a what, and a why. They have to tell a story. Here's how I would tell that story:

> The Republican Party is trying to stop you from voting. They are the party of billionaires, corporations, and Wall Street banks. Republicans know their agenda of giving tax

6 Why let facts get in the way of a sad self-justification in order to fill a bottomless well of insecurity.

breaks to the rich and paying for it by cutting health care, Medicare, and education is not popular. They know that if you are allowed to vote, they will lose power. Voter suppression is not just a strategy to keep Republicans in power. It is a strategy to ensure the corporations, lobbyists, and the rich continue to call the shots in America. Democrats believe in giving power to the people, not the powerful. The only way to unrig the system is to ensure that every eligible voter makes their voice heard. You should ask yourself, Why doesn't the Republican Party want everyone to vote?

Democrats must explain why Republicans are tryin to stop people from voting. The public has a well-worn suspicion about political motivations. They aren't surprised that a politician would do something nefarious to keep themselves in power. These lowered expectations help explain how Trump won despite several swamps worth of corruption. Therefore, talking about the larger context of why Republicans will go to such extreme lengths to remain in power, who that power benefits, and who it hurts is critical. The argument for a stronger democracy and against suppression has to be part of the larger story Democrats tell about America. It's not a side issue. It's *the* issue. Everything flows from who gets to vote. We have to make the argument proudly and repeatedly.

Democrats have to define themselves as the democracy party—the party that wants every eligible voter to vote and believes that America is at its best when all its citizens participate.

The arguments are backed up by bold proposals that demonstrate the seriousness of the argument. Automatic voter registration, vote by mail, and the other proposals I just outlined are the agenda for today. They are an antidote to the voter suppression that is happening at the state level, but in the long run, that is not enough.

Democrats need to outline a bold vision for voter expansion. These ideas won't be enacted overnight—if ever—but the purpose of having a bold vision is to shift the Overton window so that the center point of the debate is closer to voter expansion than voter suppression.

Lower the voting age to sixteen: The idea that eighteen is the voting age is not something the founders came up with. As a general rule, the founders had terrible ideas about who should vote. If we adhered to tradition, only land-owning white men would be able to vote.[7]

The voting age was twenty-one until 1971 when a constitutional amendment lowered it to eighteen to reflect the fact that eighteen-year-olds were being sent to fight in a war by politicians they couldn't vote for—or against. A similar logic suggests we should once again lower the voting age—this time to sixteen. Sixteen-year-olds can drive, work, pay taxes, and have a real stake in issues like college affordability, military interventions, and climate change. This idea is not as radical as it sounds. Some states let seventeen-year-olds vote in primaries if they will be eighteen by Election Day. Several municipalities allow sixteen-year-olds to vote in local elections, and it has worked fine.

The arguments for lowering the age are pretty simple:

- It is in the interest of the country to begin the process of being active participants in democracy as soon as possible. There is evidence that the earlier you start to vote, the more likely you are to be a consistent voter.
- There is research that shows that there is a trickle-up effect of getting young people involved in politics—it increases the political participation of their parents.

---

7 This would make the Republican Party very happy.

Opponents to lowering the voting age argue that sixteen-year-olds aren't mature enough to make such weighty decisions. To that argument, I say, HAVE YOU SEEN OUR PRESIDENT?

Are some sixteen-year-olds knuckleheads? Sure, but so are a lot of eighteen-year-olds and forty-year-olds and seventy-plus-year-old presidents. There is no maturity test for voting, and we shouldn't apply one to sixteen-year-olds that society has already decided are capable of operating two-ton motor vehicles that can kill people.

The political logic of such a proposal is ironclad for Democrats. We can define ourselves as the party that advocates for young people. We are the ones who want them in the process. These are future voters, and Democrats will have a two-year head start in showing them who's on their side.

National automatic voter registration: Here's another bold idea—every American is automatically registered to vote when they turn eighteen. If the government knows when males turn eighteen in order to ensure they register for the draft, why can't it automatically register everyone to vote? Why can't the government check tax filings against voting rolls to register the unregistered and update your address to ensure your registration is correct. The same could be done every time someone interacts with the Department of Veterans Affairs, Medicaid, and other government services. Citizens would always have the option to not vote, but shouldn't the default be registration?

Internet voting: Before the 2018 election, *Pod Save America* was in Florida for a preelection special that was going to air on HBO.[8] Jon Favreau and I were interviewing folks on the street about the election. We met a young man who told us that he wasn't planning on voting. He had a number of reasons for this

8 It's still weird that we had an HBO show. We were probably more *Arli$$* than *Game of Thrones*, but still...

decision, but one was that he worked a number of jobs, didn't have a car, and wasn't sure how he could get off work and to the polling place. Florida offers voting by mail.

"What if someone sent you a ballot?" I asked him.

"That would be cool. Wait, like in the mail? Nah, I don't check my mail. I do everything online," he responded.

Vote by mail is a very effective way of increasing turnout, and I hope every state adopts it as soon as possible. But it should be a way station toward online or mobile voting. Mail delivered in an envelope with a stamp is not a means of communication that most young people use, so we have to acknowledge that it may not be the best way to get young people to vote.

People should be able to vote online with their phone. If you can pay your taxes, buy a car, and sign up for health insurance from your phone, there is no reason that you shouldn't eventually be able to vote from your phone.

I understand the security concerns about such a proposal, especially after what the Russians did in 2016. We are not ready to make the transition yet. More work needs to be done on the security front, and we need better technology to validate who is voting. However, it is naive to think that our current system is immune to a cyberattack.

Some voting machines are online. The voter rolls are online. The Russians already tried to penetrate the computer systems of the election offices in several states. Right now, we are enduring the risk of online voting without the benefits.

We should begin preparing for that moment now.

Mandatory voting: This idea is going to sound crazy. But trust me. It just takes some time to get used to.

It is mandatory to pay taxes, register for the draft, and attend school. These are things that America has decided are a requirement for membership in our society. Why shouldn't voting be mandatory?

It's a small price to pay for the benefits of citizenship.

Mandatory voting is the law in Australia, where it works great. Those who fail to vote are subject to a modest fine. Turnout is near 100 percent, and Election Day is a fun holiday where people vote together and celebrate afterward.

Of course, to do this in America, we need to make some changes. "None of the above" would need to be an option. Election Day would have to be a holiday, and voting would have to be less of a pain in the ass than it is right now.

But ensuring that every eligible vote had an ownership stake in our country has more potential to change the direction of the country than anything else being discussed.

Getting more people to vote more often is the most simple cure for the complex set of problems that plague America. A significant majority of Americans agree more with Democrats than Republicans, but they don't vote, because their vote is suppressed by law or by indifference. Addressing that problem needs to be the absolute top priority for the Democratic Party. Literally nothing else matters. Not the message, not the policy, not the candidates. It starts with voting. As Barack Obama said before the 2018 election,

> So, if you don't like what's going on right now—and you shouldn't—do not complain. Don't hashtag. Don't get anxious. Don't retreat. Don't binge on whatever it is you're bingeing on. Don't lose yourself in ironic detachment. Don't put your head in the sand. Don't boo. Vote.

It's our job as Democrats to make voting as easy as possible.

What You Can Do to Help

- Vote.
- Go to votesaveamerica.com to find out information about voting in your state.
- Support groups like Vote.org, Election Protection, Black Votes Matter Fund, Let America Vote, and Fair Fight Action that fight against voter suppression.
- Support Fair Fight 2020, Stacey Abrams's organization to protect voting rights.
- Volunteer with Swing Left, Indivisible, Headcount, or other groups to register people to vote.
- Find five friends from high school, college, or Instagram[9] and register them to vote.
- Post on social media about voter registration deadlines, which are too arbitrary and way too early, but can be found on votesaveamerica.com
- Call/tweet/email your elected officials to demand they make voting easier and more accessible in your state.

9 There are no friends on Twitter.

CHAPTER 10

THE TYRANNY OF THE MINORITY

Barack Obama was back on the campaign trail. He wasn't in Ohio or Wisconsin[1] campaigning for himself. This time the newly reelected president was in Brooklyn campaigning for Bill de Blasio, the certain-to-be next mayor of New York. This was the first time Obama had campaigned in the Big Apple since the 2008 Democratic primary. Although he was in New York City all of the time, it was almost always to raise money, do media, or speak at the United Nations. This meant that he was always in Manhattan and rarely visited the other boroughs. Young, with a large African American population, an NBA team, and Jay-Z, Brooklyn had a claim to being the capital of Obama Nation. There might be no place in America where Barack Obama was more popular. Needless to say, Obama showing up in Brooklyn was a big deal.

Campaigning, whether in Biloxi or Brooklyn, often entails going to places with very good, very unhealthy food[2] and eating

1 Ah, the good ol' days of campaigning in Wisconsin... I'm kidding.
2 Obama often ate two bites in front of the camera and gave the rest to staff. He prefers seven almonds at a time (look up this meme).

it in front of voters and the media. After visiting a school, Obama met de Blasio at Junior's for cheesecake.[3] Normally these impromptu presidential restaurant visits are kept secret for security purposes. They are called OTRs, short for "off the record" visits. If the visit is announced in advance, the Secret Service is required to shut down the venue and search everyone and everything. In addition to costing the restaurant lots of business, the president would constantly be visiting empty restaurants. Not exactly the visual you want.

However, things don't always go as planned. As we headed over to Junior's, the Secret Service told us that word of the visit had gotten out and a very large crowd had gathered on the street. After Obama and de Blasio shook all the hands in the joint and bought the obligatory cheesecake, they greeted the crowd outside. As the president and soon-to-be mayor were headed to the presidential limo, Obama shook a woman's hand. The woman pulled Obama in close for a hug and a conversation. She explained how the Affordable Care Act had positively impacted her life. Obama turned to walk away, and she shouted, "We love you. How can we help you?"

"Move to North Dakota," Obama responded with a laugh.

Everyone who heard Obama's comment assumed it was a joke, but it wasn't. Not really.

The "North Dakota" story became a constant refrain at fundraisers. It was a way of illustrating a huge and quickly growing problem for Democrats that threatens the progressive agenda much more than the Trump presidency.[4]

Here are some very alarming facts:

---

3 A Brooklyn institution on Flatbush Avenue.

4 The important caveat with all things Trump is that I am presuming that he doesn't kill us in a Twitter fight that ends in nuclear war.

- Hillary Clinton received three million more votes than Donald Trump, yet Trump is president with the power to shape the courts and start wars because of fewer than one hundred thousand votes in three states.
- Democrats have won the popular vote in five of the last six presidential elections but only won the White House three times.
- California, which has forty million people, has the same number of senators as North Dakota, which has fewer than one million people. To put it another way, the vote of a North Dakotan is worth forty times more than the vote of a Californian.
- The Republican majority in the Senate that confirms Trump's right-wing judges and blocks progress on popular policies like gun control and a higher minimum wage is represented by a distinct minority of Americans.
- It's possible for a majority of the Senate to represent only 18 percent of the American people.

Democrats have the majority of voters but a minority of political power. Trump's win, the theft of a Supreme Court seat, a rebalancing of the courts in a conservative direction, and Trump's immunity from accountability for his criminality and corruption all flow from that fact.

That's a problem for Democrats, but also for democracy.

Most of these fund-raisers Obama attended happened in New York and California. Obama's pitch for people to move from Battery Park and Beverly Hills to Bismarck and Boise didn't get many takers.[5] In fairness, Obama was telling the story not to propose a solution but to explain why popular progressive policy ideas had not become popular progressive laws.

---

5 It got no takers.

It's important to explain to an impatient public the structural obstacles to progress. But talking is not enough. We have to do something. Urging people to move to North Dakota[6] is not the answer.[7] But there are other more radical solutions that Democrats have until recently been unwilling to contemplate. We can wait no longer. It's time to fix the Senate and abolish the Electoral College.

FIX THE SENATE

The people who work in the Senate and the reporters who cover it love the Senate. They treat the senators of today as if they were the giants of yesterday. The molasses pace of progress on urgent problems is seen as a pro, not a con. They drip in condescension when discussing the House of Representatives. The Senate lovers would never use this term, but they think of themselves as a House of Lords and the rest of Congress as a House of Commons.

Most senators view themselves as the true guardians of democracy. Presidents come and go, but the Senate is there to provide a check on popular, impulsive policy making.[8]

I worked in the Senate for four years for two senators, including the Senate minority leader. I worked for six years in the White House as Obama amassed a legislative record on par with any modern president. I am here to tell you that the Senate is fundamentally broken.

First, there are some good senators—even some very good

---

6 I lived in South Dakota twice, and it's the greater Dakota. It has Mount Rushmore, Deadwood (think Vegas meets Disney's Frontierland), and something called the Corn Palace.

7 Although it is an answer.

8 If the Senate is so great, why does every senator get to the Senate and immediately start planning their presidential campaign? Just asking…

senators,[9] but there are no giants. In most cases, the senators are former House members who ran for Senate. Winning a Senate seat doesn't make someone smarter, more deliberative, or more serious. For every John McCain and Ted Kennedy,[10] there are twenty Lindsey Grahams—an amalgamation of Frank Underwood and Selina Meyer with the ideological consistency of the Taco Bell menu.

Second, by requiring sixty votes to pass a bill, the Senate is designed to do nothing when the country urgently needs action on a wide array of priorities. Just to pick a random issue out of a hat: the planet is melting due to a climate change, and the Senate, as currently constructed, will still be deliberating a response when it's underwater.

Third, the Senate is fundamentally antidemocratic in a way that is a giant problem for Democrats. The long-term population trends are very bad for Democrats even as traditional Democratic voters become a bigger part of the overall population. Young people have been moving from smaller, more rural areas in red and purple states to cities in bigger, bluer states, giving them access to better jobs and cultural opportunities but diminishing their political power. According to one study from the University of Virginia, by 2040, 70 percent of the population will live in sixteen states, which means that the remaining 30 percent of the population will control sixty-eight Senate seats. All of this means that the political power of nonwhite voters is being dramatically diluted.

Seems suboptimal for a democracy.

Under this scenario, it's hard to see how the Democrats get to fifty Senate votes, let alone the sixty needed to pass a single bill. All of the talk of Medicare for All, the Green New Deal,

9 Again, most of them are running for president.
10 Two very flawed men who, unlike a lot of today's senators, took their job very seriously.

gun safety laws, and just about every single thing that Democrats campaigned on in 2016, 2018, and 2020 are dead on arrival even under the most optimistic electoral outcomes.

If we don't fix the Senate, it won't matter if Democrats win the presidency in 2020, 2024, or every election in this century—conservatives will continue to dictate the policies in America.[11]

ELIMINATE THE FILIBUSTER

The 2018 elections were a massive landslide for Democrats. In the House races, the Democrats won the popular vote by more than eight points—the largest margin in a midterm since Watergate and bigger than the Republican waves of 1994 or 2010—yet Democrats lost two Senate seats. To be fair, Senate Democrats were playing an incredibly tough hand. With Obama on the balley in 2012, we won seats in very Republican states like North Dakota, Indiana, and Missouri. But these states have become even more reliably Republican in the Trump era. It's fair to ask—if we can't win them during a massive pro-Democratic wave election, can we ever win them again?

In 2020, the Democrats have a chance to take back the Senate with Republicans defending seats in Maine, Arizona, Colorado, Iowa, North Carolina, Georgia, and elsewhere. But best realistic case, a newly elected Democratic president would come into office with a Democratic Senate with no more than fifty-one or fifty-two seats. A far, far cry from the sixty needed to pass a bill.

It is true that there are some legislative procedures that allow a bill to pass with a simple majority. That's how the Republicans

11 Until the planet fucking melts, because Republicans like fossil fuel money more than saving their children from climate change.

passed Trump's tax scam in 2017, and it's how the Democrats passed Obamacare in 2010, but the procedure called budget reconciliation is unwieldy, can be used only once a year, and won't work to pass much of the progressive wish list legislation under the current rules—no Green New Deal, no gun control, and no Voting Rights Act.

Obama famously told Republicans angry about his agenda that elections have consequences,[12] but the Senate rules limit those consequences.

If we win the White House and the Senate in 2020, the Senate Democrats should walk directly from the inauguration to the floor of the Senate, eliminate the filibuster, and start passing some fucking laws.

Majority rule is the basis of democracy, and it should be a pretty easy argument to win. It is certainly much easier than explaining why a minority of senators representing a distinct minority of the public can block legislation supported by the majority of the public.

Eliminating the filibuster for legislation could be done in five minutes. All it takes is a simple majority of senators to vote to change the rules.[13] We know it's easy because a version of it has been done twice in the last few years.

In 2013, the Republicans in the Senate decided that Barack Obama shouldn't be able to staff his cabinet or appoint judges.[14] President Obama had just won reelection and helped Democrats expand their Senate majority, and Republicans were pissed.[15] Since they couldn't win elections or persuade the public about the merits of their agenda, they decided to try to nullify the

---

12 Man, were they pissed.
13 How ironic!
14 Seems rational.
15 Their natural state of being when there is a Democrat in the White House.

results of the election through the filibuster. Among others, Obama had nominated Tom Perez, a very progressive civil rights lawyer, to be secretary of labor, and Gina McCarthy, a progressive environmentalist, as head of the Environmental Protection Agency. The Republicans didn't like these picks, not because there was anything wrong with Tom and Gina. There wasn't. Tom and Gina were fully qualified for the jobs with sterling records of public service. The Republicans just hate workers' rights and the idea that the government should make it harder for corporations to pollute our air and water. They pledged to block these appointments indefinitely so that Obama couldn't enact his agenda.

McConnell was also holding open seats on the DC Court of Appeals for the DC Circuit Court of Appeals, which is known as the second most important court in the land, because it's where many of the big cases are litigated before they go to the Supreme Court. If Obama was allowed to fill those seats, it would tip the balance of that court in a more liberal direction.[16]

This was an untenable and unprecedented tactic. It could not be allowed to stand.

In steps Harry Reid.

Reid was the Senate majority leader and every bit the former boxer from a small mining town in Nevada. He was tough as nails and so no-nonsense that he was famous for never saying "bye" on the phone. Once Reid was done talking, he just hung up. He had things to do and didn't have time for niceties. Despite having almost nothing in common, Reid and Obama formed an incredible partnership and friendship. Without Harry Reid, much of Obama's signature achievements never see the light of day.

Harry Reid decided enough was enough. He was not going to

---

16 Hmm, this seems oddly familiar.

let Mitch McConnell[17] and the Republicans abuse the rules to prevent a duly elected president from doing the things the voters duly elected him to do.

Reid persuaded Democrats to change the Senate rules so that the Senate could confirm all appointments to the executive branch and all judges besides the Supreme Court nominees with only fifty votes. Reid decided that lifetime appointments to the Supreme Court were so consequential that they required the consensus of sixty votes.

Of course, once Trump was elected McConnell immediately changed that rule so that Trump could confirm Neil Gorsuch to the seat stolen from Merrick Garland to preserve a five-to-four conservative majority on the court.

The next Democratic Senate majority leader should follow in the footsteps of Harry Reid and eliminate the last vestige of the filibuster and change the rules so that legislation can pass the Senate with a simple majority.

This is a surprisingly controversial position among Democrats. Everyone from Joe Biden to Bernie Sanders opposes eliminating the filibuster. The benefits of the filibuster is an article of faith among institutionalists. There are three primary arguments for keeping the filibuster.

The first argument for keeping the filibuster is that requiring sixty votes necessitates consensus building and bipartisanship.[18] If the last ten years of politics have taught us anything, it is that consensus and bipartisanship are dead. The entrenched special interests like the National Rifle Association, the health insurance industry, and oil companies are too powerful and have too

---

17 The best part about Harry Reid is that his hatred of Mitch McConnell makes my feelings toward Paul Ryan seem quaint.

18 This argument would make more sense if the most famous use of the filibuster had not been to block legislation providing civil and voting rights to African Americans.

much sway in the Republican Party to allow progressive legislation to have a shot at the requisite sixty votes. A vote to keep the filibuster is a vote against the next Democratic president's agenda.

The second argument is that eliminating the filibuster makes us no better than the Republicans who have destroyed norms and broken countless rules. Some of the people who make this argument—including a fair number of Senate Democrats—blame Harry Reid's decision to change the rules in 2013 for the sorry state of the Senate. Under this theory, all the bad stuff McConnell does is in response to Reid and the Democrats. If only the filibuster had been preserved for nominations, the Senate would be a bipartisan Shangri-la of sorts.

There are several flaws in this argument. It's dangerously naive. It incorrectly presumes that Mitch McConnell is some Senate institutionalist and not the ultimate partisan hack.[19] If Democrats had not changed the rules to confirm Obama's nominees, Mitch McConnell would have done it to confirm Trump's before Trump had finished the oath of office on Inauguration Day.

The third argument is that eliminating the filibuster is very risky. Based on the demographic trends, the Republicans are likely to control the Senate more often than Democrats. Imagine all the terrible laws Republicans could pass in that situation. This is a completely fair point. Democrats could very much live to regret eliminating the filibuster, but it's a risk I think we should still take. I don't see another path.

The best argument for eliminating the filibuster is the absence of a credible theory for passing progressive legislation with the filibuster still in place. The risk is worth it when the alternative is

---

19 The amount of willful blindness that it takes to believe this about McConnell is stunning.

allowing a conservative minority to dictate the policy agenda in America until the planet melts because that minority refuses to acknowledge the science of climate change.

FIFTY IS NOT A MAGIC NUMBER

Eliminating the filibuster will allow Democrats to pass laws when they are in charge, but it does nothing to help put them in charge more often. The entire party from grassroots activists to the DNC and everyone in between should be doing the hard work of turning more red states blue. That work is important, but will take time. In the interim, there is something we can do to make the Senate more representative and rebalance the scales in a way that advantages the Democratic Party.

Make more states.

It's not as absurd as it sounds. It's shockingly easy.[20] All it takes to admit a state to the union is votes in the Senate and House and the president's signature.

Start with Washington, DC.

The nation's capital has a population on par with Wyoming, Delaware, North Dakota, and several other states. The residents of DC pay federal taxes and have a say in the presidential election with three electoral votes, but no vote in Congress.

Time and again, DC has suffered from its second-tier status. While it has several representatives, they have no vote. The city's budget and policies are often used as a proxy war between the parties. Republicans in particular love to mess with DC, which I'm sure has nothing to do with the fact that the district is so diverse that it self-identifies as "Chocolate City."

Making DC a state would also mean two more Democratic

---

20 After we get rid of the filibuster.

senators. Hillary Clinton received 90 percent of the the vote in Washington, DC.

This is not cynical—even if it sounds that way. It's the right thing to do regardless of the impact on the Democratic Party. Washington, DC, should be a state. It's long overdue, and it's a real tragedy that it hasn't happened yet.

Besides, what do you think Trump and McConnell would do if DC voted like Kentucky?[21]

I first floated this idea on *Pod Save America* right after Justice Anthony Kennedy announced his retirement. Jon Favreau and I were discussing the larger Senate problem in the context of our inability to stop Trump from shifting the court in a conservative direction for decades.[22]

Later that day, several people reacted on Twitter and asked, "If giving DC statehood is such a good idea, why didn't Obama do it when the Democrats controlled Congress?"

There really isn't a good answer.

Democrats have long supported DC statehood. Obama supported DC statehood in the 2008 campaign. Bill Clinton even put license plates on the presidential limo that said "Taxation without Representation" to signal his support for statehood. But it's not something that was ever seriously contemplated in the two-year period when Democrats had overwhelming majorities in the House and Senate.

The problem was that it felt controversial. It would look like an aggressive attempt to consolidate our own political power. We thought of it—to the extent we thought of it at all—as dirty-pool politics that would inspire a backlash from voters.

This was a tragic error born of caution and political miscalculation. This is the exact attitude that has forced Democrats

---

21 This is a rhetorical question, you know the answer.
22 Another problem we need to solve, but more on that later.

to fight Republicans with one hand tied behind our backs for years.

Washington, DC, has the strongest claim to statehood, but not the only one.

Puerto Rico has a population of more than three million, which is more than twenty US states. The residents of Puerto Rico are already US citizens, but they have very few of the privileges of citizenship. They have no votes in Congress and can't vote in the presidential election. To highlight the absurdity of the entire situation, a Puerto Rican who moves to one of the fifty US states is eligible to vote in federal and state elections, but if they stay in Puerto Rico, no such luck.

The island nation has often been at the mercy of a federal government that takes advantage of their lack of political clout. Puerto Rico was devastated by a hurricane and a thoroughly inept response from the Trump administration in 2017. Republicans in Congress held no serious hearings to figure out what happened and did less to help the victims than in states like Florida and Texas, which weren't hit as hard.

There has been a long-running debate in Puerto Rico about the future—should they seek statehood, independence, or something else? My view is that if Puerto Rico wants to be a state, Congress should immediately make them a state and give them two senators. If they want to be an independent nation, Congress should immediately grant them independence. The choice is theirs, but the responsibility is ours.

David Faris, a political scientist and the author of *It's Time to Fight Dirty: How Democrats Can Build a Lasting Majority*, proposed eight new states. In addition to Washington, DC, and Puerto Rico, he suggests breaking up California into six smaller states. While we're at it, do we really need two Dakotas?[23]

---

23 I'm kidding (sorta).

While these ideas may go a little too far for me,[24] there is merit in broadening the discussion about remedies to the fundamentally anti-democratic nature of the Senate. The Senate is a huge problem that goes beyond Trump and we need to keep looking for more solutions.

ELECTORAL COLLEGE DROPOUT

In the run-up to the 2016 election, my overwhelming (and misguided) confidence in Hillary Clinton winning the presidency was based on a belief that she had a huge Electoral College advantage over Trump. She had multiple paths to 270 electoral votes. Trump had one—he had to win Florida, the quintessential battleground state, and Pennsylvania, Michigan, and Wisconsin, three states that had gone Democrat in every election since 1984. This was a real change from my first presidential campaign. Back in 2000, I was sitting in the Gore campaign headquarters absentmindedly playing around on the internet Al Gore invented,[25] during one of the interminable conference calls that define campaign life.[26]

I stumbled onto a site that provided a rudimentary Electoral College calculator. You clicked on the states to make them red or blue to see how to get to 270 electoral votes. In that election, the major swing states were Pennsylvania, Iowa, Wisconsin, Florida, and New Mexico.[27] As the call droned on, I started playing out various scenarios on the map.

Then it dawned on me.

---

24 I reserve the right to change my mind in the next few years.

25 Yes, I know this joke isn't original or funny, but I have been making it for years. Repetition is the key to a successful message strategy.

26 To this day, I HATE talking on the phone. Only call me if something is (literally) on fire or someone (very) close to me has died.

27 If you think nothing has changed in twenty years, West Virginia was a swing state and Virginia was not.

"Oh fuck," I said into an unmuted phone momentarily causing some confusion as people thought I had a disproportionate reaction to the congressperson who was supposed to introduce Gore.

Gore had to win ALL of the swing states to get to 270—the electoral equivalent of drawing an inside straight.

Not to spoil it, but Gore didn't draw that inside straight. He came close. He won all of those states—except Florida.[28]

The narrow Electoral College path was also John Kerry's undoing in 2004, and it seemed like it would be the fate of the Democrats for a long time. But then in 2008, Obama changed the map. He turned swing states into blue states and red states into swing states. He repeated the feat in 2012. The changing demography of the nation paired with Obama's appeal to these new emerging voting groups was credited for this shift. Many Democrats saw demography as destiny.

Sure, the Democrats would continue to have challenges in the Senate, but the country was getting younger and more diverse. Young college-educated voters were moving into fast-growing cities in states like North Carolina and Georgia. And even Texas would be blue before too long. The Republicans could be locked out of the White House for generations if they didn't change who they were and which voters they appealed to.

Another spoiler alert: that didn't happen either. Trump won the Electoral College despite the fact that Hillary Clinton received three million more votes.

Everyone had assumed that the red states of the Sun Belt and Southeast would turn blue, before the blue states of the Rust Belt turned red. Everyone was wrong. Trump won Ohio, Iowa, Wisconsin, Pennsylvania, and Michigan. Obama won these states fairly easily in 2008 and 2012. Clinton suffered through a perfect

---

28 He got kinda robbed there, too.

storm of bad news at the end of her campaign, and the margin in some of these states was razor thin. But there was undoubtedly a big shift in this part of the country, and it's one that portends some real challenges for Democrats in 2020 and beyond.

The best solution for democracy and Democrats is to eliminate the Electoral College.

Eliminating the Electoral College would be great for democracy—and Democrats. We have a huge—and growing—popular-vote advantage. Texas is on a seemingly inexorable path to being blue. In 2016, Hillary Clinton improved on Obama's margin by seven points, and in 2018, Beto O'Rourke came within a hair of being the first Democrat elected to the Senate in Texas in decades. If and when Texas becomes blue, it will be electoral checkmate. California, New York, and Texas would give Democrats 122 of the 270 electoral votes right off the bat.

But despite that fact, the Electoral College still needs to go.

The reason is very simple—the Electoral College is stupid. It's insane that we have a system that says that the person who gets fewer votes can still be president. Think of it this way: in 40 percent of the elections in the twenty-first century, the person who won the popular vote didn't get the nuclear codes. Maybe it's just me, but that seems like a giant problem.[29]

Imagine if the NBA commissioner proposed a rule that allowed a team to win a game despite scoring fewer points simply because they scored from randomly designated places on the court.

No one would stand for that. The Electoral College is even more absurd because it's the presidency, not a basketball game, at stake.

And if you don't believe me, maybe you will take the word of none other than Donald Trump. Back in 2012, when Trump

---

29 Especially since it keeps happening to Democrats.

mistakenly thought Obama had lost the popular vote,[30] he fired up the Twitter machine:

> "He [Obama] lost the popular vote by a lot and won the election. We should have a revolution in this country!"
>
> (November 6)

> "The phoney[31] electoral college made a laughing stock out of our nation. The loser one! [*sic*]"
>
> (November 6)

> "More votes equals a loss... revolution!"
>
> (November 7)

I don't say this lightly, but Trump is right.[32] He, of course, deleted these tweets four years later when the "phoney" Electoral College made a laughingstock out of our nation. Perhaps we shouldn't have elected someone who thinks *won* is spelled *one*, but I digress...

Like eliminating the filibuster or adding states to the Union, ditching the Electoral College will cause the traditionalists in both parties to howl. Republicans who agreed with Trump on the Electoral College a few years ago are now some of its biggest defenders.

There are two main arguments for keeping the Electoral College. First, its defenders argue that the founders made a specific and well-thought-out decision to choose electors over direct democracy. This is true, but the founders also made a specific and

---

30 He's so dumb.

31 The copy editor for this book points out that "phoney" is an accurate but less common spelling of the word. I refuse to believe Trump knows that fact and refuse to make the edit. The Trumpian version of Occam's razor is in any situation assume Trump will do the dumbest thing.

32 A broken clock, blah, blah, blah.

well-thought-out decision that only white male landowners could vote, so maybe they weren't perfect. America has changed a lot in 250-plus years, and we should update our political system to reflect those changes. That is not a radical notion; it's common sense.

The second argument is that if we got rid of the Electoral College, the candidates would only campaign in big cities and ignore other parts of the country. It is true that presidential campaigns are an economic boon to the "battleground" states. There are a lot of TV station owners that have second homes paid for by the millions spent on campaign ads every cycle. Campaign visits are great for local hotels and restaurants. But ensuring the even distribution of campaign dollars is a dumb reason to hang on to a system that allows the person with fewer votes to win the election.

But even that argument doesn't hold up. The Electoral College doesn't guarantee that presidential candidates campaign everywhere. It does the opposite. More than thirty of the fifty states are noncompetitive. I have worked in three presidential campaigns, and in none of those campaigns did the candidate spend any real time in Montana, North Dakota, Alabama, or Vermont. We did go to Ohio, Florida, and Pennsylvania approximately one hundred times each. Because the outcome is never in doubt in most of the country, most people feel like their votes don't count. Republicans in California and New York know that their vote will do nothing to ensure Donald Trump is reelected, and Democrats in Mississippi and Montana know that their vote will do nothing to ensure Trump is defeated.

Eliminating the Electoral College would give everyone a say in who is president. No matter where you live, no matter how red or blue your state, your vote will count. More people would feel like a part of our democracy.

It would also incentivize candidates to campaign in different places. Of course, Democrats would have reasons to go to big cities like LA and New York, because there are millions of votes there. But they would also campaign in red states that haven't been part of a presidential election in years. Democrats would barnstorm places like Nashville, New Orleans, and Louisville that haven't seen a Democratic presidential campaign this century. Republicans could do the same in upstate New York and the Republican suburbs and exurbs of the South that haven't been competitive in decades. Sparsely populated states wouldn't get a lot of campaign visits, but they don't under the current system, either. That problem is impossible to fix and shouldn't prevent the US from moving to a more democratic system.

Now that I have convinced you of the overwhelming rightness of my position, how do we get rid of the Electoral College?

Well, technically it's really, really hard. The Electoral College is outlined in the Constitution and therefore requires a constitutional amendment. That means a two-thirds vote in the House and the Senate and ratification from three-fourths of the states. The Twenty-Seventh Amendment, which was just a simple change in how Congress is paid, took two hundred years to be ratified. The Equal Rights Amendment, which takes the controversial position that civil rights may not be denied based on sex, passed Congress in 1972 but has not yet been ratified by the states.[33]

This could take a while, to say the least, but that's why Democrats have to start making the argument now. The Democrats in the House and Senate should propose the amendment. It should be part of the party platform at the 2020 Democratic National Convention, and Democratic presidential candidates should campaign on this idea.

---

33 But it's so damn close after the Democrats took control of the Virginia legislature in 2019.

The message is very simple:

> Democrats want to make America as democratic as possible. We want everyone who is eligible to get a chance to vote, and we want that vote to count. Democrats believe that the people should decide; the Republicans believe the powerful should decide.

But all is not lost: there is a way around the Constitution.[34] The National Popular Vote interstate compact is an incredibly clever idea that has been spearheaded by a Stanford computer science professor named John Koza. His organization has been working to get states to pass laws that essentially eliminate the Electoral College. As of 2019, fifteen states and Washington, DC, have adopted the compact. In those states, their electoral votes will be awarded to the candidate who wins the national popular vote, not the candidate who wins the state. For example, if the compact had been in place in Florida in 2016, Florida's twenty-nine electors would have voted for Hillary Clinton even though Trump received more votes in Florida.

The Electoral College must be ended. We just have to do the work, win some elections, and then use our power to advance democracy (and Democrats).

BREAKING SOME EGGS

A few months after the 2018 election, I was participating in a panel discussion at a book festival in Arizona. The topic of the panel was "Democracy in Danger," but the purpose was selling our books to the attendees. According to the prescribed format,

---

34 I sound like the Trump Department of Justice.

each of the participants was to address the crowd for ten minutes, followed by questions from the audience.

The first panelist up to the dais was Steven Levitsky, who had cowritten *How Democracies Die*. The subject of this truly excellent book is self-explanatory. Steven began his remarks by talking about the ways in which the Republican Party had been undermining our democratic institutions for years and how those efforts led to Trump. He tied what was happening in the US to examples around the world.

The presentation took a turn as Steven offered a warning to Democrats. Democracy, he argued, might survive what Republicans had done to date, but it would die if Democrats engaged in a retaliatory race to bottom. In a two-party system, we need at least one party that will put country over party by defending our institutions. He was concerned about the recent discussion about adding states to the union, eliminating the filibuster, changing the courts, and essentially all the other things *Pod Save America* has been screaming into microphones about for three years.

His argument was thorough, well researched, and rooted in history. It should be taken seriously by the Democratic Party as we debate the proper response to McConnell and Trump. The danger Steven spoke of is very real. The argument is also, in my humble opinion, dangerously wrong.

I had been on the book-hawking circuit for a while at that point. I had a well-worn spiel that I could have delivered in my sleep.[35] As I walked up to the podium for my presentation, I decided to do something different.

After some perfunctory remarks about what my book was about and why I wrote it, I decided to push back.

---

35 Since my daughter was three weeks old and had not yet slept longer than three consecutive hours when *Yes We (Still) Can* came out, I have almost certainly delivered that spiel in my sleep.

While I agree that Democrats shouldn't engage in the dangerous political nihilism of McConnell, turning the other cheek will be the death of democracy. America is a democracy governed by anti-democratic institutions. We are on an exorable path toward being a country where a shrinking conservative, white minority rules a growing, diverse progressive majority. If we allow that to happen, the system will collapse. We can't count on Republicans having an epiphany or doing the right thing.

It's certainly possible—as *How Democracies Die* argues—that the ideas like the ones proposed in this book will lead to even worse actions by the Republicans. The truth is no one knows what will happen. But I do know that if we do nothing, democracy as we know it will be dead.

What You Can Do to Help

- Call your senators and ask them to support ending the filibuster.
- Support groups like Moveon.org and Indivisible that are pushing Democratic politicians to support aggressive Democratic reforms.
- Move to Wyoming, Idaho, Montana, or either Dakota.
- Invite your friends to move to Wyoming, Idaho, Montana, or either Dakota.
- Push your governor to adopt the National Popular Vote compact to end the run of the Electoral College.

CHAPTER 11

DEMOCRACY FOR SALE

Barack Obama was at the time the greatest grassroots fund-raiser in the history of the Democratic Party. He fundamentally changed how campaigns raised money and was in possession of an email list of millions of people willing to keep the campaign funded with small-dollar donations.

He raised so much money in 2008 that he became the first major candidate to forgo federal matching funds and tell all the outside groups to stand down.

In 2012, Barack Obama became the first incumbent in recent memory to be outspent by the opposition. His reelection campaign was the first presidential campaign to be waged after *Citizens United* opened the floodgates to malicious special interests and avaricious billionaires.

The money problem is going to be exponentially worse in 2020. Donald Trump is raising money like we have never seen. Over the course of one weekend in the summer of 2019, Trump raised more than $30 million.

Thirty million dollars in one weekend. He raised more than many Democratic presidential candidates raised in all of 2019, and he did it in, like, six hours. He barely had to miss his favorite Fox shows.[1]

As Trump hoovers up money from hedge fund managers, oil executives, and other captains of industry, the billionaires who sat out 2016 are preparing to pour money into the election to defend their lower tax rates and freedom to pollute.

Our democracy is for sale, and under the current system, only the Republicans have the capital to buy it.

There are no easy answers, but one thing is for sure: if the Democratic Party tries to play the Republicans' game, we will certainly lose.

THE BILLIONAIRE PROBLEM

The Republicans have always had something of a fundamental money advantage. More rich people were Republicans, and corporations that hate government telling them not to kill people tend to give their money to Republicans. That advantage was mitigated by a campaign finance system that capped individual and political action committee contributions at the relatively low level of a few thousand bucks. While certainly not chump change, the law made it hard for an individual or a corporation to buy an election (or a politician) with endless spending.

This is not to say that the pre–*Citizens United* era was perfect—far from it. Campaigns were too expensive, politicians spent too much time raising money, and special interests had too much sway. But there were guardrails on the system that allowed Democrats to compete.

Citizens United changed all of that. There is no longer a

1 Who am I kidding? There is someone paid with your tax dollars whose job it is to DVR them for him. Think about that next April.

moderating influence—the more money you have, the more political power you have. This is obviously bad for democracy, but it's also fucking terrible for Democrats.

Super PACs and nonprofit groups, which can take unlimited contributions, have become more powerful than the campaigns themselves or even the national party committees. Many statewide candidates have their own super PAC, even though our porous federal laws make it illegal to coordinate with them.

Here's how fundraising for super PACs works: The candidate meets with a group of potential donors with VERY deep pockets. In the meeting, the candidate can answer questions and make the case for their election. Once the candidate is done making the pitch, they get up and leave, and then a representative from the super PAC walks into the same room still filled with the same donors and collects the checks. Some of those checks have seven or eight digits.

There are plenty examples of people living in the gray areas or outright violating campaign finance laws. There was a group of conservative organizations that were legally prohibited from communicating with each other but all just happened to work out of the same office in Virginia. Many of these groups were formed through shell organizations designed to make it impossible to know who is behind them. It was discovered in 2019 that Brad Parscale was simultaneously serving as Trump's campaign manager and a vendor to a pro-Trump super PAC, even though it would be illegal for employees of the campaign and super PAC to coordinate on political activity.

This is a truly insane way to run elections, but most politicians—Democrats included—feel compelled to play this game. Unilateral disarmament is too risky. Billionaires now run our politics, and there are a lot more Republican billionaires willing to spend a lot more money.

The most famous, of course, are the Koch brothers. David and

Charles Koch are the heirs to a Wichita-based fossil fuel fortune. They are reportedly worth $50 billion each and fund a network of political organizations that spend hundreds of millions of dollars every election to influence politics at every level, from local school boards to 1600 Pennsylvania Avenue. David Koch passed away in 2019, but Charles has pledged to continue spending his money to elect Republicans up and down the ballot.

The Koch network runs the Republican Party—they fund its largest super PAC, and they essentially control all of the data the Republican Party uses to contact voters. They are the primary reason that it's considered a mortal sin for any Republican at any level to say that climate change is real.[2]

The Koch network spent millions of dollars to advocate for the Trump tax cut. They paid for ads and lobbyists to pressure Republicans into voting for it and punish Democrats for voting against it. While the Kochs have always been advocates for lower taxes, this was more than a philosophical preference for them. They had a real stake in the outcome—an analysis from the group Americans for Tax Fairness estimated that they would reap more than $1 billion from passage of the plan.

A few days after passage, they cut a $500,000 check to Speaker Paul Ryan's[3] political action committee. They elected a Republican Congress to pass a tax cut, and then invested some of that tax cut by contributing to those same Republicans so that they could be reelected and make sure the tax cut stays in place.

Whenever anyone talks about the Kochs or any of the other less famous billionaires who fund the Republican Party and conservative causes, Democrats yell, "Where are our billionaires?"

Great question. There are a number of Democrats who are quite wealthy who give a lot of money to a lot of causes but do

---

2 It is.
3 The absolute worst...

not spend on pure politics at anywhere near the scale of their Republican counterparts.

To the extent there is an answer to this question, it is as follows:

Republican billionaires view politics as a business expense. They are spending money to make more money. They want to elect Republicans because those Republicans will cut their taxes. They want to elect Republicans because those Republicans will regulate their companies less. I'm sure even the Kochs have underlying political principles, but those principles are tied to their own personal profit. This is a point about which the Republicans are explicit. Back in 2010 when Obama and the Democrats were working on passing the most aggressive reform of Wall Street since Roosevelt, Mitch McConnell went to meet with Wall Street about the bill. He brought along one senator. Was it the top Republican on the Senate Banking Committee that was writing the bill?

No.

McConnell brought along Texas senator John Cornyn, who just happened to be heading up the Republican fundraising efforts for the upcoming election. The message was crystal clear—elect Republicans and we will protect you from these reforms so you can make more money (and put the economy at more risk).

The calculus for Democratic billionaires is different. Electing Democrats means raising their own taxes. A donation to a nonprofit is tax deductible, while a donation to a political campaign or a super PAC is not. This means that a lot of liberal giving is directed toward very worthy but nonpartisan causes like climate change, education, and reducing hunger. But ultimately the best way to deal with climate change, improve education, or reduce hunger is to elect Democrats.

Democrats also think (correctly) that political fundraising is dirty. Ask any Democrat running for office about fundraising, and the nicest thing they will say is that it is a "necessary evil." They all hate it and for good reason—it sucks. A newly elected member of Congress told me in 2019 that his day effectively ends at 1:00 p.m. That's when he heads to the campaign office for hours of "dialing for dollars" followed by fundraising receptions and networking meetings in the evening. For House members in tough districts, they have to start raising money for the next campaign the day after the election. It never stops. In addition to being exhausting, fundraising has a patina of sleaze and shame.

After the 2016 election, there was an endless series of meetings between Silicon Valley billionaires and political operatives to figure out how to respond to Trump's win. I went to a lot of these meetings, and most were hardly worth the gluten-free sandwiches they served. The meetings all arose from a sense of danger about where the country was going and guilt about what happened in 2016. Barack Obama inspired a lot of Silicon Valley types to get involved in politics for the first time. They hosted fund-raisers and dispatched their talent to work on our campaign. One of the cofounders of Facebook even quit the company to take a position on the Obama campaign. Disillusioned by the political battles of the last eight years and the drudgery of the 2016 campaign, a lot of Silicon Valley sat on the sidelines.

In one of these meetings, one of the wealthier individuals in the country was talking about the Democratic Party. He mentioned the party's failure to recruit and train candidates up and down the ballot, support grassroots groups, build party organizations in all fifty states, and wage aggressive legislative and political campaigns.

As I listened to this pretty accurate assessment of how the Democrats had ceded way too much territory, I started to get aggravated.

This individual was bemoaning the problem while possessing the means for the solution. He was complaining about getting wet from rain while holding an umbrella. When I couldn't take it anymore, I spoke up as diplomatically as I could muster.

"Your diagnosis of the problem is exactly right.[4] For far too long, Democrats and progressives have gotten our asses kicked at the fundamentals of politics. While it will take time, money, and hard work, the solution is pretty clear. Someone or a collection of someones needs to create an organization that invests in building a nationwide progressive infrastructure. It's really the only solution—the party committees are legally, structurally, and financially incapable of doing what needs to be done. And it needs to be done now if we want to have a chance to affect the 2020 election, let alone 2018."

I went on to lay out in some detail how such an organization could be structured, what it needed to do, and how it could leverage additional funding. As I spoke, I could see some heads nodding.

When I finished, one of the billionaires responded: "It sounds like you are suggesting something like a liberal version of the Koch organization."

"That's exactly what I am suggesting," I responded.

That's the moment I lost the room.

"We don't want to do that."

"The Kochs play dirty; we can't be like them."

"I don't want to be a liberal Koch."

It went on and on. There was real revulsion at the idea of getting involved in the minutiae of politics. They viewed politics as a dirty business and spending money to impact the outcome was inherently bad—even if it was completely legal and the end result would be a better, more progressive American government. In fact, one of the results of spending money within our broken campaign finance system could be changing the laws so that money has less

---

4 Telling someone they are right about something immediately before you tell them why they are wrong about everything else is one of my favorite moves.

influence on our politics. The billionaires could burn the bridge behind them.

At the time, I found this conversation incredibly disheartening. The folks in the room thought I was pushing them to be a paler shade of orange. I wasn't suggesting anyone buy an election or violate laws. I wanted them to invest in democracy, to build a Democratic Party capable of pushing forward on the very issues they cared about. Raising public awareness about climate change does little good when our politics are too rigged to do anything to save the planet.

That meeting was more than two years ago. There have been many more since. While some billionaires like Chris Sacca, Reid Hoffman, and Michael Bloomberg have invested heavily, Democrats are still outgunned. While we may win elections—like we did in 2012 and 2018—when the stars align, we continue to be at a disadvantage.

That meeting ultimately influenced how I thought about how Democrats can—and can't—fight back against conservatives in the era of Trumpism. We simply cannot succeed in a system where billionaires and corporations have this much sway.

A Democratic Party that wants to fight for democracy can't depend on an oligarchy to pay the bills. The only path forward for the Democrats is to radically change the system. We must fund the party the same way we win elections—by inspiring millions of Americans to invest in their own future.

Every Democrat supports overturning *Citizens United*, but that's not enough.

Fixing the problems created by *Citizens United* is really hard. There are only two ways to do it: One option is getting the court to reverse its opinion, which is HIGHLY unlikely under the current composition of the court.[5] The other option is the pas-

---

5 More on how we might solve this problem later.

sage of a constitutional amendment, which, as we discussed in the previous chapter, is also REALLY hard. The difficulty of the amendment process is treated as a reason to not even try.

Even if progress doesn't happen in the short or medium term, the mere act of repeatedly making the argument and organizing around a constitutional amendment will redound to the benefit of the progressive movement.

A constitutional amendment to overturn *Citizens United* is incredibly popular. A 2018 survey by the University of Maryland found that three-quarters of voters and two-thirds of Republicans supported such an amendment.

Democrats can and should continue to raise the alarm about *Citizens United* and push the constitutional amendment process at every opportunity. Make Republicans go on record opposing getting money out of politics. We shouldn't miss an opportunity to show that the official position of the Republican Party is opposed by two-thirds of its voters.

But we cannot stop there, because we cannot afford to wait any longer. Here is a list of actions Democrats can take once in power that will limit the effects of *Citizens United* while we are doing the hard work of overturning it and show voters that we are the party of reform.

POLITICS ISN'T HAMSTERDAM[6]

I was sitting at my desk during the 2008 campaign when Lauren Thorbjornsen, my very able and talented assistant, walked into my office.

"Dan, there is someone from the FEC on the phone for you."

"Um, who?" I responded with a little concern.

---

6 This isn't a typo. Look it up.

The FEC is the Federal Election Commission, the government agency that[7] regulates campaign activity. The odds that they were calling for a good reason were quite low. This was the kind of call that you want a lawyer for. The FEC can issue fines and other penalties for violations of campaign finance laws.

"Can you ask what it is about?" This was a delay tactic as I racked my brain to think about what I could possibly have done to put me in the crosshairs of the law.

After a few minutes, Lauren returned: "It's an investigator who wants to ask you some questions about a complaint you filed."

"There must be some mistake. I haven't filed an FEC complaint. Can you ask what he is talking about?"

Lauren was getting exasperated with all my prequestioning, and she had more pressing tasks than playing a literal game of telephone with me and an apparently confused bureaucrat. I told her to take a message, and I walked down to the campaign manager's office to confirm that the campaign had not filed any complaints with the FEC.

Curiousity got the better of me, and I returned the call when I got back to my desk.

"Mr. Pfeiffer, I have been assigned to investigate an FEC complaint that you filed," the official said.

"I don't really know what you are talking about. The Obama campaign hasn't filed any complaints."

"This isn't from the Obama campaign. It's a complaint against John Thune for Senate."

At this point I started laughing hysterically—if a little rudely.

"Are you serious?"

Nearly four years earlier when I was working on a Senate campaign, we had filed a complaint against our opponent for illegally coordinating with an outside group. It was so long ago that I

---

7 Theoretically.

didn't remember the details and I didn't really care. The candidate I had worked for had lost and was now in the private sector—a slap on the wrist for the guy that beat us was not really going to make me feel better about that loss.[8]

What possible good could come from enforcing campaign finance laws after the campaign is over?

The punch line here is that the Federal Election Commission is a joke by design. Congress created the FEC as part of a series of reforms passed due to Watergate, but they were careful to protect themselves. The FEC has limited authority. There are six commissioners.The even number of members means that way too many decisions are deadlocked, leading to no action. The deadlocks, which have increased dramatically in the last few years, preserve the broken status quo and incentivize all the wrong behavior.

To make matters even worse (as if that seems possible), in the run-up to the 2020 election, the vice chair of the FEC resigned. The resignation of this Republican appointee meant that the FEC lacked a quorum to even meet, let alone make rulings. And where did the recently resigned FEC commissioner go work?

A law firm famous for helping Republicans exploit loopholes in campaign finance laws in order to avoid disclosing political spending.

What a town!

A top priority for a new Democratic president and Congress should be turning the FEC into an organization that can actually do something about the rampant cheating that is happening in our politics by changing the number of commissioners, giving them more resources and more power.

---

8 To be honest, it would depend on how hard the slap was.

SHINING THE LIGHT ON DARK MONEY

Another campaign finance priority for Democrats should be shining a light on the so-called dark-money[9] groups that are major players in American politics. According to a study from the campaign reform group Issue One, these groups have spent more than $1 billion on American elections since the *Citizens United* decision. All of it secret.

While political campaigns, party committees like the Democratic and Republican national committees, and even super PACs must publicly disclose who gave them money and what they spent that money on, political nonprofits can spend millions on elections without ever disclosing a dime. Per usual in American politics, our laws make zero sense.

The fact that a wealthy person or a corporation can give unlimited sums to a super PAC is a huge problem. The fact that those donations are public at least provides a nominal measure of public accountability. The media can dig into who is supporting the politician and surmise why. The candidates who are on the receiving end of the super PAC attack ads can respond by calling out the special interest funding the ad. The employees, shareholders, and customers of the corporate interests funding the ads can respond if they disagree with the cause or person being supported.

If a new ad goes on the air in a congressional race and it's paid for by the Koch network, the public can make a rational guess that the Kochs want to elect a candidate because he or she will support their pro–fossil fuel / anti–climate change agenda.

None of this happens with the dark-money groups. They are

---

9 I'm sure my publisher is going to frown on me using my book to promote someone else's book, but Jane Mayer's *Dark Money* on this topic is a must read.

innocuously named—Americans for Prosperity, American Crossroads etc. No one knows who they are, who funded them, or why.

In response to *Citizens United*, President Obama and the Democrats tried to pass the DISCLOSE Act,[10] which would have closed the dark-money loophole and forced nonprofits to disclose their political fundraising and spending. It passed the Democratic House and had the support of a majority of Senators (all Democrats), but Mitch McConnell (R-Dark Money) filibustered the bill to death. And the rest is history.

In 2019, the Democrats passed the DISCLOSE Act, but once again, Mitch McConnell refused to take it up in the Senate because he hates democracy as much as he hates Democrats.

One of the first acts of a Democratic president with a Democratic Congress should be to pass the DISCLOSE Act.

If the filibuster has been eliminated—as it should be—this will easily pass, eliminating a Republican advantage in subsequent elections.

Ultimately, Trumpism is a Faustian bargain between corporations and the racist demagogues leading the Republican Party—if you give us tax cuts and fewer regulations, we will keep funding your racist demagoguery. The loopholes in our campaign finance laws allow the corporations to try to have their cake and eat it, too. Shining light on that financial support has the potential to cut off the financial supply lines to Trumpism.

Even if a Democratic president isn't blessed with a Democratic Senate or a Democratic Senate makes the fatal mistake of not eliminating the filibuster,[11] there are still some steps they can take:

President Obama twice considered, but ultimately abandoned,

---

10 DISCLOSE stands for Democracy Is Strengthened by Casting Light On Spending in Elections...seriously. Congress's affinity for acronyms is weird and should be stopped ASAP. (See what I did there?)

11 Essentially ceding the legislative agenda to Mitch McConnell.

an executive order to force federal contractors to disclose their political spending. A president doesn't have the authority to force disclosure for everyone—that requires an act of Congress—but he or she can impose standards on those who do business with the government as a condition of receiving a federal contract. This is an area of clear presidential authority and a way to incentivize good behavior among the large swath of corporate America that does business with the federal government. Republican opposition forced Obama to abandon the effort both times. Mitch McConnell was so hell-bent on allowing groups to spend millions in secrecy that he threatened to block the confirmation of a cabinet secretary.

At the time, I understood and supported the decision not to proceed. Working in the White House is a never-ending series of decisions among less than ideal outcomes. Because Republicans controlled the House and congressional Democrats were not super enthusiastic about this idea, we probably would have lost a fight over this executive order. However, in hindsight, I think we should have had the fight. Fighting and losing is sometimes politically preferable to surrendering in silence.

Reducing the influence of big money in American elections is one of those issues.

DRAWING A BRIGHT LINE

Sadly, it's going to take some time to solve the problem of too much money in politics. Even if everything breaks right for Democrats and somehow *Citizens United* is overturned, wealthy people will still have too much power in our politics.

The ultimate solution is full public financing of campaigns—every campaign spends the same amount, and no candidate has to raise a dime. The idea that politicians—of either party—are going to vote to spend tax dollars on campaign ads seems unlikely, no matter how good an idea it is. Therefore, Democrats are going to need to find a way to succeed in the current system without compromising our ideals.

In 2018, as the potential Democratic candidates were preparing to launch their campaigns, I tweeted something seemingly innocuous about how presidential candidates needed to forswear donations from lobbyists and corporate PACs. Twitter wasn't having it. My timeline was filled with people yelling at me for proposing that Democrats unilaterally disarm and putting purity over victory. The criticism was born from a line of thinking that Democrats play too nice and that it's a mistake to go high when Republicans go low.[12]

While I sincerely believe that lobbyists and corporations have way too much power in American politics, I wasn't taking a moral stand. I was making a political observation.

Swearing off special-interest money makes it easier to win elections and, counterintuitively, to raise money.

My view was informed by my experience working for Barack Obama and what I had seen in the 2016 and 2018 elections.

On Barack Obama's 2008 campaign, we made his decision not to accept lobbyist and corporate PAC money a central part of our message. Refusing to accept lobbyist and PAC money was pretty controversial at the time. A lot of people in Washington thought Obama was cutting himself off from money he would need to run his campaign, a rookie mistake by a political naif who hadn't yet learned the ways of Washington.

We saw it differently. Not taking lobbyist and PAC money was something that made him different from other politicians and especially Hillary Clinton, and it was consistent with his message of

---

12 Not for nothing, but every candidate refused lobbyist and PAC contributions.

change. He mentioned it on the stump at every stop, and it helped him raise an astounding half a billion dollars online, mostly in small donations.

When Obama won the nomination, he directed the DNC to stop taking lobbyist and PAC money. As president, he wouldn't appear at a fund-raiser if they accepted lobbyist and PAC money at the event. This remained a point of dispute in Washington. The rest of the party refused to follow his lead—the Senate and House campaign arms and most members of Congress continued to raise money from lobbyists and PACs. As much as they desperately wanted Obama's help fundraising, the congressional leadership was always annoyed that they had to turn the lobbyists away from the fundraising events featuring the president.

As Obama's presidency wore on, the DNC started to champ at the bit of Obama's fundraising restrictions. The DNC was struggling to get out of debt from Obama's reelection campaign. Hillary Clinton was preparing to run for president in 2016, and her allies at the DNC wanted to make sure the DNC was well funded. Clinton was planning to accept lobbyist money during her forthcoming presidential campaign.

David Simas, Obama's White House political director, came to me with a request from then DNC chair Congresswoman Debbie Wasserman Schultz. My immediate reaction was that breaking faith with a core campaign promise would be a political disaster for Obama. Simas told me that Schultz was likely to raise it with Obama when the president appeared at a DNC fund-raiser in the coming days. I headed down to the Oval Office to make the case to Obama for why he should reject her request out of hand. I felt pressure to deliver on this because when I became senior advisor, David Plouffe told me that it was my responsibility to be the voice of the '08 campaign in the White House. I was supposed to try to keep the faith with the promises Obama made on the trail. This became more important as the years went on. The promises felt more distant, and the number of White House senior staff members who had been on board when the campaign launched had dwindled to a handful.

Obama was sympathetic to the DNC's predicament. They were in debt due to his reelection. Most of the party leadership had no objection to money from lobbyists and PACs, but he believed in his original promise and wasn't ready to abandon it with a few years left in his term.

The DNC continued to push aggressively to begin accepting lobbyist and PAC money. They prepared charts showing how much money they could raise. Every time it came up, I would again run down to the Oval Office to remind Obama why this was a bad idea. If Clinton's allies and others in the party wanted to change the rules, they should be the ones to do it. Obama shouldn't take the hit for it.

Obama held out until February 2016—a year after I left the White House. Hillary was poised to become the nominee, and by tradition she would take over the DNC after she clinched the necessary delegates. At this point, Clinton had been accepting lobbyist contributions for her campaign for over a year. The walk back of Obama-era fundraising rules was inevitable.

Within days of the change being made, the DNC hired a fundraiser to focus exclusively on PACs, and invites to a fundraising event were sent to every Democratic lobbyist in town.

What the Clinton campaign and the DNC failed to realize is that the political damage of appearing to be indebted to lobbyists and corporations was more hurtful than the extra money was helpful.

In 2016, Bernie Sanders used Clinton's fundraising practices against her in a surprisingly strong primary challenge. It's not just that he was able to land political attacks; his purity helped him raise record sums in online donations. In 2018, Beto O'Rourke raised an unprecedented $80 million for his 2018 Texas Senate race following a similar path. In 2019, Elizabeth Warren and Sanders went one step further and swore off all in-person fundraisers for their campaigns. Both raised more than most candidates pursuing the more traditional path.

The lesson here is that taking a righteous stand on who funds one's campaign is worth more than a press release and a line in a stump speech; it's a necessary step to tapping into the grassroots donor base of the party.

Democrats will never find enough munificent billionaires to compete with the Kochs and their ilk. A Democratic Party that depends on wealthy tech executives and hedge fund managers to fund our GOTV efforts and advertising campaigns will never be able to embrace the sort of populist economic policies that the country needs and the millennial voters who are poised to dominate politics demand.

Winning in politics requires showing a contrast. The Republicans are a wholly owned subsidiary of corporate America. Our ability to make that case to voters is hampered if we are also seen to be in the thrall of the same interests. The ability to raise real money from real people depends on showing those people that they have actual ownership of the campaign. The days of being able to court corporate executives on a Monday and send out a grassroots email on a Tuesday have come to an end.

There are really only two options in the current system—try to court the high-dollar donors and billionaires or build a grassroots fundraising base that allows Democrats to compete against the GOP money machine. There might have been a time when one could try to do both, but the politics have shifted.

Democrats have to choose, and the choice is clear.

What You Can Do to Help

- Support candidates who reject money from corporate PACs and lobbyists.
- Call your local officials and ask them to reject money from corporate PACs and lobbyists.
- Bundling isn't just for rich assholes—raise money from the people in your network to support your candidate of choice.
- Support groups like End Citizens United that are trying to reduce the influence of money in politics.
- Set up recurring donations for down ballot candidates with organizations like Run for Something and Sister District.

CHAPTER 12

INJUSTICE FOR ALL: AN ARGUMENT FOR COURT REFORM

There have been a lot of really bad days since Trump became president—there was the day he pulled out of the Paris climate change accords, the day he called neo-Nazis "very fine people," and the day he told four congresswomen of color to "go back home." Trump's presidency is a parade of seemingly never-ending horribles. Much of the last few years has been a battle between the hopelessness of today and the hope for a better tomorrow. But if I had to pick the worst day since Trump took over, I would pick the day Anthony Kennedy resigned from the Supreme Court.

That was a day the hopelessness won.

At the end of every recent Supreme Court term, there has been rampant speculation that Kennedy was going to retire. Every time, this sent the press into a frenzy and progressives into a panic.

Kennedy had been the swing vote on the court for years. He was appointed by Reagan but had sided with the four liberal justices on some key rulings, including cases to legalize same-sex marriage and uphold *Roe v. Wade*.

As the lawsuit to overturn Obama's health-care law wound its way to the Supreme Court, it was believed by most observers that the fate of the law was in Kennedy's hands. During this period, Obama would often joke about offering to mow Kennedy's lawn, wash his car, and perform other assorted chores. Someone who knew Kennedy passed along that he didn't appreciate the jokes, so they stopped immediately.[1]

By the time the summer of 2018 had come around, there had been enough false alarms about Kennedy resigning that I didn't pay much attention to the rumor mill spinning up again. Besides, it's very rare for a Supreme Court justice to decide to resign so close to an election.

I was working in the dank former garage of my San Francisco apartment that served as my office and homemade podcasting studio. This was right after my first book came out, and I was recording an interview with a local radio station when the news broke. Normally when I am recording the podcast or doing anything else that requires using my brain,[2] I turn off the notifications on my computer. I simply don't have the discipline to not look at my texts, and I don't have the concentration to read my texts and simultaneously speak coherently. That morning I had forgotten to put the computer in do-not-disturb mode.

I had been doing hours of book interviews every day for weeks at this point. I had most of my answers down pat and was on autopilot when the messages started to pour in. The first text came from the long-running text chain I have had with my *Pod Save America* cohosts Jon Favreau, Tommy Vietor, and our good friends and Obama administration colleagues Ben Rhodes and Cody Keenan.

Because I couldn't help myself, I clicked over...

"Fuck," read the first text.

---

1 Maybe Obama told the joke one too many times, because Kennedy voted to gut the law.

2 Like writing this book.

"Motherfucker" soon followed from someone else.

Then a text from my wife came in. I clicked over to that, too.

"Shit."[3]

I saw a bunch of emails and a few more texts come in. Something was happening, and obviously I couldn't NOT know what it was.

I went to Twitter.[4]

Motherfucker.

I saw the news. Anthony Kennedy was retiring. I felt like someone had kicked me in the gut. I quickly ended the interview and started to read what happened and think about what it all meant. I finally caught up with my text chains of Democratic despair.

My response to everyone was something like, "Goodbye Obamacare, Roe, and everything else we care about. Hello, *Citizens United*, a bunch of procorporation stuff, and oh yeah, we are fucked for decades."

Overdramatic?

Actually no.

The sense that everything bad Trump does can be fixed is the primary reason most Democrats haven't left the country or crawled under the bed since 2016. Executive orders can be torn up, legislation can be repealed, and treaties can be rejoined. The next president can say Trump's famous tagline to everyone from Jared Kushner to the lobbyist running the EPA to the white nationalists staffing the Department of Homeland Security. Don't get me wrong—it will take a lot of work and even more time to repair the damage Trump and the Republicans have done to America. But we can hold on to the idea that this is a moment in time and at some point it will be over.

---

3 Our daughter was one month old at the time, so this text could easily have just been a status report.

4 Twitter: where you go to confirm your worst fears.

But a Supreme Court appointment is not something that can be easily fixed. The impact will be felt for decades. Kennedy's seat wasn't just *a* seat; it was *the* seat. Replacing Kennedy with Kavanaugh puts everything Democrats care about at risk. The chances of a progressive majority on the court in the near future are now somewhere between slim and no fucking way.

To give you a sense of just how bad this situation is, my daughter Kyla was about a month old when Kennedy retired. When Brett Kavanaugh, Kennedy's even more conservative replacement, is the same age as Ruth Bader Ginsburg, Kyla will be thirty-two years old.

Thirty-two years old.

It all feels so deeply unfair. Mitch McConnell stole a Supreme Court seat from Obama that would have given progressives a five-to-four majority for the first time in decades. Donald Trump lost the popular vote. He is a walking asterisk, and now he gets to shift the court to the right for the foreseeable future. It gets worse. The two oldest justices and therefore the most likely to retire next are Ginsburg and Stephen Breyer—liberals appointed by Bill Clinton.

This is about more than partisan point-shaving—lives are at stake. Democracy is at stake. If *Roe* is overturned, women will lose their lives because they don't have access to safe medical procedures. The new Trump Supreme Court has already said it's okay to gerrymander entire populations out of elections. They will uphold *Citizens United*, and much of Barack Obama's legacy is up in the air, not to mention whatever progressive legislation a future Democratic president passes.

Brett Kavanaugh being on the court is a moral travesty and political disaster. Kavanaugh is not some conservative legal jurist in the mold of Scalia or Bork.

He is a Republican political operative whose views are dependent not on legal principles, but political opportunism. Kavanaugh was incredibly aggressive in the pursuit of a Democratic president when he worked for Ken Starr on the never-ending investigation into Bill Clinton. He pushed to investigate whether former White House deputy counsel Vince Foster had been murdered, even though several previous investigations had ruled his death a suicide. But years later, Kavanaugh changed his position and wrote a law review article that said a sitting president shouldn't be investigated while in office.[5] Brett Kavanaugh's role is not to advocate for the original intentions of the founders in the eighteenth century; it is to advocate for whatever helps the Republican Party in the here and now.

Kavanaugh was credibly accused of sexual assault. Christine Blasey Ford—his accuser—testified before the Senate despite threats on her life and family. Her account was credible and powerful. The Republicans ignored her, short-circuited the investigation, and confirmed him anyway.[6] For decades, we will look back and wonder how someone accused of sexual assault was given a lifetime appointment on the Supreme Court in the middle of the #MeToo movement. Imagine what that says to the millions of victims of sexual assault in this country.[7] It's disgusting, and the Republicans consider it one of their greatest accomplishments.

Of all the Obama speeches over the years, the line I have thought about the most since Trump was elected comes from Obama's speech on the fiftieth anniversary of the March on Washington, where Martin Luther King delivered the "I Have a Dream" speech: "The March on Washington teaches us that we are not trapped by the mistakes of history; that we are masters of

---

5 And if you don't think this is why Trump picked him for the court, I have a case of Trump steaks to sell you.

6 Kavanaugh also threatened revenge on the Democrats who believed Dr. Ford, which isn't exactly the temperament you want in a justice.

7 Kavanaugh isn't even the only sitting Supreme Court justice confirmed after credible accusations of sexual misconduct.

our fate," Obama said. "That's the lesson of our past. That's the promise of tomorrow—that in the face of impossible odds, people who love their country can change it."

The idea that we are "masters of our fate" is how I stay positive during this very dark period in American history. Whenever Trump did something that hurt someone or said something that offended everyone, there was something we could do. It was possible to turn the anger into activism, to undo the damage and right the wrong. Marching, donating, canvassing, and ultimately voting was a solution. Even if the odds were long and the payoffs distant, there was something that could be done. This time was different.

After Kennedy retired and Kavanaugh was confirmed, someone asked me whether there was anything that could be done.

My answer:

"Suffer."[8]

No amount of activism was going to change the fact that conservatives controlled the Supreme Court for potentially decades. Even a massive landslide in 2020 would have zero effect. The fact that we were not "masters of our fate" was deeply depressing.

Under the current rules and accepted norms of politics, my initial reaction was correct. We are fucked, and there is nothing to do about it. But it doesn't have to be this way. Democrats don't have to accept the status quo.

We can be masters of our fate. We can reform the court to undo the damage done by Trump and make it more responsive to the majority of Americans.

If you believe that we need to repair American democracy, you need a plan to fix the courts.

---

8 In addition to suffering, the Democrats in Congress could begin impeachment hearings on Kavanaugh, which would allow them to investigate the allegations and the efforts by the Trump White House and Department of Justice to quash the investigation.

COURT REFORM, NOT COURT PACKING

In general, establishment Democrats[9] have become more open to aggressive responses to Trumpism with every passing day. It wasn't that long ago that discussion of eliminating the filibuster or abolishing the Electoral College was verboten. Now, they are discussed on the campaign trail and in the halls of Congress. But if you mention changing the composition of the Supreme Court—or court packing, as it is commonly known—even some of the most ardent reformers go running for the exits.

But court packing, which we should call court reform because it is a more accurate and appealing term, isn't radical at all. It is much more achievable than people think. Court reform is more moral, democratic, and constitutional than the measures undertaken by Mitch McConnell and Donald Trump to change the composition of the federal judiciary.

There is nothing unconstitutional or unprecedented about changing the Supreme Court. The Constitution says nothing about how many justices should be on the Supreme Court. It's up to Congress, and they have had a hard time making up their minds over the years. Congress passed a law in 1801 saying there should be five justices. It was increased to seven in 1807. In 1837, they passed a law to make it nine justices, and then in 1863, they made it ten. And then Congress reduced the number to seven again in 1866 to prevent impeached president Andrew Johnson[10] from naming any new Supreme Court justices before he left office. In 1869, they changed the number back to nine. Obviously, there is ample precedent to change the number and even precedent to change the number in response to a political crisis in the country. Trumpism is a political crisis.

---

9 Of which I consider myself one, despite living far from DC and not having worn a tie in years.

10 Seems like a relevant historical example.

Much of the stigma associated with court reform[11] is nearly a century old. President Franklin Roosevelt (in)famously proposed "packing the courts" by adding six new justices as a response to the Supreme Court repeatedly overturning his New Deal initiatives. FDR's plan went down in flames, and generations of politicians were taught that messing with the courts is akin to political suicide. Of course, Roosevelt is one of the most accomplished Democratic presidents, and there are warning signs in his failure. However, the implosion of FDR's court-packing plan—besides allowing it to be called court packing[12]—may have had more to do with how he sold the idea than the idea itself. Instead of being forthright about the nature and purpose of his plan, Roosevelt sold it to the public and Congress as a measure to deal with an aging Supreme Court by adding a justice for every justice who turned seventy[13] and didn't retire. The lesson is not that court reform is a sure political loser; it is that you can't advocate major reform on a false premise.

I have three words for the folks who cling to the idea that the Supreme Court should be left alone because it is an independent institution above politics—*Bush v. Gore.*[14] The Supreme Court has always been political. It has been at the center of some of the most contentious issues in American history from civil rights to abortion to marriage equality, but the day five justices appointed by Republicans handed the presidency to a Republican who lost the popular vote was the day we all should have realized that politicians wear black robes, too.[15]

A 2019 poll by Quinnipiac University found that only 38

---

11 We are going to make this a thing—work with me.
12 See above.
13 Based on the Democratic leadership these days, seventy is the new thirty (this is also a problem, FWIW).
14 The people who say *v.* isn't a word are the same ones who correct others' grammar on Twitter. Get a life.
15 And apparently some of them wear white robes, too.

percent of respondents believe the Supreme Court is motivated mainly by the law. There is good reason for this. A 2014 study by the conservative *Washington Times* found that on the Federal Courts "Democratic appointees ruled in favor of Obamacare more than 90 percent of the time, while Republican appointees ruled against it nearly 80 percent of the time." This statistic is even more staggering when you consider that independent legal scholars overwhelmingly believed that the legal arguments against Obamacare were specious at best.

If the Supreme Court is going to be the final arbiter of political questions like whether the government can guarantee health care for its citizens, Democrats cannot allow Republicans to hijack the court. The court cannot be a conservative veto on the progressive policies supported by the majority of Americans.

WHAT COURT REFORM LOOKS LIKE

Reforming the courts is about more than righting the wrong of McConnell's theft of a Supreme Court seat.[16] The problem with the Supreme Court is that its composition is a game of chance. The ability of a president to shape the court is unrelated to anything other than the health and whims of the justices who happen to be serving when a president gets into office. Some presidents get multiple appointments because justices got ill, passed away, or decided to retire during their four or eight years. Other presidents get no appointments. Four of the nine justices currently serving on the court were appointed by presidents that the majority of Americans voted against.[17]

---

16 Although that would be reason enough.

17 Yes, Bush's two appointments came in his second term, but he wouldn't have been there without an Electoral College fluke in 2000.

Norm Ornstein, a political commentator and political scientist, put it best in a column in the *Atlantic*: "The policy future of the country depends as much on the actuarial tables and the luck of the draw for presidents as it does on the larger trends in politics and society."

Too often, Democratic presidents come out on the short end of this legal lottery. Eleven of the last fifteen Supreme Court appointments have been made by Republican presidents.

Our polarized, dysfunctional Congress means the Supreme Court is too powerful to be left to chance. Justices serve lifetime appointments, and most serve on the court for decades. They are getting appointed at younger ages and serving longer tenures. There is a yawning dissonance between what the public wants in the moment and the ideological leanings of the Supreme Court. America will have a Supreme Court that reflects Donald Trump's politics for decades after Trump returns to reality TV or emigrates to Russia to be closer to Putin.

The current five-to-four conservative majority is irrevocably tainted by Mitch McConnell's theft of one of Obama's appointments. A Democratic president with a Democratic Senate and no filibuster should address this problem by adding two justices. The obvious risk to that approach is that we are going to end up in a bidding war. When Republicans have the Senate, they will just add two more justices. But why stop at two? Why not add five? Or ten? But the theft of a Supreme Court seat cannot stand.

Republicans abusing their political power is like rain in Seattle. You know it's coming, you can't stop it from happening, and you can't let it stop you from doing what you need to do. Grab an umbrella, get out of the house, and get to work.[18] Republican malfeasance is not a reason to walk away from court reform. It is

18 This metaphor is lame, but it works. Do you have a better one?

THE reason to reform the courts, but to do it in a smart way that strengthens our hand against the inevitable response.

Such a plan would change the number of justices but also put in place term limits. While changing the composition of the court is politically controversial, getting rid of lifetime appointments for Supreme Court justices is quite popular. A 2015 Reuters poll found that 66 percent of Americans supported a ten-year term limit, while only 17 percent supported lifetime appointments. Judicial term limits is an idea so bipartisan that even Ted Cruz has been open to it.[19]

Yale Law School professors Dan Epps and Ganesh Sitaraman proposed a court-reform plan that has been praised by presidential candidates Pete Buttigieg and Beto O'Rourke, among others. Under their plan, the court would be made up of five justices appointed by Democrats and five appointed by Republicans serving lifetime terms and another five from lower courts. The last five would be agreed upon unanimously by the other ten and would serve one-year, nonrenewable terms.

This plan has a lot of substantive and political appeal but would require amending the Constitution. There is no specific reference to lifetime tenure in the Constitution, which actually says judges "shall hold their offices during good behaviour." While this interpretation has never been tested in a court of law, it would be up to judges who benefit from a cushy lifetime gig to say otherwise. Therefore, it seems unlikely to be changed any way other than a Constitutional amendment.

Fix the Court, a nonpartisan group that advocates for—you guessed it—fixing the court, is pushing a plan by a group of law professors that is a possible work-around. Under this plan,

---

19 My guess is that it wouldn't poll as high if people knew about Cruz's support, since Ted Cruz being an insufferable ass is one of the few things Republicans and Democrats can agree on in these polarized times.

justices would be relegated to senior status after eighteen years and brought in to break ties or temporarily fill unexpected vacancies.

These are just two of a growing number of proposals that have the benefit of addressing the short-term problem of McConnell's shenanigans and a longer crisis of an overly political and too-powerful court. The Democratic Party needs to adopt one of these plans, make it part of the party platform, and campaign like hell on it.

MAKING THE (COURT) CASE

In October 2016, I was at a college in Pennsylvania to participate in a discussion with students about the upcoming election.

As I was getting ready to leave, a group of students cautiously approached me. After some small talk, they got to the heart of the matter.

"We are considering voting for Jill Stein in November," one of them told me, referring to the Green Party candidate for president. I worked for Al Gore when Ralph Nader, who like Stein ran on the Green Party ticket, helped hand the presidency to George W. Bush. Gore's loss led to multiple wars, a financial crisis, ballooning debt, and an American city under water. Needless to say, I was triggered.

"Do you mind if I ask you why? In many ways, a vote for Jill Stein is a vote for Trump,"[20] I responded as politely as possible.

"We supported Bernie in the primary, and we want to get rid of *Citizens United*," another answered.[21]

---

20 Actually, in every way.

21 Despite the prevailing narrative in certain quarters of the Democratic Party, Bernie Sanders's supporters voted for Hillary Clinton in 2016 at a higher rate than Hillary Clinton's supporters voted for Barack Obama in 2008.

Hmm, this seemed promising.

"Hillary also wants to get rid of *Citizens United*."

They were more than a little surprised at my declaration.

"How do you know? Bernie promised to only put people on the Supreme Court who would overturn *Citizens United*. Clinton didn't promise that."

"I don't know how else to say this, but there is zero chance that Clinton would ever put someone on the court that supports *Citizens United*. I would bet my life on it. Besides, if Trump wins, he will appoint a justice who is pro–*Citizens United*, and he will tip the court in a conservative direction for decades," I said.

"If she felt so strongly about it, why didn't she say it?"

I kept arguing. Everyone else had exited the auditorium, and I had a long drive ahead of me. As we parted ways, they promised to keep an open mind about voting for Hillary Clinton. But if I had to guess, they voted for Jill Stein.

Trump won Pennsylvania by forty-four thousand votes. Jill Stein got forty-nine thousand votes in Pennsylvania.[22]

In hindsight, I should have changed my flight and stayed in that auditorium until they signed a blood oath to vote for Clinton. To be fair, Hillary did actually say she would apply an anti–*Citizens United* litmus on her court picks, but she first said it at a private fund-raiser, and it was never a major part of her platform. Clinton's approach and the response of these students speak to the bigger problem: Democrats have until recently been unwilling to make the courts a major issue with long-standing substantive and political consequences for the country. It's a major reason why Trump is president and Hillary Clinton isn't.

Making the courts an issue that matters to Democratic voters must be a priority. The randomness of the opportunity to shape the Supreme Court is probably a reason it is less of a priority

---

22 Womp, womp.

for Democratic voters. A push for court reform would make the courts front and center as an issue in every election. It would be a chance to talk about why the courts matter and which issues are at stake. The only way Democrats win elections is by convincing non- and recalcitrant voters to turn out.[23] The best way to do that is to raise the stakes in the election. Court reform is a way to do that.

Enacting a court-reform plan is going to be hard, and it will take time. There is a lot of work to do to convince Democratic politicians, let alone the public at large. As an example, even Bernie Sanders, who self-identifies as a revolutionary, finds messing with the Supreme Court to be a little too revolutionary for his tastes. Whenever there was an issue where the odds of success were long but the cause was just, Obama would often tell us to push forward because "it was better to get caught trying."

Democrats need to get caught trying to fix the courts.

---

23 I'm going to say this over and over again until the media, pundits, and too many Democratic consultants stop fetishizing white "swing voters" over new voters and nonvoters of color.

CHAPTER 13

A DEMOCRATIC (RE)UNION

In his first two years in the White House, Barack Obama racked up a series of legislative achievements that surpasses every modern president except Lyndon Johnson and Franklin Delano Roosevelt: the Affordable Care Act, Wall Street reform, the Recovery Act, a huge middle-class tax cut, equal-pay legislation, expanding the Children's Health Insurance Program, ending Don't Ask, Don't Tell.

This list goes on and on. But politics being what it is, I rarely get asked about the things Obama did. People always ask about the things he didn't do.

If you asked a lot of my former colleagues about the things they regret not getting done before the Republicans took over and put a stop to "legislating," they would respond with climate change legislation, immigration reform, and gun control.[1]

I have a different answer.

Don't get me wrong—those are all incredibly worthy, lifesaving causes. The planet is melting, a shocking number of Americans die

---

1 I would add to the list banning the necktie and establishing national casual Friday.

daily from gun violence, and every day of the Trump presidency is a painful reminder of the need to fix our broken immigration system. If I could wave a wand, I would do all of those things and more. But they don't haunt me as much, because I don't think they were necessarily achievable, even with those huge Democratic majorities.

There is no doubt we could have pushed more and fought harder. The failure to make guns a bigger issue in the first term haunts me on a daily basis. However, I believe we would have run into a harsh political reality. It was a very different Democratic Party back then—especially in the Senate. Take climate change, for instance: of the fifty-nine Democratic senators, two were from coal-producing West Virginia, two were from oil-producing North Dakota, and one was from oil-producing Alaska.

On guns, the Democratic caucus was filled with members from gun-loving states from across the South and the Plains states. Immigration was much more complicated politically back then.

Even with Obama's prodigious political talents, electoral mandate, and huge majorities, I am not convinced passing these bills was possible. But there is one bill from that period that haunts me, because I believe that we could have gotten it done.

The Employee Free Choice Act.

When I give this answer, the questioners asking about regrets usually respond with, "Huh?"

The Employee Free Choice Act, or Card Check, as it is known, is a law that makes it easier for unions to organize work sites. The law would force an employer to recognize a union if a majority of the workers signed cards indicating their desire for one, make it easier for workers to get their employers to enter a binding arbitration process, and penalize employers who discriminated against workers who wanted to unionize. Strengthening unions is good for the economy and protects workers against the often vulture-like instincts of large corporations. And it's good for the Democratic Party. For decades, labor unions and Democrats have been allies in the fight for workers' rights. Unions have been major funders of Democratic campaigns and have provided the foot soldiers for Democratic get-out-the-vote efforts.

Card Check was the fortuitous marriage of smart policy and good politics.

So, why didn't it happen?

The protracted battle over health care took too much time and emptied the tank of political resolve. While Card Check was achievable, it wasn't an easy vote. Lots of Democrats were afraid of the backlash that would come from being seen as doing a favor for unions in the midst of an economic crisis.

The Chamber of Commerce and other corporate-funded groups pledged to run millions of dollars in ads against anyone who voted for it.[2]

The political reticence to take a tough vote that would strengthen a core part of the Democratic coalition is indicative of the larger problem of the Democratic approach to political power. Building, maintaining, and strengthening coalitions is what successful politics is all about, it's how you get power and it's how you keep that power.

Now contrast our approach to that of the Republicans. The National Rifle Association is to the Republican Party what labor unions are to the Democratic Party.[3] The National Rifle Association spends millions on the Republican Party—they contribute to their campaign coffers; they run ads and turn gun owners into campaign foot soldiers. The NRA even ran a pro-Republican TV

---

2 They did anyway, which should be a lesson to all involved. The Republicans are coming after you, no matter what you do, so you might as well vote for what you think is right.

3 Of course, labor unions fight for workers, and the NRA is a neofascist organization that fights for the right of gun manufacturers to make a profit off people dying. Harsh? Maybe. True? Definitely.

network for a while.[4] The NRA brands itself as an association of hunters and hobbyists who love the Second Amendment and America.[5] But that is a bullshit cover story. The NRA receives a significant amount of its funding from gun manufacturers. They rise and fall with the amount of weapons that are sold in America. It is in the financial interest of the NRA to ensure that as many guns as possible are sold in America. When they lie and say that Obama and Clinton are coming to get your guns, it is to encourage a panic in the market. People go buy more guns and the NRA gets more money. Since the Republican Party depends on the NRA, they have the same incentives. The Republican Party always stands with the NRA, no matter how unpopular (or immoral). In the wake of the horrendous shooting at Sandy Hook Elementary, commonsense gun-control measures like universal background checks polled at 90 percent.[6] But the Republican Party nearly unanimously defeated a bipartisan effort to pass these laws because it's what the NRA wanted. The Republican House of Representatives wouldn't even bring up the bill for a vote. Instead, they tried to pass bills to make it easier to carry a concealed weapon and bring a gun to a national park. They also stopped efforts to prevent people on the terrorist watch list from buying guns. All of these efforts were unpopular in the moment, but the Republicans knew that protecting a member of their coalition in the long term was worth some short-term pain.

Back in the early 2000s, the Republican Party was worried about the future of the NRA. The tobacco industry had been a major funder of the Republican Party. In exchange, they (with the help of Democrats from the South) protected the tobacco industry from the regulation that would be appropriate for an

---

4 NRATV made Fox look like PBS.

5 In that order.

6 Who are the 10 percent who think there shouldn't be background checks? Criminals and Republican members of Congress.

industry that was aggressively marketing a highly addictive and lethal product to children while lying to the public and the government about the health effects.[7] Antismoking advocates turned to the courts after being stymied in Congress. A series of high-profile lawsuits that uncovered nefarious conduct and delivered financially devastating jury verdicts made the tobacco industry politically toxic and crippled their ability to be a major political player.

In reaction to a Congress that was largely sponsored by the NRA, gun-control activists decided to follow this model against the gun industry, filing lawsuit after lawsuit implicating the gun manufacturers in the epidemic of gun violence that plagues America. If these lawsuits succeeded, they would devastate the gun manufacturers, bankrupt the NRA, and deny the Republican Party a major stream of campaign funding.

The Republicans in Congress sprung to action—they passed the Protection of Lawful Commerce in Arms Act, an unprecedented piece of legislation to grant the gun manufacturers immunity from legal liability. The Congress made the gun industry virtually un-suable. The victims of gun violence would have no legal recourse to seek damages from the companies that profited off tragedy. This was a historically outrageous gift to a special interest that funds the Republican Party and bears a measure of responsibility for an untold number of deaths over decades. But here's the part that will blow your mind—the Democrats helped them pass it. And not just a few Democrats—a lot of Democrats.

Why would the Democrats be the architects of their own destruction?

The answer is not great.

---

7 Ah, those aggressive nanny-state Democrats trying to stop kids from smoking.

The first time this legislation came up was in 2004. At the time, I was working for Tom Daschle, the Senate minority leader from South Dakota. Daschle was in the middle of an incredibly tough race for reelection. South Dakota is a very Republican state that loves its guns. The opening day of pheasant-hunting season is a de facto holiday. As the most prominent elected Democrat in the country, Daschle had become the face of the anti-Bush "resistance" and the target of an onslaught of political attacks from the White House and the Republican Party. He was Re-public-an enemy number one, and it was taking a toll at home. The debate in our office about the legislation was vigorous, to say the least. The issue was not as clear-cut as it would seem. The version before the Senate included an extension of the Assault Weapons Ban—the legislation that puts forward the crazy idea that people shouldn't be able to walk into a sporting goods store and buy a weapon of war.

The Republicans (and the NRA)[8] were vehemently opposed to an assault weapons ban for reasons that defy common sense. Packaging the Assault Weapons Ban with immunity for gun manufacturers seemed like the only way to pass the ban with Republican control of the Senate, House, and White House. But the ultimate reasons that drove Daschle and some other Democrats to support the bill were fear and naivete. Fear of the political repercussions of opposing the NRA and a naive hope that doing what the NRA wanted meant the NRA would oppose them less aggressively going forward.

Guess what?

It didn't work.

The legislation that Daschle voted for never became law because of Republican opposition to the inclusion of the assault weapons ban.[9] The NRA still went all in to defeat Daschle.

8 Same thing.
9 Which has still never been extended. It has been legal for an eighteen-

They spent heavily, pulled no punches, and portrayed Daschle as vehemently antigun, even though he supported their top policy priority.

The NRA is one of the most evil and effective forces in politics, and Democrats have no one to blame but themselves.

Why did I tell this very old and potentially overly long story?[10] Because I think it says everything about how Democrats and Republicans have approached politics in the past and what needs to change in the future.

Democrats have missed opportunities to strengthen their allies, like labor unions, and have helped Republicans strengthen their allies, like the NRA.

Republicans, on the other hand, will do anything and everything to increase their political power—even when it means taking a short-term political hit. At the same time they were helping the NRA, the Republicans engaged in a multi-million-dollar campaign to decimate the political influence of organized labor. While Republicans have a sincere opposition to the idea that workers should have power, the primary purpose of their antilabor efforts is to make it harder for Democrats to win elections. As you might have guessed, the Koch brothers were the major funders of the efforts to hurt labor unions. Wisconsin, under Governor Scott Walker, was the laboratory where the Right pioneered a lot of these efforts. Walker is a pretty empty suit who ran for president in 2016 and got his clock cleaned by...Jeb Bush.[11] As soon as Walker was elected in 2010, he passed a series of laws to restrict the rights of public employees, including teachers, to collectively bargain. These laws had their intended purpose—driving

---

year-old to buy assault weapons in large portions of America for fifteen years.

10 My editor, who hates my old stories, is really going to hate this part. If you are reading this, I won an argument or he gave up on me.

11 Yes, he lost to a man with very low energy.

down wages and causing union membership to plummet. According to a 2015 report in the *Washington Post*, the Wisconsin branches of the two biggest teachers' unions—the National Education Association and the American Federation of Teachers—lost a third and a half of their members, respectively. The state employees union saw a reduction of 70 percent within a few years. Across the country, Republican governors followed the Koch-Wisconsin playbook, passing right-to-work laws to make it harder for unions to organize and bargain.

In a very short period of time, unions have gone from a central piece of the Democratic coalition to a political afterthought come election time. Back in the 1950s, one in three workers was in a union. Today, that number is one in ten.

It's time to reverse the trend, fight back with vigor, and put forward a strategy to help strengthen unions.

Workers' rights must be at the center of the Democratic agenda.

Since Trump's election, there has been a renewed focus on workers' rights. Schumer and Pelosi introduced an ambitious pro-union agenda in 2017 after Trump was elected. Among the 2020 Democratic candidates, Bernie Sanders has been the most vocal and aggressive on issues of workers' rights—with Elizabeth Warren right behind him. Many of the presidential candidates have supported the fast-food workers fighting for a livable wage. This is very important progress, but there is more work to do.

One of the lessons I have learned the hard way in my years in politics is that you can't sneak big change in through customs. If you want to do something when you are in government, you have to talk about it when you are on the campaign trail. The campaign is the best opportunity politicians have to build public support for their agendas. This may seem counterintuitive, but it's harder to make the case when in office, because voters too often tune out once the voting is over. When we were in the White House, Vice President Biden used to say, "Compare me to the alternative, not the Almighty." The campaign is when you get to be compared to the alternative. In this case, the alternative is a bunch of plutocrats in populist clothing.

STEP ONE: PRIORITIZE CARD CHECK

This seems like a patently obvious thing for the next Democratic president to do within the proverbial "first hundred days" of the administration. Yet, there have been promises to put Card Check at the top of the agenda. When *Pod Save America* interviews presidential candidates, we always ask them how they prioritize legislation. It's one thing to say you support a tax cut, immigration reform, the Green New Deal, and the hundreds of other plans on your website. There is a lot of overlap between the Democratic candidates in every primary on what plans they support, but the more important question is which plans they will prioritize. Generally, a president's first bill has the best chance of becoming law, the next bill has the second-best chance, and it goes on from there.

The next Democratic president must prioritize the Employee Free Choice Act. It would be the most dramatic step to help unions in decades. If it isn't at the top of the priority list, Card Check will end up on the regret list four or eight[12] years later.

STEP TWO: TAKE ON RIGHT-TO-WORK LAWS

Right to work is one of the most Orwellian terms in all of politics. Right-to-work laws don't give people the right to work; they take power from workers and give it to corporations. Traditionally,

12 God willing.

every member contributes to the union because they benefit from the wages and benefits negotiated by the union. Right-to-work laws deny unions necessary funding.

More than half of states have right-to-work laws on the books. Several passed in the last decade when the Republican Party and the Koch brothers made marginalizing unions a top political priority. Reversing this trend needs to be at the top of the Democratic To Do list.

There is a bill sitting in Congress sponsored by more than two hundred Democrats that would do just that. The Protecting the Right to Organize, or PRO, Act[13] would mitigate many of the worst aspects of right-to-work laws (and generally shitty behavior from management) by giving workers the private right to sue employers, authorizing real penalties for violations of workers' rights, and ensuring that unions can collect fees from employers to cover the cost of their negotiations. The last provision goes right to the heart of the intent of the right-to-work laws.

Even if you are not persuaded by the substance of the PRO Act, think of it this way—there are few things that would piss off the Republicans and their funders more than passing this bill. That in and of itself is a reason to do it.[14]

There is another route to accomplish some of the goals of the PRO Act. Where Democrats control the legislatures and governors' offices, they should repeal any right-to-work laws and pass pro-union provisions like the ones in the PRO Act. Unfortunately, for the reasons discussed throughout the book, the Democrats don't (yet) have enough power.

However, about half of US states have some form of ballot initiative process where it is possible to circumvent the Koch subsidiaries who run a lot of state government. In those states,

---

13 There we go with the terrible Congressional acronyms.

14 I know this is petty, but just imagine Jim Jordan angry. Okay, bad example.

you can go put an initiative on the ballot, and let the voters decide.[15]

Missouri is not exactly a liberal utopia. Trump won Missouri by eighteen points in 2016. The governor is a Republican. Both senators are Republican. Missouri has eight members of Congress, and six of them are Republican. It's a red state, getting redder every single day. In 2017, Missouri passed an antiunion/procorporation right-to-work law. The unions and others in the state got enough signatures to put a measure on the 2018 ballot to repeal the law. Given the partisan leanings of the state and the conventional wisdom that being for unions was bad politics, this initiative seemed like a long shot...at best.

As it turns out, the conventional wisdom was wrong.[16] Sixty-eight percent of Missouri voters voted to repeal the antiunion law. If it can happen in Missouri, it can happen anywhere.

STEP THREE: GIVE WORKERS A SEAT AT THE TABLE

Utah senator/former Massachusetts governor/failed presidential candidate/dressage champion Mitt Romney has many skills.[17] But first and foremost among his myriad talents is accidentally saying the quiet part of conservatism out loud. Everyone remembers his 47 percent gaffe during the 2012 election. There was also the time he said he didn't care about the very poor. Asking me to pick a favorite Romney gaffe[18] is like asking a parent to pick their favorite child. But if I had to pick, I would choose the following one.

---

15 Democracy! Who woulda thunk it?

16 Something that is "conventional wisdom" is always wrong. When something is right, it's just called "wisdom."

17 JK—he isn't particularly skilled; he is just handsome, rich, and the son of a famous also rich person.

18 I have tried for years to brand Romney gaffes as Mitticisms, but it has YET to catch on.

The Iowa State Fair is one of the great events in all of politics. In addition to eating literally anything you want deep-fried on a stick, you get to interact with presidential candidates. Traditionally, candidates visit the "soapbox" where they address the fairgoers and take some questions. Romney, per usual, was as cool as the side of the pillow you are sleeping on, and got into an argument with an attendee.

At some point in the argument, Romney blurted out, "Corporations are people, my friend."

This was the perfect Romney gaffe.[19] It was yet another disastrous moment in an even more disastrous campaign. The man could sound like he was reading an astrophysics textbook when talking about the struggles of people in the economy, but if you talk out of school about the legal obligations of large corporations, Mitt Romney will fight you.[20] Our campaign—and most of the media—had a lot of fun with Romney's statement, using it as another example of a candidate whose policies put the interests of corporations over working people.

The point of this Romney story is twofold. First, dancing on Mitt's political grave one more time now that he is a senator who backs Trump on a regular basis despite the occasional sad tweet. Second, technically—and I mean VERY technically—Romney was right. Corporations in the eyes of the law have similar rights to people in the eyes of the law.

Senator Elizabeth Warren's Accountable Capitalism Act turns Romney's point on its head.[21] As Matt Yglesias wrote on Vox: "If corporations are going to have the legal rights of persons, they should be expected to act like decent citizens who uphold their fair share of the social contract and not act like sociopaths

---

19 Mitticism?
20 "My friend" is Romney for "Hey, asshole!"
21 Points for no cheesy acronym names.

whose sole obligation is profitability." Warren's plan would require corporations of a certain size to apply for corporate citizenship, which would carry with it obligations to more than the bottom lines of the shareholders. Under Warren's plan, workers would get the opportunity to elect 40 percent of the board of directors. For all the various economic proposals that are bandied around in politics—tax cuts, tax increases, tax credits, etc.—giving workers a seat at the able could do the most to make American capitalism more worker friendly. To give you an example of how this plan would make a difference, just think back to the Trump tax cut of 2018. During passage of the bill, Trump, congressional Republicans, and other noted liars promised that the giant tax cut for corporations who already had record profits would mean higher wages for American workers. Except, that's not what happened. As soon as the tax law passed, the corporations who had promised higher wages used the money for stock buybacks, which made rich investors richer and did nothing for workers.[22]

Democrats need to focus on empowering workers as opposed to courting the donations of the investors and CEOs that are getting rich at the expense of the workers.

STEP FOUR: ORGANIZING THE GIG ECONOMY

Uber, Lyft, Instacart, and so many other Silicon Valley companies are changing what it means to be an American worker. Many people have taken advantage of the "side hustle"[23] offered by these services, enjoying the opportunity to earn some extra money on a

---

22 Great job, Paul Ryan!

23 I am using this term ironically. The fact that I have to point that out suggests I may not be doing it well.

flexible schedule. But with that flexibility comes limited autonomy and no security or benefits.

Uber et al. don't consider their drivers and delivery personnel to be employees, which means they don't have to pay payroll taxes or Social Security. It also means these companies don't have to provide health care, pensions, sick days, family leave, or other benefits that are traditionally given to workers. This transformation promises to further undermine the very idea of work and exacerbate rapidly growing economic inequality.

This growing population of workers is in desperate need of the advocacy a union provides, and they represent the future for the American labor movement. It should be a priority for Democrats to help these workers by enacting policies to make it easier for workers in the gig economy to organize. This would require Democratic politicians to be as willing to confront their allies in Silicon Valley as they are to confront their adversaries at the oil companies. In 2015, Hillary Clinton gave an economic policy address as part of her presidential campaign. Buried in the speech was a comment on how the internet was changing the economy. "This on-demand, or so-called 'gig economy,' is creating exciting opportunities and unleashing innovation. But it's also raising hard questions about workplace protections and what a good job will look like in the future," she said. "Fair pay and fair scheduling, paid family leave and earned sick days, child care are essential to our competitiveness and growth."

Silicon Valley screamed bloody murder—how dare a Democrat attack them! There was criticism from Democrats, including the author of this book, who were concerned that Hillary was ceding the party's future-oriented image for retrograde policies.

However, Hillary Clinton was right.

Democrats have come a long way in our willingness to call out Silicon Valley since Clinton's forewarning. In recent years, Facebook and Twitter have been on the front lines of the destruction of democracy through the algorithmic perversion of our discourse. Uber was revealed to be a pit of toxic masculinity and poor management. And Democrats have focused more on the negative impacts of the transformational technology coming out of Silicon Valley.

Yet for all of the tough rhetoric coming out on the campaign trail, many Democrats are still making a beeline to the Bay Area to hobnob with tech founders and executives to fill their campaign coffers. The folks who started Google, Facebook, and the rest were frequent visitors to the Obama White House. Former executives from these companies took huge pay cuts to work in the administration and bring government from the dark ages to the age of the internet. And after Obama left the White House, a lot of his former staffers went to work in Silicon Valley. Large swaths of the folks who worked for me in the Obama White House are now employed by Facebook, Airbnb, and the rest. I went to work for GoFundMe, a venture capital–backed online fundraising company. For the most part, the people who work in tech and in Democratic politics agree on a lot—climate change, LGBTQ rights, and immigration reform. The folks in tech are our donors, friends, and former colleagues, but we have to be willing to lose some friendships and donations.

Facebook, Google, and Amazon are now some of the most powerful corporations in the world. They are disrupting democracy, putting smaller companies out of business, and exacerbating economic inequality. There is no question that these tech giants need to be subject to more aggressive regulating scrutiny—including looking at whether they are monopolies that should be broken up.

This is particularly true when it comes to workers' rights. Democrats must support policies that help the workers in the gig economy. We must be their voice. For better or worse (and it's probably worse), the Uber model of work is likely the future for a lot of Americans.

If Democrats don't stand for those workers, nobody else will.

In 2019, California passed a landmark law that made it harder for companies to classify their workers as independent contractors. The law ensures gig workers are treated more fairly and received more benefits.

What was the response from the industry?

They declared the law didn't apply to them and wouldn't abide by it and pledged to spend tens of millions of dollars to put an initiative on the ballot to overturn the law.

If Democrats want to be true to our populist roots, we need an agenda that addresses the needs of the workers of the new economy. In 2016, Senator Elizabeth Warren proposed a three-part plan to support the workers in the gig economy. First, require that the companies that employ these workers deduct payroll taxes to ensure that the workers are paying into Social Security. Second, provide a form of catastrophic insurance in case they become injured or ill and are unable to work. Third, make paid leave available to all of these workers. The goal of proposals like Warren's is to ensure that workers in the new economy have some of the protections that were fundamental to the old economy.

Nationally, Democrats should support laws to force employers to treat contractors like employees. These laws are popular. A poll by the liberal think tank Data for Progress found people supported such laws by twenty points.

This idea needs to be at the center of the Democratic platform. Efforts to unionize these workers should have the full and vocal backing of the party. Democrats should be the voice of the workers hurt by the tech revolution much as we were the voice of the workers hurt by the industrial revolution.

Every day, Democratic politicians and progressives come out with new and better ideas to protect workers and promote unions. The ones outlined in this chapter are a sampling of what can and should be done. The party is moving in the right direction on the campaign trail, but it needs to happen in the halls of Congress and in the White House once we have the power to turn these ideas into laws.

DANCE WITH THE VOTERS WHO BRUNG YOU

It's fair to ask why I wrote a whole chapter on this topic.[24]

The story of Democrats and labor is a parable for how the conservatives came to dominate politics in America. Republicans saw unions as core to the strength of the Democratic Party—particularly in the Midwestern states that decide presidential elections. So they ran a multipronged strategy to weaken the unions and therefore weaken the Democrats. It was a twofer. Weakening unions helped Republicans win elections and helped put money in the pockets of Republican donors, who in turn gave more money to Republicans.

Democrats were too reticent to use political power to fight back. We were afraid of Fox News and the Republican attack ads. Too many of us sat there and watched the Republicans and the Kochs strike a blow to the Democratic base.

The greatest trick the Republicans ever pulled was convincing Democrats to be scared of their friends.

This is what Reagan did with his racist "welfare queen" rhetoric. George H. W. Bush built on this strategy with his racist Willie Horton attacks in 1988. This was all part of an effort to separate the Democratic Party from the African American community that was supporting Democrats by huge margins. They wanted to make standing with African Americans and African American leaders politically toxic. This was so successful that by

---

24 It's a question my editor has asked repeatedly.

the time Bill Clinton was running for president, he felt like he needed his Sister Souljah moment. Then in 1996, he felt like he needed to sign an onerous and overly conservative welfare law to win reelection.[25]

But Republicans aren't only trying to convince voters; they are trying to scare Democratic politicians from doing things that are in their political interest. There is an old saying in Washington: The only people who believe Republican talking points are Democratic politicians.[26]

This has been the Republican strategy for decades—demonize the voters that Democrats depend on in the hope that they can make it politically toxic for Democrats to stand with their own supporters.

That can never happen again. We have to stand with, fight for, and strengthen the Democratic coalition. If we don't stand up for our friends, they won't stand up for us.

What You Can Do to Help

- Call your members of Congress and ask them to support the Employee Free Choice Act, the PRO Act, and other bills to help strengthen unions.
- Support local efforts to overturn right-to-work laws, as was done in Missouri.
- Patronize businesses that are unionized where possible.
- Push back on social media against antiunion propaganda.

25 This decision was bad at the time and looks even worse now.
26 To be honest, I have been trying to make this an old saying for a decade.

CHAPTER 14

#NEVERTRUMP . . . AGAIN

Other than an affection for good walks spoiled,[1] Donald J. Trump and Barack H. Obama would seem to have nothing in common. Obama grew up in Hawaii, raised by a single mother who struggled at times. Trump was born into a wealthy New York family. Obama is an award-winning author. Trump doesn't read books. Obama ran on hope. Trump ran on hate. Obama is a black man from the South Side of Chicago. Trump is a racist.

But there is one through line in their candidacies: they both ran as reformers seeking to fix a broken Washington.

Obama ensured that his administration operated in a manner consistent with his campaign promises as a reformer. One of his first acts was to sign an executive order that put in place unprecedented reforms, including

- banning federal lobbyists from working in his administration;
- banning his staff from lobbying his administration;
- requiring his staff to recuse themselves from issues they worked on in the private sector; and

---

1 I am 99 percent sure Trump does not walk on the golf course or anywhere else. He would make Lindsey Graham give him a piggyback if he could.

- repealing a Bush administration policy that made it easier to keep government information from the public.

While we were far from perfect—a fact that the White House press corps enjoyed pointing out[2]—we did our best to live up to these ideals every day we walked into the White House. And as has been noted repeatedly over the last few years, Obama left the White House without a scandal.[3] But despite Obama's efforts, Washington itself remained awfully swampy.

Trump, on the other hand, didn't even try to live up to his "drain the swamp" rhetoric. His campaign chair, deputy campaign chair, lawyer, national security advisor, political consigliere, and foreign policy advisor were all found guilty of a potpourri of crimes. Most spent time in prison. Trump was essentially named an unindicted coconspirator in a felony for using campaign funds to pay hush money to women who had affairs with Trump.[4] His EPA administrator, secretary of the interior, and secretary of veterans affairs all resigned in scandal. His administration is being run by lobbyists who are doing the bidding of their once and future special interest employers. Instead of draining the swamp as he decried on the campaign, Trump has used the federal government to line his own pockets by directing government spending to his hotels and golf resorts.

Trump has refused to release his tax returns. His administration engages in unprecedented secrecy while suppressing science and ordering government agencies to deny climate change and lie about hurricanes.[5]

---

2 The press doesn't give presidents points for trying.

3 If you don't count the tan suit. (I do.)

4 This sentence is amazing when you consider that Trump is (a) still in office and (b) has a 90-plus percent approval rating with Republican voters—especially evangelical Christians, who I am told take morality seriously.

5 As a nation, we should pledge to never, ever forget the time Trump used a sharpie to alter a hurricane map to make one of his insane tweets "accurate."

After spending years and many, many tweets decrying Barack Obama's very traditional use of presidential power, Trump has been at least "authoritarian curious." He declared a national emergency to try to build the border wall that Congress refused to fund. Trump has also contemplated bypassing Congress to cut taxes for wealthy investors, ending the idea that people born in America are citizens, and pardoning himself of crimes he committed in the 2016 election. Who could forget the time that Trump "hereby ordered" via tweet that all US companies stop doing business with China?

Trump has gotten away with all of it. The lying, the lawbreaking, the corruption, and the crimes have all gone unpunished. There has been little to no accountability.

This fact says more about America than it does about Trump.

Let's be honest: Trump is not some criminal mastermind.[6] He commits his crimes out in the open for the world to see. Were he not president, he would end up on one of those BuzzFeed lists of "America's dumbest criminals," like the kids who post pictures on Instagram of all the things they shoplifted, while tagging the store where they did the shoplifting. He isn't "Teflon Don." For most of Trump's tenure, his poll numbers have been historically bad. He is the first president in the history of the Gallup Poll to never reach 50 percent approval in their first three years in office.

To the extent that there is a silver lining or two in the very dark cloud of Trump's presidency, it's the realization that the laws and regulations that surround presidents and their power are deeply flawed. They presume a measure of good faith on behalf of the president and his party.

Some like to say that the system didn't anticipate someone like Trump, but that's not really true. Trump is exactly who the

---

6 He intimidated a witness in a criminal investigation on Twitter, which is just an incredibly stupid thing to do—except he got away with it.

founders anticipated when they put the impeachment and Twenty-Fifth Amendment procedures in the Constitution. They imagined a situation where a person lacking the morals or capacity for the job of president won a presidential election.[7] Richard Nixon's decision to resign rather than be impeached during Watergate was proof the system worked.

What the system didn't anticipate was the outright corruption of one of the two political parties. Nixon only agreed to resign when a group of Republican senators and members of Congress went to the White House to tell him to resign. Despite a Cheesecake Factory menu worth of crimes, the position of the Republican Party in the Trump era has been willful blindness. They have let Trump get away with everything. They view their constitutional responsibilities of checks and balances as options, not obligations. If Mitch McConnell had been the leader of the Senate during Watergate, Nixon would have finished out his term, and the Republican Party would have named several airports after him.

There is an assumption in our political system that when push comes to shove, our elected officials will put country over party. Every day of the Trump era proves this notion to be dangerously naive. Our institutions are not up to the task of dealing with this president and this Republican Party. They have found the loopholes and aggressively exploited them to amass political power.

The final part of a Democratic Party effort to repair our democracy is a plan to protect our country from a future Trump. We need to strengthen our institutions, close the loopholes, and enshrine norms into law.

---

7 Maybe they didn't imagine a person who was both too corrupt AND too stupid to be president.

POWER-LESS, NOT POWER-FULL

Every president seemingly becomes more powerful than the previous one. The continual expansion of presidential powers is certainly tied to a Congress that is too broken to do the most fundamental parts of its job. The simple act of funding government operations brings Congress to the precipice of collapse every year. More often than not, they forgo making decisions and just pass a bill to extend the previous year's budget. This inaction pushes more authority and decision-making power onto the president. Another problem is the cycle of reversed incentives. When a party is out of the White House, they decry the expanding powers of the president. When they win the White House, they become vigorous defenders of the inherent powers of the presidency.

Donald Trump is certainly not a paragon of ideological consistency, but his tweets about presidential power when Obama was president are a sight to behold.

For example, when Obama was preparing to take executive action to deal with a portion of the broken immigration system, Trump tweeted, "Repubs must not allow Pres Obama to subvert the Constitution of the US for his own benefit & because he is unable to negotiate w/ Congress."[8]

To his credit, President Obama was very thoughtful about uses of presidential power.[9] He certainly used it when needed, especially with a recalcitrant and incompetent Congress. I was a big advocate for the "pen and phone" strategy in his second term that continually highlighted presidential action in the face of Congressional inaction. He aggressively used his regulatory authority to clean up our air and water, make our food and workplaces safer, make our economy fairer, and reduce carbon pollution to save our

8 I'm truly shocked he knew how to use the ampersand in a sentence.

9 I am biased, but also correct in this instance at least.

planet. The policies may have been aggressive, but these were traditional uses of presidential power. Even the more controversial efforts to protect some undocumented immigrants from deportation were within the long-established powers of the presidency.

But for all of his enthusiasm for his pen and his phone, President Obama twice shied away from pushing the limits of presidential power. During the 2011 debt-ceiling standoff, Obama was presented with the option of simply ignoring Congress and paying the bills anyway. The theory underlying this option included the Treasury Department minting a trillion-dollar coin.

I know it sounds crazy, but here is a summary of this plan from the decidedly uncrazy Matt O'Brien writing in the *Atlantic*:

> It sounds nuts. But there's a loophole that actually lets the Treasury create coins in whatever value it wants, even $1 trillion. It's all straightforward enough. The Treasury would create one of these coins, deposit it at the Federal Reserve, and use the new money in its account to pay our bills if the debt ceiling isn't increased.

This trillion-dollar coin would have solved all of our problems, but Obama decided not to push the envelope of his own power. He was very concerned about the precedent it would set.

A few years later, Obama was contemplating a military strike against the Syrian regime in response to a horrific chemical weapons attack directed at Syrian civilians that opposed the Assad regime. As a staffer whose primary responsibilities were domestic in nature, I had no window into the planning or timing of the military response. I was, however, charged with working with the national security team on how, when, and where Obama would explain his decision to the public.

The assumption in Washington was that Obama, like nearly every president before him, would ask for congressional forgiveness rather than permission. Despite the passage of the War Powers Act after the Vietnam War, presidents with the agreement of the courts had adopted an "ask for forgiveness rather than permission" approach to the use of military force. That was certainly the direction Obama was headed until he received a letter.

A bipartisan group of members of Congress had sent Obama a letter demanding that he seek congressional approval before striking Syria. This letter hit home for Obama, who rose to prominence as an opponent of the Iraq War and George W. Bush's aggressive use of executive power in the "War on Terror."

As Obama said to me on the night he abandoned the idea of a unilateral strike, "I kept thinking to myself, if I was still in the Senate—not the White House—I would have signed that letter."

Obama made the decision to seek congressional approval, because he wanted to be the rare president who didn't want more power. He also wanted to throw the ball back in the lap of Congress, which had been a very willing partner in expanding presidential power. Ever since the vast majority of Congress got it so wrong on Iraq, they had been working hard to avoid taking tough votes.[10]

The response to Obama's decision on Syria was very telling. First, Congress was unable to come to a decision. The Republicans who had been yelling at Obama for not being tougher on Assad from the safety of cable news sets all found excuses to oppose the president. The Washington, DC–based media, which fetishizes missile strikes and thirsts for war, savaged Obama for his decision. In their myopic view, a president choosing not to use power was a sign of weakness, not strength.

Absent action, the expansion of presidential power is going to continue because no one has an incentive to curb it. Presidents want power because they want to do things. Statements and

---

10 While reserving the right to complain ex post facto.

plaintive tweets aside, Congress as an institution wants a powerful executive because it shields them from having to make politically perilous decisions; and the media equates power with strength and restraint with weakness.

Donald Trump is the most authoritarian president to date, but he won't be the last. He has shown that there are few consequences to ignoring Congress—an institution with the approval ratings of ringworm. Trump doing dictator cosplay while live-tweeting *Fox & Friends* and alternately feuding with Debra Messing, Don Lemon, and Morning Mika is not the Republican president that scares me the most. It's the next authoritarian Republican president who is smarter and less easily distracted that we should all be afraid of.

AN AGENDA OF RESTRAINT

The best—and perhaps only—way to reduce presidential power is for a Democratic president to work with a Democratic Congress to put that restraint into law.

The first step would be to repeal the Authorization for Use of Military Force (AUMF) that was passed in 2001 to target the perpetrators of 9/11. This authorization has been used as the legal basis for the "War on Terror" for nearly two decades. It justifies drone strikes in Libya and Somalia. It's why there are troops serving in Afghanistan who were in diapers on 9/11. It's how the Obama and Trump administrations were able to conduct thousands of air strikes against ISIS without congressional approval. The Trump administration has even floated leaning on the 2001 AUMF to justify military strikes against Iran. Repealing the 2001 AUMF would limit the ability of future presidents to conduct military strikes and send US men and women into harm's way without a public debate and a congressional vote.

The second step would be to repeal the National Emergencies Act. This law was passed in the 1970s to ostensibly rein in presidential power by putting some limits on the extraordinary powers that presidents claim during a "national emergency." The law requires public disclosure, periodic reports, an annual expiration, and requires Congress to meet every six months to consider a vote to terminate the state of emergency.

You might be surprised to learn that you not only are living in a state of emergency—you are living in thirty states of emergency. President Trump invoked a state of emergency in order to fund the construction of his much ballyhooed border wall after Congress refused to fund this useless vanity project. Therefore, in clear contravention of Congress's will, Trump declared a state of emergency, which allowed him to steal money from the Pentagon to build the wall.[11] Going against type, even Republicans in Congress decided to do something about Trump stealing their lunch money. They voted to block his emergency declaration—this is one of the only times Congress has ever used the power it gave itself in the National Emergencies Act. Alas, Trump vetoed the bill, and just enough Republicans stuck with him that the fake national emergency stayed real.

Despite Congress trying to do the right thing, the result is the ultimate argument for changing the law. The two-thirds threshold to override a veto is simply too high in a polarized Congress. There is almost nothing that the mind could conjure that would cause that many Republicans to stand in Trump's way. If a president needs new powers to deal with an emergency, he or she should have to ask Congress for them. Some argue that this system cannot work, because Congress is too slow.

11 You may remember that Trump promised that Mexico would pay for the wall, which rolls off the tongue better than, "We are going to build the wall and pay for it by defunding schools and childcare centers for US troops." I'm no pollster, but...

That is a fair concern, although Congress did move quite (and too) quickly to give President Bush a blank check of executive power after 9/11.

These steps are just the beginning of a larger effort to rebalance the scales between the three branches of government. Future Democratic Congresses should also look seriously at reforming the War Powers Act to ensure a greater role for Congress in decisions around the use of military force. This is especially important with the rise of drones and cyber warfare actions that take place out of sight and under the auspices of covert action.

The substantive benefits of this approach are obvious every day Trump is in office, but there are political benefits as well. Imagine what it would say to a cynical public if a president reduced his or her own power.

The most important thing for a Democratic Congress to do—if they want to be credible to voters—is be consistent. If and when a Democratic president pushes the envelope, they have to speak out. They cannot follow the Republican formula of sending periodic sad tweets and then enabling authoritarian behavior. That approach breeds cynicism about politics and politicians. Cynicism is the friend of the Republican Party that can only win with diminished turnout. It is the enemy of a Democratic Party that depends on new voters turning out because they think their vote will mean real change.

LAWS > NORMS

It has long been a tradition that presidential candidates release their tax returns. These releases give the public an opportunity to delve into the finances and potential conflicts of interests of a possible president. There is no law requiring that they do so. I am not naive enough to think that candidates volunteer for this financial colonoscopy out of the goodness of their hearts. They release their tax returns because they believe the public will punish them for refusing.

Back in the 2012 campaign, Mitt Romney initially refused to abide by the decades-long tradition of presidential candidates releasing years of tax returns. Romney is fabulously wealthy thanks to buying struggling companies and harvesting them for profit and parts during a long career as a private-equity executive. His wealth was an issue in the campaign, and he was very resistant to providing the public with more information about this Achilles' heel. He faced tremendous blowback from the public, the press, and even members of his own party.

Romney eventually relented, but it was too little, too late.[12] He released two years of returns—far fewer than the decade of returns that most candidates release—and they happened to be the two years he was running for president, not the years he was working in private equity. As painful as the release of a treasure trove of data reminding voters about his wealth was, Romney concluded that the cost of hiding the information was greater.

Romney's experience proved that not releasing one's tax returns was a politically unsustainable position for a presidential candidate.

Then Trump came along.

In 2016, Donald Trump steadfastly refused to release his tax returns. He claimed the fact that he was under an audit prevented him from releasing his returns. There has never been any evidence that Trump is actually under audit.[13] There is nothing that prevents someone under audit from releasing their tax returns.

---

12 "Too little, too late" should be emblazoned on the Romney family crest. It's a perfect summary of his political career.

13 And plenty of evidence that he is a liar.

Trump presumably made the same political calculation as other candidates, but he concluded the political cost of releasing his tax returns was worse than the cost of hiding them. There is speculation that Trump didn't want to release his returns because they would reveal that he is much less wealthy than he claims. Either way, Trump didn't release his returns.

Trump bucked tradition and won. The lesson was taught.

Depending on tradition is not enough. Presidential candidates should be required by law to release ten years of tax returns at least nine months before the election. Heck, why stop at the president? Every candidate for federal office should be required to do so.

Congressional Democrats made requiring the release of tax returns part of the first bill they passed in 2019, and they should do so again when there is a Democratic president to sign it. In the interim, states like California are passing laws requiring the release of tax returns to appear on the ballot in that state. Trump has no chance of winning in California, so he won't feel compelled to release his returns. However, other more competitive states could follow this path, and the next time there is an open Republican primary, the candidates will need to appear on the California ballot. These efforts make clear that Democrats are fighting to give the public access to information, while Republicans are fighting to hide it.

The Trump presidency has provided a detailed map of the loopholes in our laws. It's a reminder that we cannot depend on intrinsic morality or a sense of shame for our politicians to do the right thing. Norms and traditions are clearly not enough. The Democratic Party should advance an agenda that enshrines our norms into laws and ensures presidents are accountable for their actions.

I imagine there might be some resistance to some of these ideas. Some will argue that Trump is a once-in-a-lifetime problem.

Others could be resistant because they involve adding teeth to the laws that could be used against a Democrat in office.

Anyone who thinks the next Republican president won't be a smarter, more dangerous version of Trump has been sleepwalking through the last few years. If Democrats spend years decrying Trump's corruption and then don't do anything to clean up Washington, they deserve to lose.

Some ideas:

- **Strengthen the Hatch Act:** The Hatch Act is the law that is supposed to ensure that federal government officials are not doing politics on the taxpayer dime. When I worked in the White House, I lived in mortal fear of breaking that law. There were lawyers in the White House counsel's office whose whole job was making sure people like me stayed on the right side of the law. As it turns out, my fears were for naught. Kellyanne Conway, who has the same title I did while in the White House,[14] has violated the law willy-nilly for three years. After several warnings, the office responsible for enforcing the Hatch Act had enough. It was time to act. They reached into the armory and pulled out the biggest weapon available.

  A letter to President Trump *recommending* that he fire Conway. Trump, of course, refused to do so. Conway stayed on the job and continues to campaign for Trump on the public dime.

  This is another example of the naivete at the heart of the political system. The law worked previously because it depended on the capacity for shame. I didn't want to violate the law not because I was afraid of prison,[15] but because I

---

14 While we had the same title, her duties seem to consist only of occasionally yelling at Chris Cuomo.

15 I am.

didn't want to embarrass President Obama. I also knew that President Obama would not look kindly at rampant lawbreaking from one of his staff[16] and would certainly have fired me if he had received such a letter. The system doesn't work when the folks involved are incapable of shame. Therefore, the law needs more teeth, a true enforcement mechanism, and real penalties for violations. The law is broken if a top advisor to the president can break it on a daily basis with no consequences.

The second problem with the Hatch Act is that there is a giant loophole. Do you know who isn't covered by the Hatch Act?

The president of the United States.

Yes, the law preventing public officials from campaigning on the job excludes the candidate who would do the campaigning.

There was a reason behind this decision at the time, but it hasn't really stood the test of time. In the Obama White House, lawyers reviewed every official speech to make sure that there was no language in them that could possibly be construed as "political activity." This included endorsements of candidates, encouraging people to vote or donate to a campaign, or criticism of a political opponent on the ballot. The reason for the diligence is that a campaign is required to pay a portion of the costs for presidential travel if an event is deemed political. Air Force One, the presidential motorcade, and the rest of the traveling circus are quite expensive. We didn't want our campaign or some other campaign to get stuck with a very large bill. Trump, on the other hand, violates this stricture on nearly every trip he takes. There are no consequences.

---

16 How quaint.

This needs to change. Making the president liable for the crimes he commits would be a start.

- **Require presidents to divest:** Federal officials are required to follow pretty rigorous conflict-of-interest rules. The Office of Government Ethics reviews their financial holdings to ensure there are no conflicts. If a conflict exists, they are required to divest. For example, someone whose job includes making policy about self-driving cars would not be allowed to own stock in Uber and Lyft. There are also annual financial disclosure reports that must be filed and made public.

  There is, however, no law prohibiting the president from having a financial conflict of interest. The only such law is the emoluments provision of the Constitution, but that deals with money from foreign governments. Nothing stops Trump from owning hotels, golf resorts, wineries, and schlocky apparel businesses that potentially benefit from his decision making.

  In the past, this never mattered—every previous president voluntarily divested from any potential conflicts. President Jimmy Carter even famously put his peanut farm in a blind trust to stay above reproach. Trump refused to divest from his businesses. He continually makes decisions that benefit his bottom line. He steers millions of taxpayer dollars to his hotels. Every time he stays at Mar-a-Lago, the Secret Service, White House staff, and military aides that travel with the president stay at his hotel. The government pays for those rooms with taxpayer dollars that go right into Trump's pocket.

  If any other government official acted this way, they would be headed to jail. We can no longer depend on a sense of decency in our president. We can no longer depend on pressure from the media and the public to force presidents to do the right thing. Conflict-of-interest laws must apply to the president. It's as simple as that.

- **No more get-out-of-jail-free cards:** Trump's presidential crime spree is enabled by the fact that we treat our presidents as being above the law. The US presidency comes with a plane, armed guards, a pretty sweet house, and a get-out-of-jail-free card.

  The Mueller report is crystal clear that Trump went to extreme efforts to obstruct the Russia investigation. Many legal observers believe that if Trump were a private citizen, he would have been indicted. Trump also would have been indicted and likely prosecuted for a scam to pay hush money to cover up his affairs.

  But he is president, so he escapes consequences. A sitting president cannot be indicted; therefore, our sitting president hasn't been indicted of the crimes he has committed. This presidential immunity isn't in the Constitution. It isn't even a law. It's from a memo written before I was born. In 1973, the Office of Legal Counsel within the Justice Department came to this conclusion during Watergate. It is notable that Nixon's administration officials were the ones who decided that Nixon couldn't be indicted. The opinion was reaffirmed in 2000 after Bill Clinton was impeached. Despite the conflict of interests of the authors of the original memo and those who seconded it, there are good reasons for this policy. The Constitution designates impeachment as the mechanism for holding presidents accountable for wrongdoing.

  The impeachment process was rendered null and void by a closely divided Senate and an overtly partisan Republican Party. Removing a president requires two-thirds of the Senate. This means approximately half of Republicans would need to vote to remove Trump for crimes. I am relatively confident that if Trump were caught on tape loading bricks of gold stolen from Fort Knox into the trunk of his car, even Senate Republicans would vote against removing him from office.[17] If removal from office is not a viable option no matter how heinous the crime, then the president is above the law.

This policy creates some perverse incentives. Trump committed crimes to win the election. If those crimes had been unsuccessful and he lost, Trump would be indicted. But because the crimes were successful, Trump can't be indicted.[18] What sense does that make?

The next Democratic president should rescind the OLC memo. This move would have real credibility with the public because they would be theoretically exposing themselves to legal jeopardy.[19] A president saying that he or she is not above the law would also have the benefit of being very good politics.

Trump has proven that the consequences for dishonesty, corruption, and criminality are few and far between. A future Democratic administration could easily be tempted to color outside the lines or live in the grayer areas of the law. Trump has shown how an "end justifies the means" approach to government can work.[20] Under this approach, why would Democrats close the barn door after the mule escaped?[21]

Closing the loophole that Trump exploited is the right thing to do, which, frankly, is reason enough. No president—Republican

---

17 Ted Cruz would lead the defense yelling, "Fake News," Susan Collins would wrestle with the decision publicly before siding with Trump, and Joe Manchin would also vote with Trump just to rub it in our face that we are stuck with him.

18 Staying out of jail is also a strong incentive for Trump to commit more crimes to get reelected.

19 Don't commit crimes in the White House. Don't. It's not that hard.

20 I specifically avoided using the term *successful* here, because Trump's only real success to date is staying in office/out of jail.

21 Think about it.

or Democrat—should be above the law. But pushing for these reforms is ultimately good politics for Democrats.

A Trump-lite approach would foster cynicism among the very voters Democrats need to turn out. This is my ten millionth reminder that Democrats depend on making politics inspiring enough that new and less likely voters turn out, and Republicans depend on making politics cynical enough to turn off those same voters.

Obama and Trump both proved the most powerful message in American politics is "change." Americans are rightly angry about what is happening (and not happening) in Washington. They want something different and better. This is particularly true of the younger voters that were raised on 9/11, Iraq, Katrina, a financial crisis, the Republican backlash to Obama, and now Trump. They have been living in one of the most tumultuous periods in American history, but our politics have been too small for the big challenges that shaped their lives.

If the Democratic Party wants to earn the support of this group of voters we have to be seen as the ones who will fix the broken politics system. And we can't be a party that runs on fixing the broken system and then benefits from it once we are in office. We have to resist the gravitational pull of the status quo.

Republicans are the party that views democracy as an impediment to their political goals. They have proven time and again that they will trample the best American traditions to hold on to power. Weak institutions make this easier. We cannot play their game. We will not win.

If we can't learn that lesson from the shit show in the White House, then what was the point?

CONCLUSION

YES WE (STILL) CAN

Thanks to *Pod Save America*, I have had the opportunity to travel all over the country since Trump took office. We have been to states as blue as Massachusetts and New York and as red as Utah and South Carolina. These visits have been an eye-opening and consistent source of rejuvenation amid the daily disasters of the Trump era.

People in America have every right to be angry. There is a racist clown in the White House doing the bidding of his donors even though the majority of Americans voted against him. But there is nothing angry about the people I have met at our shows. They are activists who channeled their anger into action.

They are also wannabe optimists. Everywhere we go, people ask us to stay hopeful, because hope for a better tomorrow fuels the activism of today.

This is where it gets hard.

One of the challenges of talking about politics in the Trump era is finding the right balance between honesty and hope. The idea that defeating Trump is the beginning, not the end, can be deeply depressing. I wish I could say that Trump was an aberration or that his election was a glitch in an otherwise well-functioning system. The truth about the Republican Party and what they have done to our democracy is hard to hear.

But we have to be brutally honest about the situation we are in and who we are dealing with—as unpleasant as that may be.

This book contains a number of ideas that will make some folks in Washington queasy. Many of them are ideas I would have rejected out of hand before Trump knocked the blinders off my eyes. But my approach to this moment of crisis in our democracy—like my approach to a lot of my life over the last decade—is informed by a lesson Barack Obama taught me.

It's easy to forget, but there was a moment when it seemed likely that Barack Obama would be a one-term president. The summer of 2011 was brutal. Obama was bruised and battered by a budget battle with the Republicans that damaged the economy, caused the US credit rating to be downgraded for the first time in history, and led to pretty much everyone from the Far Right to the Far Left being pissed at him.

Obama's poll numbers were a Trumpian level of terrible. All of official Washington was calling for a mass firing of Obama's staff. The monthly jobs report for August 2011 reported that the US economy had created exactly zero jobs,[1] and Obama's prime-time speech to Congress was bumped from prime time to make room for a Republican debate... on MSNBC.

The mood in the White House was dark.

With this backdrop, Obama called a meeting of his political advisors. We met on a weekend in the East Wing of the White House. Everyone was dressed in the awkward weekend attire of people who wear business attire for a living. This was a big meeting by Obama standards. Most of the White House senior staff, the leadership of the reelection campaign, and even some of his old friends

---

1 This news was so absurdly and specifically bad that when it came out, all I could do was laugh.

were present. The ostensible purpose of the meeting was to regroup from the summer from hell and plot out the fall and winter. But Obama had another reason to gather the troops. He had a message for us.

Obama kicked off the meeting by thanking us all for coming into the office on what would have been a rare weekend day off, but he quickly cut to the chase:

> If the election were held today, I would probably lose. The economy isn't going to miraculously get better. There isn't going to be a grand bargain. The stakes were high in the last election, but they are higher this time. Where we can make substantive progress we will, but I want to spend from now to the election drawing big distinctions and picking clear fights. I want the American people to see the two very different visions for this country. If I go down, I'm not going down like a punk.[2]

The president had given us our marching orders: get our heads out of our asses, stop playing it safe, go big, and run a campaign that matched the moment.

In the coming months, Obama would lay out a huge jobs package, stare down the Republicans in a fight over taxes, give a campaign-defining speech on economic inequality, and go against the advice of nearly everyone in politics and endorse the legalization of same-sex marriage.

This strategy worked. We won reelection in an electoral landslide and ran a campaign of which we could all be proud.

The lesson Obama taught me was that when you have every-

---

2 Someone in this overly large meeting leaked Obama's remarks to the authors of the campaign book *Double Down*. My recollection of what Obama said is different than the leaker's, who was never identified but definitely sucks.

thing to lose, the only way to succeed is to run like you have nothing to lose.

Obama's message in 2012 is even truer today. The stakes are exponentially higher. Playing political prevent defense where we hope Trump falls under the weight of his corruption and incompetence is doomed to fail.

Despite all of the preemptive compromise from Democrats in Washington, and the cautious centrism from the pundit class, I am hopeful about the future of the Democratic Party.

I have spent the last few years meeting the people who are making change in their community. People who didn't wait for someone in Washington to tell them what to do. People who are unafraid to fail. Whenever things get dark and depressing, these encounters are what keep me hopeful. Ironically, the election of America's worst citizen unlocked a wave of citizenship.

I think about the students I met from Parkland, Florida, who turned tragedy into a nationwide movement to pass gun safety laws.

I think about Ady Barkan who was diagnosed with a terminal disease and decided to spend whatever time he had left fighting to ensure that everyone in America has access to health care.

I think about Amanda Litman, who could have gone on vacation or taken a lucrative consulting job, after working on Hillary Clinton's campaign, but instead started an organization that is helping thousands of people run for office all across America.

I think about Tamar Masseh, a mother from the South Side of Chicago who responded to gun violence in her neighborhood not by hiding in the house, but by standing on the street with an army of fellow moms to stare down the violence.

All across the country, there are people who are showing us the path forward. They are fighting back with the fierce urgency of now. They embrace the audacity of Obama. They are fighting like there is no tomorrow, because they know if they don't fight, there will be no tomorrow.

They are the future of the Democratic Party and the country. If we follow their lead, we will beat Trump, fix our democracy, and make sure that this era was nothing more than a detour from the path to a more perfect union.

They are why I still believe that "yes, we can."

As Barack Obama ended his stump speech in 2008, "Now, let's go change the world."

BONUS CONTENT

A PAUL RYAN RANT FOR THE PEOPLE IN THE BACK

If you listen to *Pod Save America*, you know I have very strong feelings about former Republican House Speaker Paul Ryan. I have been known to rant about him from time to time.

During our annual holiday mailbag episode in 2018, Michael Martinez, who produces *Pod Save America*, surprised me with a supercut of my rants about Paul Ryan. This was the last podcast that we would record before Paul Ryan ambled out of Congress into historical obsolescence.

In the moment, I was a little horrified. I don't like to hear my own voice,[1] and I thought I sounded a bit like a lunatic, especially when I heard myself call Paul Ryan an "incompetent fuckstick." But despite my fear that I was becoming a caricature of myself, I stand by every word I said.[2]

This is not a bit. I hate Paul Ryan,[3] and I have for a long time.

---

1 Huge flaw if you stumble into a career in podcasting. I have to leave the room when my wife listens to the podcast at home.

2 Even *fuckstick,* which is a terrible word that I had never said or really thought about before it came tumbling out of my mouth discussing Paul Ryan trying to take health care away from Americans for shits and giggles.

3 To be clear, I hate Paul Ryan the politician. I don't know Paul Ryan the

The lanky, sad-eyed Wisconsinite who is the star of the *West Wing* episode playing in his own head is everything wrong with the Republican Party. I have hated him for going on a decade. In other words, I hated Paul Ryan long before it was en vogue to hate Paul Ryan.

Back in 2011, Paul Ryan showed who he was. The Republicans had just taken over Congress. Ryan, who was the chair of the Budget Committee, was fashioning himself a rising star and intellectual leader of the Republican Party.[4] Ryan told a Horatio Alger story of an Ayn Rand–loving Capitol Hill staffer that used to wait tables at Tortilla Coast,[5] a Mexican eatery on Capitol Hill, who rose to the pinnacle of Republican politics.

Ryan unveiled the "Ryan plan," which privatized Medicare, slashed Medicaid, cut food stamps, and generally made life worse for poor Americans in the name of deficit reduction. And oh yeah, the rich didn't have to pay one extra dime in taxes, because why should we ask the wealthy to sacrifice when we can just take from the poor? Ryan talked about his plan as a response to a crisis of debts and deficits that threatened to plummet America into a financial crisis. This was, of course, bullshit and merely a justification to cut government spending to those who need it most.

President Obama, as a Democrat and a human being, was horrified by the inherent cruelty in Ryan's plan and irked by the way the media was lionizing Ryan for the courage of proposing ripping health care away from poor people. Ryan was also lying through his Crest Whitestrips[6] about the impacts of his plan.

---

person, but by all accounts he is an affable guy who loves his family. I am, however, more interested in how a politician treats other people's families, and on that measure Paul Ryan is an epic failure.

4 A lot like being the tallest of the Seven Dwarfs or the best show on CBS or the smartest Trump White House staffer—you get the point.

5 I spent a lot of hours at Tortilla Coast because they had an affordable happy hour, but the food sucked.

6 I am shocked the fact-checkers didn't ding me for this, because I know nothing about his dental hygiene.

Obama is an orator by nature, and his first instinct in moments like these is to give a speech. He wanted to explain what Ryan was doing and set up a contrast between Ryan's plan (shitty) and Obama's plan (good).

We put a speech about the economy on the schedule and booked the auditorium at George Washington University. The White House Legislative Affairs staff apparently didn't read the copies of the speech being circulated and followed protocol and invited the chairs and ranking members of the relevant congressional committees to the speech. Ryan accepted the invitation—a fact that was not shared with the communications team.

The legislative affairs team also sat Ryan in the front row, another fact that was not shared with the communications team. The first person who knew what was in the speech to find out Ryan was sitting in the front row was Barack Obama, who discovered this fact when he arrived at the podium and saw Ryan sitting there, staring right back at him.

Obama thought to himself, "Well, this is awkward." But what else was there to do but give the speech? The president spent about forty-five minutes politely and accurately ripping Ryan's plan to shreds. Ryan got visibly upset and stormed off in sadness and anger. Ryan didn't rebut the substance of Obama's critique—the speech was factually accurate and fair. He whined about the etiquette and told Obama economic advisor Gene Sperling that Obama "had poisoned the well" for future deals.

Ryan, who has spent most of his time in Congress branding himself an "ideas man," was unwilling and—frankly—unable to debate his ideas. His arrogance and sense of entitlement was more than a little off-putting. I had been reading for years stenography bordering on hagiography about Paul Ryan from Washington reporters. If this was the best the Republicans had to offer, they didn't have much to offer. It was clear that the press was so desperate for a smart, serious Republican to fill in the second part of its both-sides narratives that it had puffed up an empty suit beyond recognition.

Strike one.

Flash forward about five months: Obama was secretly negotiating with the Republican House Speaker John Boehner over a so-called grand-bargain budget deal. This deal would have resolved a budget standoff that was threatening a very fragile economy and would have provided economic aid to struggling families in the near term in exchange for reducing the deficit in the long term.[7] After several fits and starts, Boehner called Obama to tell him the deal was dead. And who was the person holding the bloody knife?

Paul Ryan.

What was Ryan's reason? A disagreement on policy?

No. He thought it was a pretty fair deal.

Politics.

Boehner told Obama that Ryan opposed the deal because it would "guarantee Obama's reelection."

Talk about poisoning the well.

Strike two.

Flash forward again to 2016.[8] Paul Ryan continued on his path of failing up and became the Speaker of the House. He spent much of the previous year's election talking down Trump. Ryan, to his credit, called out Trump for some of his racist remarks. He also canceled a campaign event with Trump after the infamous *Access Hollywood* tape came out. Ryan and his aides were very clear to

---

7 This proposed deal has received a lot of criticism, much of it fair, both at the time and in the years since, but our goal was to get funding to create jobs and grow the economy, and we had to trade something that the Republicans wanted. People of good faith can disagree with Obama's approach to these budget negotiations, but we can all agree that Paul Ryan sucks.

8 We are going to skip over Ryan's embarrassing run as Romney's vice presidential pick. Needless to say, he sucked at that, too.

everyone who would listen that he privately thought Trump was corrupt, a fraud, and unfit intellectually and temperamentally for the office of president. And how did Ryan express these grave concerns about the man vying for access to the nuclear codes?

He voted for Trump. Paul Ryan voted for someone he thought was dangerously immoral and outrageously stupid to lead the country, because he would rather support a racist, corrupt idiot than a Democrat.

Things only got worse once Trump won. Paul Ryan refused to criticize Trump or hold him accountable for literally anything. Despite a record-breaking number of scandals, Ryan prohibited the House committees from doing oversight. The House Intelligence Committee's investigation into Russian interference in the 2016 election was not focused on Russia or its many connections to the Trump campaign. Devin Nunes, the chairman, used the committee's resources to prove the insane conspiracy theories that came out of the mouths of the biggest kooks on Fox News and the dark corners of the internet. When thousands of Puerto Ricans died due to governmental mismanagement of the response to Hurricane Maria, the Republicans held zero hearings to find out what happened. They didn't look into the corrupt practices of Trump's EPA administrator, VA secretary, secretary of the interior, or any of the other Trump officials that resigned in scandal. Paul Ryan clearly believes that checks and balances only matter when the president is a Democrat.

And in perhaps the perfect example of Ryan's fetid fecklessness, when Trump praised the Nazis that marched in Charlottesville as "very fine people," Paul Ryan finally had enough. He called together his press staff[9] and went further than before. He was so upset about Trump's patently offensive comment that he had

---

9 I was shocked when this happened because his press staff had basically gone on vacation and stopped responding to questions from reporters.

to express his concerns publicly. His office issued a statement in response to the burgeoning controversy emerging from the Oval Office.

The idea that Ryan was going to say something about Trump was exciting for the Never Trump conservatives who were desperately hoping that their one-time hero would reclaim his place as the voice of non-Trump conservatism.[10]

Like Charlie Brown with the football, they would be fooled yet again.

Ryan's statement simply reiterated his opposition to Nazism[11] and never mentioned Trump's comment. I guess it says something about the party in the Trump era that Republican politicians felt a need to denounce Nazism. Even at Trump's lowest moment, Paul Ryan couldn't muster the courage to take a stand.

Why did Ryan do this if he didn't like Trump? I think there are two reasons that go beyond the fact that he has the moral fortitude of Jell-O.

Paul Ryan is a Republican first and an American second. I know that seems like a harsh thing to say, but what else can you say about someone that would rather support a dangerously unfit Republican over a Democrat? Ryan believed he had to bend the knee to Trump and let Trump do whatever Trump wanted—legal, quasi-legal, or outright illegal—in order to stay in power. What was best for the Republican Party trumped[12] what was best for America. Party over country is Paul Ryan's approach.[13] The cruel irony of this is that Paul Ryan degraded himself and sold his soul to help Republicans in the 2018 elections, and they got destroyed anyway.

---

10 I honestly hate myself for using such a trite cliché

11 Which is like putting out a statement that says, "Water is wet."

12 I also hate myself for this pun.

13 If Paul Ryan had a Tupacesque tattoo, it would say "GOP LIFE." This is a terrible joke, but I can't get the image out of my head, and now neither can you.

Paul Ryan's raison d'être is taking health care away from poor people. I know this also seems like a harsh thing to say about someone, but it is also true. If you don't believe me, listen to Paul Ryan himself. Back in 2017, when the Republicans were trying for the zillionth time to repeal the Affordable Care Act, Paul Ryan sat with Rich Lowry, the editor of the conservative publication *National Review*. Lowry asked Ryan about his proposed cuts to Medicaid, the government health insurance program for the poorest Americans. Republicans have long hated Medicaid because... it is the government health insurance program for the poorest Americans. The Congressional Budget Office had estimated that if the Republican cuts went into place, fourteen million people would lose their health insurance.

Ryan, unbowed by the horrific impact of his policy, told Lowry, "We have been dreaming of this since I have been around, since you and I were drinking at a keg."[14]

If taking health care from poor people was life goal number 1, cutting taxes for rich people was life goal number 1A. In the 2017 tax-cut legislation, Ryan finally achieved his dream of lowering Apple's tax burden, which, in his mind, justified his support of Trump.

Whatever it takes to help one sleep at night.

In Trump, Ryan saw a vehicle to achieve his cruel policy goals. He would tolerate—and even enable—the racism if it meant he could pursue conservative policy. Racism is fine. Corruption is fine. Siding with Russia over the US is fine. If—and only if—you agree to right-wing policies to make the rich richer and the poor poorer. The policies themselves are gross, but the trade-offs being made for the sake of those policies is beyond the pale.

People who are not already part of the "hate Paul Ryan" movement may read this and say, "Sure, Dan, Paul Ryan seems terrible,

---

14 Ryan doesn't seem like a fun hang in his college days.

but is he really worse than the rest of the Republicans? Why do you hate him more than Marco Rubio, Mitch McConnell, or a dozen others?"

Great question. I will be the first to admit my hate for Ryan is not entirely rational. It has been pointed out to me that I get more worked up about Ryan than Trump.

I rant about Ryan so much that I wouldn't be shocked to find my name on a watch list in the headquarters of the Capitol Police. There are very good reasons to hate Marco Rubio, McConnell, and dozens of other Republicans. I couldn't argue with someone who said they hated Maine senator Susan Collins for lying about her support for *Roe v. Wade* and voting to confirm Brett Kavanaugh.[15] I wouldn't quibble if you picked avowed white supremacist Steve King as your least favorite GOPer. And I wouldn't complain about some choosing doltish fail son-in-law Jared Kushner for showing us what would have happened if Cousin Greg from *Succession* worked in the White House.[16]

I hate Ryan the most because he had the power to make things better, and he chose not to out of a combination of cowardice and amoral partisanship. When the going got tough, he ran away. He retired from Congress instead of fighting for a better country or even a better Republican Party.

McConnell, for example, knows he is a bad guy. He proudly wears the black hat. He even calls himself the Grim Reaper.[17] Ryan thinks he is on the right side of history. He thinks he is the protagonist in the Trump era. To the extent he recognizes that he erred, he is convinced beyond a shadow of a doubt those errors were not his fault.

---

15 Kavanaugh seems like someone who hung around the keg with Ryan.

16 Kendall, who is not a rocket scientist, is too smart to be Kushner, and Roman has too much personality for Kushner, who is basically a first-generation *Westworld* robot missing a personality chip (and yes, I recognize this is a massively mixed HBO metaphor).

17 He also calls himself "Cocaine Mitch," which is a topic for another day.

As he was preparing to leave Congress, Ryan engaged in a never-ending farewell tour of speeches and press interviews. This was the final effort to try to turn the chicken shit of his tenure into chicken salad.

In a discussion with conservative columnist Jonah Goldberg, Ryan made an impassioned plea to his party to stand up to the Alt-Right—the euphemism du jour for the white nationalist movement that had taken over the Republican Party.

"Intellectually do everything you can to defeat the alt-right. It is identity politics, it is antithetical to what we believe, and it's a hijacking of our terms.... We have to go back and fight for our ground and re-win these ideas and marginalize these guys as best we can to the corners," Ryan told Goldberg.

If you can ignore the fact that Ryan did nothing in his tenure to take on the Alt-Right and that his super PAC ran ads in the 2018 election that were so racist they might make Steve Bannon blush, Ryan delivered his answer with such a sad sincerity that it was almost believable. He seemed, for the moment at least, as a man truly saddened by what had become of the party to which he had dedicated his life.

However, once again, Paul Ryan revealed himself as one of the great frauds in modern political history. His quest to take on the Alt-Right ended the moment he ambled off the stage.

His first move after leaving Congress?

Joining the board of Fox News's parent company, which is the engine of the Alt-Right and white nationalism in American politics. He didn't take on the Alt-Right; he decided to profit off it.

This—among so many other reasons—is why Paul Ryan is the absolute fucking worst.

ACKNOWLEDGMENTS

Un-Trumping America would never have gone from a figment of an idea to an actual book without the unending support of Sean Desmond. It is hard to imagine a smarter, more supportive, and more patient publisher. Working with Sean since my first book has been a real privilege. Sean is supported by an amazing team at Twelve, including Rachel Kambury, Paul Samuelson, Dan Modlin, Brian McLendon, and Jarrod Taylor. It's safe to say that I would never have had the opportunity to write books without the guidance and support of David Larabell and CAA, who believed in me as an author long before I typed my first word.

Alyssa Mastromonaco has been my closest friend and confidant since the first day of the Obama campaign, when I passed her test for new people by volunteering to take on an unexciting task. For more than a decade she has listened to me, looked out for me, and made me laugh when I needed it most. She was an invaluable sounding board for this book.

Kristin Bartoloni and Alex Platkin at Silver Street Strategies are the best researchers in the business and have been keeping all of Obama world factual for years. I rejected only one of their research flags, and it was about Tom Brady's support for Donald Trump.[1]

I don't know that I ever had a real vision of what my professional

1 The reasons for this should be obvious to everyone who is (a) not from Boston and (b) has a soul.

life would look like after the White House, but I am positive it never included podcasting. The entire *Pod Save America* experience has been an unexpected gift. None of it would be possible without Jon Favreau, Jon Lovett, and Tommy Vietor and their bold decision to give up everything and start a progressive media company as a way to make an impact in the Trump era. While I talk[2] into a microphone a couple of times a week, Jon, Jon, and Tommy are building a next-generation media company that is moving the political conversation in America away from Fox News and toward reality. Every time I visit the Crooked Media headquarters, I am inspired by the dozens of smart, motivated, and idealistic young people that make the company go. In particular I want to thank Sarah Wick, Tanya Somanader, Shaniqua McClendon, Travis Helwig, Michael Martinez, Jordan Waller, Elisa Gutierrez, Kyle Seglin, Jesse McLean, and Andrew Chadwick.

Meeting our listeners has been one of the best parts of cohosting *Pod Save America*. To a person, they have been smart, friendly, and inspiring. So many of them are engaged in politics for the first time and channeling their anger and angst into activism. In these dark political times, they give me hope.

I remain eternally grateful to Barack Obama for the tremendous opportunities he gave me. Working for him on the 2008 campaign and in the White House was the privilege and honor of a lifetime. The people I met on that campaign and in the White House remain my friends and family more than a decade later. I will always be immensely proud to be a member of Team Obama. It's easy to forget amid all the Trumpian tweets, but it wasn't that long ago that we had a smart, decent president staffed by talented people who tried to do the most good for the most people with the time given to them by the voters. It happened then and it can happen again.

---

2 Sometimes yell.

Finally, and most important, none of this possible without Howli. She has been my partner in every way—supporting me, pushing me, reading and rereading every word in this book. I have no idea where I would be without her and am so grateful we found each other. Our family has gotten bigger, and our life exponentially fuller with the addition of our daughter, Kyla. I am a very lucky man.

ABOUT THE AUTHOR

Dan Pfeiffer is the #1 *New York Times* bestselling author of *Yes We (Still) Can* and a cohost of *Pod Save America*. One of Barack Obama's longest-serving advisors, he was White House director of communications (2009–2013) and senior advisor to the president (2013–2015). He currently lives in the Bay Area with his wife, Howli, and their daughter, Kyla.